Daughter
of a Thousand
STARS

a MEMOIR

D1568754

HAJAH KANDEH

Daughter of a Thousand Stars: A Memoir
Published by Divine Right Publishing
San Francisco, CA

ISBN: 978-0-578-87123-3
Personal Memoir

Cover and Interior design by Victoria Wolf,
wolfdesignandmarketing.com

Printed in the United States of America.

DIVINE RIGHT
PUBLISHING

Dedicated to God, who has made all things possible,
to all those living in the shadows, and to every
person who suffers in silence.

For my son, mama's heart, who gives
me the greatest reason to try.

To All of You

To all of you who have loved me into being
at unexpected times in random places;
To all of you who have opened your hearts
accepted, even welcomed, my woundedness,
thank you for loving me into being.
To all of you who have loved me into being,
though I was neither kin nor kind,
for bending the rules, going out of your way,
for doing things you never had to do,
thank you for rearing me into being.
To all of you who have believed me into being
for seeing something when there was nothing left to see,
for believing in me when I could no longer believe in myself,
thank you for inspiring me into being.
To all of you who have gathered my broken bones
and helped me to my feet,
thank you for standing me into being.

*All sorrows can be borne if we put them in
a story or tell a story about them.*

~Isak Dinesen, author of *Out of Africa*

Acknowledgments

WRITING THIS BOOK has been the hardest thing I have ever done. It required me to use all of the challenged parts of me: my attention, focus, physical challenges with pain and other discomforts, computer skills, the hardships of living on the edge with no money and waking up each day to deal with all the reasons I should just give up. I want to thank God for giving me the courage to persevere and push through. I want to thank all of the amazing people listed here without whom this book would have remained only another dream.

To Randy Peyser, you don't sell books; you birth dreams! Thank you for being.

To my editor, Diane Eaton, you're a master at your craft, and I am in awe! Thank you for your incredible brilliance, which shines through these pages. I will never have enough words to thank you.

To Polly Letofsky and my tribe at My Word Publishing, you've set the bar way up for self-publishing. Your expertise and generosity know no bounds and I will never find the words to thank you.

To Victoria Wolf at Wolf Design and Marketing, my book cover is a glimpse into your genius as an artist. Thank you for creating a cover that not only compliments, but completes my story.

To my brothers, D.J. and Robert N., with gratitude and love, you were my first sources of light and joy, and, through it all, you have never given up hope for me.

To Mimi, who showed me that love trumps biology, thank you for being my mother.

To Mrs. Simmons, thank you for typing those first few chapters.

To Ariane, angel, guide, and rock, thank you for being so much more than a therapist and for always reminding me that God has a plan.

To Aunty Gloria, you're the best! Thank you for loving me in spite of myself.

To Pastor Peter, Prophetess Honor Sade, thank you for knowing the God you serve and introducing him to me. I will be eternally grateful.

To Reverend Doctor Ernestine Sanders "Auntie" for blessing me with your prayers and tender love. I know you're smiling down on me from heaven.

To Aunty Eleanor, thank you for the first seven years of my life. I owe you big.

To Tanis, my greatest gift from cancer, your friendship is a resting place. Thank you for making magic for me.

To Marcet-Marie, my first friend in America, you will always be in my heart. Your laughter has sustained me over the years.

To Gina, my newest friend, for giving me your light and

believing in your soul-sister whom you have yet to meet.

To mama Tarpeh for going without food or drink to seek God's face for me. I love you.

To my friend Carmen, thank you, hermosa, for your care packages that include your beautiful heart.

To Olivia, for making room for my son and me at your family's table so we would not always be alone on Thanksgiving. Wafaa, I did it! Thank you for knowing I could.

To Ayla and Birhan, who never said no when I needed to borrow a few dollars.

To all my doctors who have gone beyond the call of duty to give me a chance at life. To Vigya and Tarsha Dhiman for working tireless pro bono hours on my website and media platforms, I could never repay you. Thank you.

For My old friends from childhood and the new ones I have made—you know yourselves. I appreciate you more than you'll ever know.

To Alberta, Aunty Sylvia, and all of you who have prayed for me, loved me, and accepted me.

To my sisters, the Kay Queens, who showed up just in the nick of time to bring me back home.

To Anne (Sibana), you were and will forever be a huge part of my story.

To my mother, who gave me life without which I would not have a story to tell.

To papa, thank you for giving me your heart.

Introduction

LIFE CAN BE QUITE MIRACULOUS, but the road to one's miracles is often a circuitous route, not a straight line.

I wish more than anything that I had an easy story to tell. But this is my story, and it is a journey where the most difficult and unexpected twists and turns occurred first, before I was led to the sweetest of miracles.

Why would anyone feel inclined to believe that the world wants to hear their story? I have often wondered about the hubris of those of us who write about ourselves. Yet, a case can be made for stories. Stories are the pulse of every society, the unwitting custodians of our history. How else can we trace where we came from and what lessons, if any, we can learn from the past? As long as humans exist, there will be a need and a place for stories.

I share my story in the hopes that you, too, will live out your own story discovering that you are stronger than you think. While the particulars of our stories may be different, we have all known suffering. It is our humanity that unites us and gives us hope.

Daughter of a Thousand Stars has been a long time coming. I have always wanted to write the story of my life, and while there are echoes of the many other stories I have dreamed of telling but never got to, *Daughter of a Thousand Stars* is the one I am meant to tell. And although I may never be completely comfortable in the telling of it, it is time to do so.

Everything in the book is true, even as there were times when I have wished it were not so.

Some names have been changed to protect the privacy of the people who are part of this story.

CHAPTER 1

Echoes of Childhood

I WAS BORN IN KONO, the heart of the diamond mines in Sierra Leone, West Africa. My childhood is a blur. Like a vast expanse of desert, I only remember landmarks.

By the time I was eleven, I had been defiled, mutilated, battered, sent away to boarding school, lost my papa, and had my name changed to assume the name of my mother's then-current husband.

Most of what I recall after those experiences got buried in the deepest recesses of my mind so that I could bear the demands of living in the shadow of trauma. Like other survivors, I did what I needed to do to keep putting one foot in front of the other. Blanking out thought. Numbing oneself into forgetfulness. Anesthetizing one's heart to bear the demands of a wounded psyche. Tools.

I did not know it then, but my concept of time is almost non-existent. I do not remember years; I remember events. Some people can tell you clearly who they were or what they did at age five, or six, or nine. I can't. I remember highlights. Like hearing words spoken in my ears: "You're a bastard, a whore. You'll never amount to anything." I remember sounds like musical notes reverberating in my ears from being slapped so hard my eardrums shook. I remember the flash of lightning darting across my eyes and the taste of my own blood from the tender child-flesh breaking under the force of an enraged adult's hand. I remember hiding so far away inside myself that it would take me more than three decades to begin the journey of finding my way back home to me. I remember feeling all wrong, trying to understand why, and wondering how I was going to make myself right somehow.

I worshipped the ground my mother walked on. No one was more beautiful; no one could compare. She was my sun, and I woke up to her radiance. I lived for the moments when I was in some way connected to her. It could have been something as simple as watching her in conversation or rummaging through her purse looking for coins to tip a young errand boy, or laying out her freshly ironed, bubble-gum pink uniform for work the next day. I was simply happy around her, craving each moment alone with her, however small. I did not even mind the burning onion tears as I peeled, washed, and cut the soft bulbs into clumsy chunks and then dropped them into a delicious pot of something she was cooking. My mother was a great cook. She had come back, and though things were not as I would have wanted, I hoped they would change if I changed. I was going to be the best child, the brightest, the funniest, the most hard-working, the politest. I would do well in school and respect my elders. I would listen and do as I was told without talking back. I would not steal or play with boys or tell lies. I had witnessed adults practicing "give me this, and I will give you that." As in, "Don't hit me, and I will pretend I didn't see you sneaking in at 4:00 a.m., reeking of alcohol, bad choices, and cheap perfume."

I would be the perfect child. Then all my troubles would go away, including my mother's new man. I would be alone with her, and she would love me again.

I have been asking the people who cared for me when I was little to fill in the gaps for me so I can piece together my broken selves. I do not remember most of my childhood, and the parts I do remember, I often want to forget.

Before she met my stepfather, I am told my mother had made up her mind to continue her studies—even after she had shamed her family with a pregnancy. She was barely old enough to understand the seriousness of being responsible for a child, yet she was bright and knew that she could still make something of her life if she chose to. Having a child did not have to mean the end of her dreams, she thought. So she left me with her younger sister, Emmah, and my biological grandmother's younger sister. My grandmother's sister had lost all her children during childbirth so my grandmother gave my mother to her to parent. I did not know this then, she was my grandmother. I did not learn any differently until I got to college.

I was named after her. My aunt tells me she was happy to take on the job of caring for me, even after my grandfather died, which was shortly after my mother left. She had left home for the city to attend The Technical Institute, a school that prepared young women for a career in accounting or to be a private secretary to a high-powered executive. My grandmother was too grief-stricken to parent anyone. My aunt told me that I was like her own child since she had not yet given birth to Bakar, her son. In a tender voice, she told me that I had been an intelligent, warm child whom everybody liked. I asked her to tell me if she had noticed anything "wrong" with me while I lived with her, as I tried desperately to trace the origins of my misfortunes. Perhaps I had been unlucky even then. She was puzzled by my query and told me, "No." Only that I was a sickly child and got anemic as soon as I fell ill, which scared her no end. It was Africa. Many children die from simple, preventable diseases that people in the Western world would be shocked by—diarrhea, bronchitis, a cold.

My aunt was a young woman herself when she took on caretaking me; she was self-assured and mature for her age, and she adored me. Much later, she was proud to tell me that she shopped for me at the most expensive boutiques in town—shops that catered to the rich mine owners that lived there or visited—the town that had the most diamonds in all of Sierra Leone. The town where I was born. I could feel her smiling through the phone . "You were like my handbag," she said. "I took you everywhere with me." I hastened her along her story, wanting to know more. "Tell me, did I have any friends? What did I like to eat ?" I was unsettled by the emotions that washed over me as we talked. I had called her from San Francisco once I decided I needed some facts before I gave any more thought to writing this story. I fought to stop the dam from bursting open and drowning us both as I started to discover that someone other than my papa had not only loved me but wanted me, too. She told me I took part in school concerts, and she recited some lines from my first school play nearly four decades ago. "It was great watching you on stage. Sometimes I got so carried away, I would scream 'That's my child!' when you did something especially funny or clever, and the audience burst into wild applause."

After we talked, I was confused and scared about what I might learn from the others I was contacting to tell me their version of my childhood. I am not sure what I had expected to discover in my conversation with my aunt, but it wasn't that I had been normal in some ways after all.

My aunt loved Bollywood films and took me with her to see them a lot when I had been in her care. Some of my happiest memories are about going to a matinee with her in the middle of a hot afternoon to watch three-, sometimes four-hour-long Indian films. We chewed on roast beef and drank ice-cold Fanta as we waited with anticipation for the movie to begin. I loved the tender, mouthwatering pieces of fillet marinated in peanut butter, tomato paste, and a puree of sweet peppers, onion, and garlic, skewered, then slowly roasted over hot coals. She bought them from the smiling street food vendor, whispering in my ear that "She's the only one whose food I trust. She's clean."

I was dazzled by the brightly colored costumes and the beautifully choreographed dance numbers that constituted most of the Bollywood films. The men always wooed the women through song and dance. It was enthralling. The hero, however, always seemed to have some tragedy unfolding: the loss of a father, a sibling, his home. Sometimes the tragedy was due to some natural disaster, and sometimes it was at the hand of criminals who were following the orders of the local mafia boss for an unpaid debt or some other reason. Sometimes it was punishment for shared affection for the village belle.

Our hero expressed his sorrow and longing through music, and then always vowed to avenge the wrong. Most people in the theatre would cry right along with him as haunting sounds from the sitar played out his heartbreak. It was always shocking for me to see grown men cry, but I cannot say I didn't like the sight of it. The films were always driven by two themes—revenge and love. Of the hundreds of movies I watched, the storylines never veered much from those two. Still, I was never bored.

I got into trouble one weekend when *Disco Dancer*, a movie that had been rumored to be the best Bollywood movie ever released, came into town. I was as filled with excitement as my aunt, the movie buff, was. She could talk of nothing but the film. But when I shared my excitement and anticipation, she closed up. She told me in no uncertain terms, "You're not going."

I could not believe it. How could she do that to me? She had been the one to introduce me to Amitabh Bachchan, Hema Malini, Shashi Kapoor—the Sophia Lorens, Clarke Gables, Audrey Hepburns, and Meryl Streeps of Bollywood! She was going with her friends, she told me. Messages had been sent back and forth between them to coordinate everything. They would all meet at the cinema near the ticket line. Every attempt I made to plead my case in the ensuing weeks was met with a stony, "I have already told you—you're not going." I turned into a bundle of nerves and probably dropped a pound or two from anxiety.

After that, you could not have found a better-behaved girl anywhere. I did everything I could to please my aunt and get in her good graces so that she would change her mind and take me to the movie. At last, the day came. My aunt was too excited to eat the delicious cassava leaves that had been prepared for lunch that day and started getting dressed hours before the show. I took two bites of rice, scrambled quickly to my feet, hastily threw water over me to pass for a shower, and got dressed.

Looking bright and colorful and brimming with excitement in my favorite purple dress, I rushed to my aunt's room and breathlessly shouted, "I am ready! Let's go!" She looked at me as if I were some creature from another planet.

"Ready? For what? Where are you going? What are you ready for? Why are you all dressed up?"

The questions came fast and hard and left me disconcerted. I could feel my confidence dwindling. "For the film," I managed, all smiles.

"Didn't I tell you you're not going?" she snapped.

I started to protest. She ignored me and, with finality, told me to go change my clothes and go play with my cousins. She did not want to hear another word about me going anywhere.

Why would she go with all her friends to the most anticipated movie of all time and not take me? The unfairness of grown-ups.

I started crying. Between sobs, I asked, "Why can't I come too? Everybody is going except me."

"Not 'everybody' is going. Do you see other children here? I don't blame you. I am the one who has spoiled you. But you must stop this nonsense," she yelled. I sniffed, blowing my nose loudly in the sleeve of my dress, crying even harder.

"From now on, you're not going to any more matinees with me."

At that moment, I hated my aunt. The threat of not getting to see my favorite characters hung heavy on me, but I had more pressing matters at hand. I had to see *Disco Dancer*. I went out to the veranda and paced back and forth, trying to figure out what to do. Suddenly, I had an idea. I rushed back into my aunt's room and told her I was feeling sick all of a sudden.

"I think I have a fever. Feel my forehead. See how hot I am?"

She looked at me carefully, softened for a second, and then the moment passed. She became quiet and seemed deflated. I had gotten her. I smiled to myself. I watched as a bird watches its prey while my aunt sat heavily on the edge of the only chair in the room. She kicked off her leather thongs, which had left deep grooves on the tops of her feet, like tire marks of a tractor on a dirt road.

We sat side by side in silence in the stuffy room. After what seemed like an eternity, she stood up and put her hand on my shoulder. A sly smile quickly crossed her face, then, just as quickly, disappeared. It was replaced by a gentle, sympathetic voice, complete with a concerned frown.

"I am sorry, mama. See. You can't go now," she said in saccharine tones. "You're not well. You must stay home and lie down. When I come back, I will make some peppe soup for you. Ok?"

Peppe soup, the Sierra Leonean cure-all bone broth, is so hot with cayenne and chilies that it kills any virus or bacteria lurking around. It also burns the lining inside your nostrils, not to mention how it lights your rear end on fire in the unfortunate event you need to use the bathroom soon after drinking it. "I don't want any peppe soup," I shouted, angry with myself for having been so stupid. If only I had not said anything about being sick. In Africa, you usually get preferential treatment from everyone when you are burning up with fever from malaria.

I went into hysterics. "I want to come with you! The fever is gone now. Touch my skin," I said, lifting up my dress, grabbing her hand, and laying it on my chest, desperate to prove my wellness.

She lost all patience and raised her voice. "I know what you're trying to do. You want me to be late and miss the show. There is going to be a long line to get tickets. I am not arguing with you anymore. This conversation is over." There was something hard and sharp in her tone, which worried me. Her voice insisted on no further argument.

My mind raced. What was I going to do? I knew I could not persuade my aunt, and I knew I was going to watch the film. Then it hit me. It was a big risk, but I had no other choice.

My aunt left the house dressed up in the Indian outfit she had bought at Mr. Rajani's shop, excitement in her every step. The dress looked like it must have weighed a ton from the way she was straining to carry it in her arms, carefully, as one would carry a fat baby—afraid of dropping it. I had gone with her when she bought the dress—reluctantly. A trip to Mr. Rajani's shop made you fodder for the neighborhood kids and their siblings. They would wrinkle their nose when you walked by to stave off the smell of garam masala that trailed behind you hours after. The spices were so pungent that you only had to be in the room for a few minutes before the smell clung to you and followed you everywhere. It was as if the angel of spices had been assigned to you for that day. I hated going to that shop.

I waited until my aunt had walked a little distance, then I followed, running to catch up, but remaining unseen. I followed at a safe distance, and each time I felt she suspected someone was following her, I hid between houses and tiptoed around anything that remotely looked like it might make noise and draw attention to me.

My aunt and I traveled like this until we got to the movie house, where we found more than a thousand people waiting in line. For the first time, I panicked. Never had I seen so many people in one place at the same time—99% of whom were grown-ups. My heart was pounding and sweat was coursing down my back.

I caught a glimpse of my purple dress in the glass window of a broken-down van parked on the street and saw that it had streaks of black lines running down the back from sweat and adrenalin. I was afraid to get lost in the crowd, so I tried to get close to my aunt somehow. I did not want her to see me before the moment I had wanted to magically appear. There were already a lot of people between us, and since I was short in a sea of adults, I could not see those ahead of me. I kept track of her only by her brightly colored Sari with its tiny shiny sequins that sparkled like hundreds of small suns each time she moved. I started elbowing people out of the way as my panic grew and stayed close but still undetectable behind my aunt and the friends she found once we got to the cinema.

We slowly inched our way through the throng of people until, at last, my aunt was next in line at the counter.

"How many?" the ticket seller asked in a dull voice.

"Two," I answered, stepping out from behind my aunt. I smiled confidently at the dusky young man who looked tired and hungry and seemed resigned to a long afternoon of dealing with hundreds of irate, overheated people. My aunt looked down as though she had seen a ghost. With shock and disbelief, she watched me as I stepped out of the line and stood beside her. She hesitated a little but knew she was cornered. She had to let me come with her. There was no way she would tell me to go out in that crowd and walk back home by myself.

People were already grumbling. "Mrs., are you going to pay and go? Why are you standing there holding up the line?"

In the few seconds my aunt had taken to look at me and let me know I was toast once we got home, anger had settled in her normally pretty round face, making her almost ugly. She counted the money wordlessly, paid, then grabbed my hand and roughly pulled me behind her. I did not care. I made it. I let out a huge sigh and smiled to myself, feeling happy. *I will deal with the consequences later,* I told myself.

We walked up the stairs briskly; someone in the hot, dark, crowded room looked at our tickets with a flashlight and ushered us to our seats. I sank in my seat and stared straight ahead. I could not risk glancing over at my aunt's face. I sat stiff as a corpse, counting the seconds for the lights to be dimmed and for the projector to be turned on to start the film. Then the unthinkable happened. I needed to pee. Badly.

What was I going to do? No way was I going to tell my aunt I needed the bathroom. I was in enough trouble as it was already. Having to ask her to take me to the nasty room where ammonia had seeped into the floors and walls, and no amount of scrubbing could get rid of its stench was one thing. Asking all those people in our row to stand up and make way while they grumble as we shoved past them through the tiny space between seats was not going to happen. I knew that I had pushed enough for one day. I sat down and sank deeper into my seat, rubbing my legs together as I waited and prayed for each scene that followed to be action-packed and loud.

I waited for what seemed like forever until there was finally a car chase between the police and the hero. High screeching sounds reverberated through the speakers in the walls as tires squealed from rubbing against asphalt and going at speeds faster than was safe. Gunshots, dramatic music, loud screaming from the passersby who were fleeing the oncoming cars that seemed to be flying straight at them—and I gave my bladder permission to let go. It did, the warm liquid bathing me in pleasure.

In that dimly lit room, watching *Disco Dancer,* my wet clothes sticking to me, sitting in that worn, scratchy leather seat, I felt an exhilaration I had never experienced before. It was as though the film, the sounds, the people in the room, and I had all become one.

These days, when I meet an Indian person, I am eager to say, "Miranam" and a few other of my favorite phrases that I picked up from the Bollywood movies of my childhood. The shift in their attitude is always electric. What starts as a simple "hello" morphs into comparing movie lists and favorite actors. Sometimes we exchange recipes and, on occasion, telephone numbers. This act of meeting people on their turf, connecting with them in their world, and the magic that ensues keeps my heart open and eager to explore even more cultures. In these brief exchanges, something wonderful happens. None of the usual separators of color, race, or religious status come into play as we giggle over some silly scene and argue over whose favorite actor is better-looking. We just simply become people with a shared interest. I relish these experiences.

This was another memory of childhood that I never forgot.

It was one of many glorious moon-lit nights in Africa—the kind you see painted in pictures or captured on screen. Fireflies were out in large numbers, flying so close sometimes you could almost catch them as they danced. It was as if the world was happy with itself that night and, from deep within its heart, glowed. The sky was bright with thousands of stars shining like smiles creating an otherworldly feel. Perhaps some ancestors were right up there with them winking at us too.

In our culture elders always pour libations on special occasions. One day, curious, I asked my grandmother why they did this. She looked at me with a gentle smile on her lips and whispered, "The dead are always with us, watching over us, and we must never forget them."

Lily Bongo, one of my great aunts, had been admitted to the hospital, and my mother and I were going to visit her. Strangely, we did not meet anyone on the road, as though God had given us permission to have the whole universe to ourselves. I held my mother's hand, swinging to some silent music, laughing, feeling like a princess whose every wish had been granted. We continued this way for a while when, suddenly, something sharp cut into my foot, and I screamed out. The enchantment was broken.

My mother looked down worriedly and asked what the matter was. I pointed to my foot, and there, crawling away, was a scorpion. I had been bitten. She picked me up and put me on her back, which is typical of the way African mothers carry their young. Blood coursed down my foot as my mother ran. She knew scorpions are dangerous and their poison can be fatal. I felt the bones of her hips as I bounced up and down her back as she ran hard and fast towards the very hospital where we were going to visit my aunt. After the initial shock and pain of the sting, I felt nothing except the most profound feeling of happiness. I was on my mother's back. I was safe. She loves me. She is running with me so that something bad does not happen to me. I am the luckiest child in this magical world. Pain forgotten, I felt alive. Whole. Right.

I still have the scar from that night, although it has faded and is much smaller now. Yet, I am still chasing that sublime feeling of being loved, being wanted by my mother. It seems that no amount of self-loving and self-mothering, encouraged by my therapists over the years, has succeeded in ending that chase. Since that night, I have never again felt that happiness, that joy, that connectedness, and oneness with her—that feeling of being her world, her everything, her child.

Perhaps it was that night that set the tone for me to stop trusting things that look right and feel good. Something catastrophic will happen for sure. My life will continuously play out the scenario of happiness, catastrophe, happiness, catastrophe. Have I attracted this mad dance to myself by my belief born from that incident with the scorpion those many years ago? Is it simply the nature of life to give you one thing and take another, to give you happiness, then replace it with grief?

My papa had what millennials would call "swag." He had swagger. Not much is known about his family except that his father had come from Mali to trade in Sierra Leone, where he met my grandmother. My father had one brother and four sisters. My father was often fondly called "Chairman." He was a tall, handsome, charismatic man whom the ladies loved. He loved them, too, as is evidenced by the 29 children they bore him. I am one of them.

By the time my father met my teenage mom, swept her off her feet, and got her pregnant, he'd had other children by wives who lived with him. My mother lived with her parents. She never became one of his wives. She and I never lived with him and his family: my stepsisters and stepbrothers. We lived at my grandmother and grandfather's house then and I was brought to my father and his family on weekends or holidays to visit. Every Friday, the chauffer Pascal would pick me up from school. I would have my bag already packed, ready to go. I lived for those moments when the white Mercedes pulled up, and Pascal, dressed in his white uniform and white gloves, got out to let me in the air-conditioned car. I would sink into the plush leather seats and let out a long sigh as if I had been holding my breath from Monday until Friday when I was finally on my way to see my papa. In some ways, I was.

Seeing my papa was not always guaranteed. There were gaps that sometimes lasted for years. When my mother got pregnant, she was 18 and unprepared for it. My mother's parents had sent her to an exclusive high school for girls and spared no expense for her education and comfort. Telling them she had gotten pregnant by an older Muslim man with wives and children was difficult. My grandparents were Christians, and she had brought shame to them since they had such high hopes for her.

I am not surprised she was not exactly looking forward to having me. By the time I was born, my father had ten children, all girls. Yet, as in many parts of the world, boys are coveted in Africa. They are prized possessions that bear the family name and maintain its legacy and bloodline. Girls just get married, go to live with their husband's family, and assume their husband's name. They do not have much value. So, when my father's sister consulted with a medicine man about my imminent birth and was told my mother was going to bear a boy, my father was ecstatic and spared no expense in preparing for my birth. At least one of them had wanted me.

I was born weighing 10 pounds, 11 ounces in a private hospital. A girl. My mother had her own room, which had the comforts of electricity and enough well-trained staff on duty at all times. These were a big deal in Africa then. Corpses were often left t⸍ rot in government hospitals because of sporadic blacko⸍ one could smell the stench of decomposing flesh Sometimes the wards were packed dormitories th⸍

prison camps. I have asked my mother countless times, and her answer is always the same.

"How did my father react when he was told I was not the boy he had been expecting so eagerly?"

"He was happy."

"Happy? Not disappointed?" I asked each time in disbelief.

"Not in the least," she responded every time. "Perhaps he was on the inside, but if he was, he never showed it." She's given the same response each of the several dozen times I have asked her over the years.

My papa accepted my birth. Although I was a girl, I looked very much like him and "had the heart of a man," he would say with pride. In a way, I was the boy he had always wanted. Years later, when I would meet bad men that I trusted too quickly and hoped would be generous and loving like my papa, they would tell me I had the heart of a man, meaning, stubborn and too strong.

Over the years, I have asked my mother to repeat the story of my birth, just so I can hear her tell me that my father wanted me. It was never lost on me that he could have shunned me, walked out on me, or walked out on us. He did not, although it would have been easy. It would have been understandable. He had no need for another girl; he had ten already. On the contrary, soon after I was born, his older sister brought a gold ring that she had made especially for me. The ring had to be strung on thick black thread and tied around my wrist to support my baby finger from the weight of it. I wore that ring until I was about two when I dipped my hand in a hot steaming pot of rice pap, a kind of baby porridge most African babies are fed. I put my hand in the still-boiling pot, trying to reach for it, while my mother had her back turned for a second. I must have been very hungry. My finger swelled around the ring, and I was rushed to the hospital where the ring was cut off. I still have the scar on the middle finger of my left hand.

Papa announced my birth to his wives and their children. It was a conscious choice of his to acknowledge me as his child. Otherwise, my half-sisters would have had no knowledge of my existence since we did not live in the same household, and I was not borne of one of Papa's legal marriages. Papa also made sure my siblings had a relationship with me, even though I did not live with them. They came to visit me from time to time, stopping at my grandmother's supermarket that doubled as a bar, often giving them whatever goodies they fancied. Papa bought the finest things for me and lavished my grandparents with gifts. Everyone looked forward to his visits. As soon as my relatives who were living in my grandmother's house or in surrounding houses saw my father's car pull up, they would run to him, each recounting what they had done for me that day. They only had to say they had carried me on their back for a stroll, ran an errand for my mother, or washed my baby clothes before my father's hands were in his pockets to reward them. We had no washing machines back then.

I was nicknamed "Hajah show" because I was always dressed to the nines, often insisting on wearing white as Papa did. But as I was often playing with my cousins and friends on mostly unpaved and dusty roads and backyards, I got dirty and did not like it. It was common to have my outfits changed a few times a day because I could not abide any stain on my pristine clothes.

Those first few years, my father's love gave me confidence. I was a precocious little girl, and I like to believe it is because I knew I was wanted, loved. Not denied like children in my circumstances often are, because technically, I was considered a bastard in our culture. My mother had me out of wedlock.

In my father's eyes, however, I was another Mandingo princess—his princess. I was treated just like the other children whose mothers he was married to. Nothing was held back from me. His only regret was that my mother's parents wouldn't let me live with him and his families. Polygamous homes are common in Africa. But since I looked so much like my papa, who had loved my mother so much, my grandparents were afraid that if I went to live with him, there would be jealousy among the wives, and I might get poisoned or voodooed. So, I went back and forth between my mother's family and Papa's house until my mother came back from her studies with a certificate and a new man. She took me from my aunt—my primary caretaker for the first eight years of my life.

While she had been studying in the city, 223 miles away, my mother came to see me some weekends or when she was on holiday. I do not remember her visits. The few family memories I have before my mother came back for good were fond ones of Papa, who sometimes took me to visit his Lebanese friends who lived across the street from my grandmother. I liked going with him because Munira, the daughter of one of the men, was my friend and always seemed happy to see me. Her and her younger sister took great pride in showing me around their big house each time I visited. We played with dolls with long shiny hair and ate kebbe-a pocket made with bulgur wheat , minced meat and Middle Eastern spices. They were delicious. Papa and his friends drank thick black coffee and talked and laughed and perhaps even did some business. We could hear them from the veranda. On Fridays, when I went for my weekend visits with Papa, I did the rounds of greeting all the wives and siblings. It was a long process because each wife had their own house in the huge compound papa had built to accommodate his very large family. Afterward, I would run into what was the main house where papa's quarters were.

When I entered my father's opulent bedroom, it was as if I had stepped into another world. The first thing that hit me was the welcome coolness of the room. His bed was the width of a mid-size room, and I would climb in and jump up and down until I got tired and then flop down like a rag doll, spent. Sometimes I fell asleep. Other times, my sisters were there, and we would create such a raucous, which Papa never seemed to mind. I guess when you have that many children, you develop superhuman abilities to block out noise and manage the endless demands they make.

Even though he was always surrounded by so many people, Papa always made sure he gave me his attention while I visited. As for me, I left everyone and everything behind when I was there with him. As soon as I saw him, I would hug him tightly as though he would disappear if I let go, like smoke between my fingers. There was innocence and joy in those embraces. I had not yet learned to fear grown men alone with small children. I had not yet had the need to scan my surroundings and ask questions or run. My eyes had not yet taken on the guarded look of children with secrets and invisible wounds.

Papa smelled of cigars and love and a hint of Campari, his favorite drink. "Tell me what you did in school today!" Papa's deep baritone would wash over me, and I, happy as a clam, told him stories. I told him about my teachers—the ones I liked and the ones I didn't. I told him about my friends, the ones who had been nice or mean. I talked about anything and everything. Sometimes I acted out plays we had done at school. I talked while he listened, smoked a Cuban cigar, and sipped his Campari.

Sometimes he took me to his office, and I would sit with him while he worked. Papa was a diamond magnate who had never had a formal education, yet there was no one smarter or savvier.

He traveled the world and always moved in circles of the most sophisticated and accomplished people. Women everywhere loved him. I even have a sister whose mother is white. Papa always dressed in the traditional embroidered loose gown and pants worn in hot climates by princes and rich men. He wore only white. I never saw him in another color.

Papa practiced Islam and went to the mosque for Jum'ah, a congregational prayer that Muslims hold on Fridays. Every Friday, he had a cow killed and distributed among the poor. It was not unusual to find him sitting on the floor in a circle eating from the same tray of food with men of all socioeconomic backgrounds. He treated everyone the same. You could only tell he was monied by the easy air about him.

One Friday, I found him sitting with a group of beggars. They had just finished eating together. I stared at him without announcing my presence for a long time in quiet pride and disbelief. He was my father. This man who was friends with big men and business partners, with important people and not-so-important people. He was my papa, and I loved him.

My sisters told me that the president of Sierra Leone visited Papa once and stayed in his home for a few days. They gushed about all the special foods and activities they enjoyed during the visit and how proud they had been to tell their friends at school that their papa was friends with the president of the country. How I envied them. Sometimes being the outside child means you miss out on a lot.

An African father's pride is to have a respectable family ask for the hand of his daughter in marriage. A woman who is not married and does not have a child suffers a sad fate, for she will be talked about, shunned, and sometimes labeled a witch. It is not what a parent wants for their daughter. A good dowry, a good bride-price, a good family name—these are symbolic of a family's success with having secured the future of their child by a good marriage. My father believed in education, so he sent all of his daughters to the best schools. In this and so many other ways, my papa was different. Most African men reserve education only for their boys.

I loved it when he took me places with him and showed me off. I sat among his friends—men who ran the government and determined destinies. I listened to their conversations with rapt attention and soaked in the plush atmosphere at the Whiskey A Go Go in Kono, my father's favorite club, with its heavy velvet curtains and well-dressed patrons. I knew even then that being allowed in this testosterone-dominated world was a great show of my father's indulgent affection for me.

Papa took great pride in telling his friends how clever I was. He told them that one day I was going to become his lawyer. "Look at her," he often said, "she is bold, talkative, and smart and always comes first in her class. She will make a very good lawyer and save me money when she grows up." They would all laugh and clink their glasses, drinking to my future successful law career.

In Africa, children are usually seen and not heard. A child or woman is only in the company of men to serve. Otherwise, they are usually expected to disappear quietly after the necessary, albeit unwelcome, interruption of bringing in food or fulfilling some other request.

But in Africa, people also give money to show love and affection, and Papa's friends demonstrated their affection for me with wads of notes they gave me for "lunch" each time they saw me, calling me their "book woman." At birth, you get money. You get married; you are given money. Someone dies, same thing. The best gift my father gave me was the high regard that he and his friends showed me in those early years of my life.

One afternoon, I was in Papa's office when somebody came to sell him diamonds. He looked at me, showed me the stones, and asked me how much I thought they were worth. I walked over to the safe and gathered as many bundles of Sierra Leone leones as I could and gave them to him. He looked at me and laughed indulgently. "Mama, if you keep giving away our money like that, soon we will be poor." (The term "mama" is used to show adoration and reverence for the grandmother, but it is also often used to show how much a parent loves their child by putting them on the same pedestal as their mother.) Papa gave the man all the money I had handed him. I do not think I have ever felt more important.

Papa had a great sense of humor and often teased me, too, saying, "You are so ugly you look like a man," referring to my features that were so unmistakably like his own. I was very much my father's daughter even though I had the dark brown, almost black, hue of my mother.

"Look at your teeth," he said, pointing to my unformed baby teeth. "Who is going to marry you? I would have to buy a house and a car and add some money to that and beg someone to take you off my hands." We would both collapse into laughter from his teasing. Memories of such moments with him held me together after he died, and the world shifted beneath my feet.

We did not have too much time together. I did not have enough of him before he was taken from me, but when I was with him, he made me feel special and more than loved—valued. When the circumstances of my life began to whittle me down to something unrecognizable and strip me of everything good, I would remember that I had once been valued by my papa and his friends. It helped me put one foot in front of another and survive a life that no longer seemed to have meaning.

All my father's children bear his very distinctive features; I am no exception. I have his big heart, but I am stubborn like him, too. Boyfriends I have had who've said as much are not wrong. I remember my first disagreement with my papa—it would be my last, too. I went for my usual weekend visit when I learned that Papa had taken a new wife. Many things had changed drastically. His attention was now firmly on her and children. Where before, there was some kind of harmonious chaos with his many wives and children, now there was tension you could cut through with a knife. Nobody was laughing. Worry was etched on every wife's face, and sadness, too. I felt it. I felt the subtle and not-so-subtle change in my papa. One day, I went to visit papa. It was a day that would change things between us forever. I greeted the wives as usual, and I greeted his new wife, too. I called her "Aunty." Papa did not like that. In polygamous homes in Sierra Leone and a few other parts of Africa, you are supposed to refer to all the wives of your father as "mama" or mother. It is a sign of respect. So, papa told me to greet her again and call her mama X. I refused and said she was not my mother. Papa got angry with me; I was defying him, embarrassing him even, by not doing as he had asked in front of his wives.

In most homes, no child would do that and survive. You would practically be skinned alive. Such defiance is not heard of and certainly not tolerated. He neither yelled at me nor hit me, which would have been the standard response of an African parent, especially a father. I told him I wanted to be taken back home to my mother and grandparents. He said, "Ok, if that is what you wish." The driver took me home. I was sad and angry, nothing like that had ever happened before.

I did not visit him for a long while after that. His new woman had changed our world. Papa was living solely for her and the children she bore him. He had chosen her, and it broke my heart. It was as if the rest of us no longer existed.

I saw my father just once more. I had gone with my mother to the blacksmith's shop in downtown Kono, where I was having a cast iron pot made so I would learn to cook. That was my one condition to learn to cook: a pot made especially for me that no one else would cook in but me. At that time, somewhere between eight and ten years old, I could still make certain demands on my mother's ever-shifting love.

My father and I met by chance; we were both surprised to see each other. He made his driver stop, got out of his car, leaned against the familiar Mercedes, and beckoned me to get in. I stood across the street from him and said, "No." He tried asking me other things, but I was sullen and did not want to talk to him. He asked me if I had changed my mind. I didn't ask him about what. We both understood what he was referring to. I hadn't changed my position and wouldn't go across the street to meet him. I was still angry with him, still holding the hard stance that petulant children take when they don't get their way. He stood and waited with the driver for quite some time, looking at me with an unreadable expression on his face. Then, without looking back, I turned and walked away.

A couple of years later, after someone told me that Papa had died, I played that scenario over and over again in my head. My last encounter with him had ended with me walking away, sad and angry. How I wish I could have parted from him differently. Had I broken his heart by walking away? Did he even care? Someone had already taken my place. He did not want me anymore. These are the things I told myself to make his loss bearable.

I can still smell strong coffee and the unmistakably elegant scent of pure Cuban tobacco when I look at the only photo I have of my papa.

Decades later, when I reconnected with some of my sisters. They shared their stories including some that gave me clarity. In a polygamous home such as my father's, it was not uncommon for a jealous stepmother to do black magic and use witchcraft to put a curse on the other wives' children. They were never to amount to anything and their destinies would be shaped by misfortune and failure. I lived that curse whether one or more wife was the reason for it or not.

CHAPTER 2

What's in a Name?

"Because it is my name! Because I cannot have
another in my life! Because I lie and sign myself to lies!
Because I am not worth the dust on the feet of them that
hang! How may I live without my name? I have
given you my soul; leave me my name!
~Arthur Miller, The Crucible

THERE IS A REASON EVEN PAGANS KNEW to name their children after gods. A name defines a person, and ancient peoples understood this. A name, like a face, is something one must carry everywhere, something that heralds or hinders one's entrance into a particular place or community.

Sometimes your name is the only thing others have to judge you by before they meet you. In Nigeria, the name "Ayomide" in Yoruba means "my joy has arrived;" "Imani" in Swahili means "faith;" "Nyandebo" from the Mende in Sierra Leone means "beautiful one." Each of these names speaks to the importance and symbolism of names. "Remilekun," meaning "stop my grief, " is given to a Yoruba child whose parents have had miscarriages or several children die. The parents name a child born under these circumstances this way and hope that this particular child will be the one to put an end to their pain by living and not dying like the others before him.

A name can also be a curse.

In Sierra Leonean culture, one is referred to as the "child of So-and-So." You are identified by your father's name, and your place in society is established because of your name. Marriages are often arranged based on lineage, so there is no you without your father's name. Children who are denied by their biological fathers because they are the product of an extra-marital affair are called "basta-pikin"—bastard. In essence: unwanted. They are irrefutable proof of indiscretions no one wants to admit to. This negation essentially erases any sense of who the child is as a person. It also leaves the child with no claim to any inheritance once the father dies. He or she is not recognized as a legitimate heir.

In my adolescent years after my father had been gone for a few years, my mother struggled with the financial demands of my education. When I returned from boarding school one holiday, my mother told me she had no money to pay my school fees for the next school year. She gathered my report cards, and we made rounds to some of my father's old friends to ask for help. She told them how well I was doing in school, showed them my results, and proudly shared that I had in fact just won a scholarship to go abroad for the summer. I had come in first among hundreds of children who had taken the foreign language exams. It was a huge deal. Not many people in Sierra Leone ever get to travel abroad, especially not when they are children. Papa's friends were happy and proud for me. They remarked about how grown up I was and said that they were not really surprised by my school results. "Lamin always said she was going to do well. We are still waiting for her to become a lawyer!" My throat filled, and I fought the tears, the pain, and the embarrassment of having to beg for money and wishing papa had never died in the first place. They gave my mother money for my school fees as some of their comrades who had not known my father looked on askance, confused. Papa's friends simply responded, "She is Lamin Simbakoro's daughter."

Once they remarry, most women in Africa who have one or more child outside of wedlock change the child's name to their current husband's name, serving two purposes. First, it is an effort to send a message to the new husband that they are giving them all they have, including their children. But it's also an effort to minimize the ridicule—or in some cases, very persistent negative feedback—from the husband's family who might not like the idea of their son taking care of someone else's children. There is also the irrefutable fact that their son has married a woman who was not a virgin and might even be "loose." To avoid being sentenced to single parenthood in a society that is very much against unmarried women, these women instead sacrifice their children, robbing them of their identity and any sense of belonging. After all, the children are rarely accepted by the new husband's family, and neither are they a part of their birth father's any longer since they are now called by another man's name.

Since my last name was changed to my stepfather's, I no longer had access to the power behind my father's name. And I no longer had access to my siblings or anything that defined me.

I grew up believing I had no value without my name and, because I had no value, I gave myself away casually, never asking for what I needed, usually simply happy to be acknowledged. No one ever had to earn my trust or deserve my love. I was worth nothing, so I expected nothing from anyone.

My circumstances changed even more after my father died and my mother remarried. In exchange for innocence, I was given a dream life. In exchange for my name, I got a pass that allowed me entrance into a world of private clubs, fancy cars, and the kind of life the kids in *Ferris Bueller's Day Off* lived. My stepfather was an engineer at the most renowned mining company at the time in Sierra Leone. Since I now bore his name, I had access to his line of credit and a host of other privileges. I only had to tell people that I was his child. I was Aladdin, and my stepfather's name was my genie.

The families who lived in the lavish bungalows of the National Diamond Mining Company were the envy of everyone who was not a part of that very exclusive world. It was as if the rich lifestyle of the wealthy and privileged in America had been lifted up like a portable home, transplanted in Sierra Leone, along with golf-courses, swiss bank accounts, and private chefs. Movie nights at the private movie house down the main drag of the huge down-town area; big birthday celebrations; overdone Christmas parties; bus drivers picking up families right in front of their house with just one telephone call; and stuffy, snobbish, rich kids in a world closed off to those who did not belong.

We had our own supermarkets as big as the Walmarts in America but with the pedigree of Whole Foods. We ate cornflakes and drank chocolate milk. We shopped in air-conditioned aisles while our schoolmates walked barefoot in the sweltering heat to the local markets after being at school all day—there to pick up a few cups of rice and a bottle of palm oil to spread on the rice if they were lucky and the little money they had covered it. Palm oil can be expensive; sometimes salt on rice was all they could afford. We sipped ice-cold Coca Cola in tall glasses that the well-dressed waiters brought us. We gave a glimpse of our world to the children we would sometimes invite to play, who would otherwise never walk into a ballroom or a members-only club party.

We would go to Yengema Club, the most popular of the clubs after school and ask the uniformed chefs to make us club sandwiches and whatever else we wanted. After, we would be handed a bill on which we signed our fathers' names, and their accounts would be charged for whatever we had spent. We would make a great show of it as our invited guests looked on in awe, noticing that no money had left our hands to pay for the food and drinks we had ordered all afternoon, sometimes barely even touching them.

We played tennis, squash, and endless board games. My friend Sibana was a master Scrabble player, and she always beat the boys, even up until we went to college. I never developed her passion for it.

The grown-ups played golf on the private course, which Sibana and I sometimes vandalized by peeing behind the well-tended bushes, laughing and praying the grounds men did not see us. On really hot days, we would lounge by the pool, making exaggerated moves with our bony hips, sashaying like we'd seen the older girls do, hoping that the boys would look at us.

Sibana was not a part of this group. She always seemed complete and contained within herself, and, for all the years I have known her, I have never seen her peddle her wares in exchange for love. Perhaps that was why I wanted to be so much like her and why I always wanted to be around her. Maybe some of her self-assuredness would rub off on me. Every year, the company had lavish Christmas parties and presents which a very blond Santa in a sea of African children would give out. I always felt out of place and uncomfortable when my name was called to shake Santa's hand and get my present. I felt like a fraud knowing that although I had his name, I was not my stepfather's child and had no right to get a present. I was my papa's child and would always be, and deep inside, it hurt to no longer be called by his name.

I began to hate my mother then. She had taken the only thing I had left that gave my life definition.

One Christmas, after the presents had been opened and families were socializing with music, food, dancing, I escaped unnoticed and walked out to the lawn so I could sit on the swing and watch the pool. I always liked the blue of the pool, perhaps because it mirrored the blue of my soul. I saw a couple of other kids scattered about, and though I really did not want company, it was nice to ask someone to push me on the swing. The creaking rhythmic sound of the swing felt strangely comforting, and the creaking drowned out the laughter in the hall.

"Push me higher," I told the little brown girl with the bright yellow ribbons in her pigtails. She had wandered over to me, and I wondered why she wasn't inside with the others. Perhaps she, too, had secrets. She pushed me, and again I told her to push harder as I enjoyed the rush of cool breeze against my face and the feeling of being lifted and carried away.

"Push with all your strength!" I shouted, almost laughing. It was the closest to feeling happy I had come in a long time. I wanted to fly far away, straight into the sky, but she was taking too long.

"Push!" I begged. She pushed. She was surprisingly strong for one so little. Then I flew off the swing and fell hard on my arm.

I heard screams—some were my own, and some must have been from the other children who had seen me fall. Someone alerted the parents that there had been an accident on the swing, and most of them came running to look for their child.

I heard someone say, "That arm is definitely broken." I suppose the angle looked unnatural, even from an untrained eye. It was. I had broken my arm very badly in several places and had to wear a cement cast that covered my whole arm for six months in 90-degree plus weather. But what hurt the most was not the hell of wearing that heavy, uncomfortable cast in sweltering heat. It was not the excruciating pain and sleeplessness of the first few weeks if I held my arm a certain way. It was not trying the agony of trying to scratch the itch in places I couldn't reach or the embarrassment and shame I felt each time I went to the bathroom and someone had to help me clean myself. It was the fact that I had called attention to myself that hurt the most. All I had wanted was to be invisible.

There was one use of my card with my stepfather's name on it that did bring me joy. It was the only thing in the uneven exchange that kept me somewhat sane. It gave me access to the library. I would run to the library after school every day, scour the shelves like a hungry dog, and lose myself in the rows and rows of books in the ornate hall. I could never have enough. I discovered worlds that were magical, happy, and hopeful. I discovered worlds that were not like mine. I discovered beautiful worlds. I read almost everything I could lay my hands on and checked out as many books as I was allowed to. In the beginning, I read Agatha Christie and Virginia Andrews. Sibana introduced me to her and loved her books.

Sibana, like my books, was life for me. She was not just my friend. We connected in ways that every lonely child needs at that tender blooming of young womanhood. She was like the sister I never had—without the rivalry and with all the benefits. She was my doppelganger—another word she taught me. A dead ringer for Angela Bassett, she had her legendary cheekbones, cat eyes, and skin the color of caramel.

Sibana opened new worlds to me. She had lived in America and was well-traveled and very sophisticated. I wanted to sound like her—proper, British, smart , confident. Once, we were looking at a perfume ad by Gucci, and I told her excitedly, "I like that Goosey ad! The models are so perfect!" She smiled and patiently explained that, in Latin or Italian, words like "Gucci" aren't pronounced like they are spelled. I made many such mistakes, but she never laughed at me or made fun of me as children often do. I learned. Embarrassed sometimes, yet happy, I knew that this friend offered an opportunity; I had a lot to learn from her. We read a lot and exchanged books. I would never have read Virginia Andrews had it not been for her.

Those nuanced descriptions of trapped children finally coming out of the attic and into the light had some psychological impact. Perhaps one day, I too would come out of my own attic. I read hundreds of books from all different genres. I read the classics and poetry and politics. I spent countless hours lost in the funny Nigerian comics about pa Jimoh and boy Alinco, an unwitting playboy who always got into trouble. They were hilarious and entertaining, never serious. I was not aware of many African writers. I devoured Chinua Achebe's classic, *Things Fall Apart* and Ola Rotimi's *The Gods Are Not To Blame* wanted more. I loved *So Long A Letter* by Mariama Ba, the only female African writer I knew of. If there had been more African writers, or if their works had been as readily available, I doubt I would have been as drawn. We humans are curious about the unfamiliar. I read about Marilyn Monroe and became obsessed, but my favorite book of all was *The Arabian Nights*. I must have read it dozens of times, and, to this day, I still go back to some of the stories I could never get enough of.

I have a copy of an old special edition I found in an old bookstore and have given it to my son. We have read some of the stories together. I loved the language as a child and the morals behind the stories. The acts of valor and bravery, romance, and reverence, seduced me. I loved that people could live and die for ideals. I loved imagining myself a Bedouin princess being carried off by my prince because he was bold and bad and wanted me above all. He would risk everything for me. I wanted someone to risk everything for me.

I read Barbara Cartland and was swept away. What was an African girl doing reading books about countesses in powdered wigs, fainting spells, rich princes, ball gowns, and love? What did I know of such worlds? I read *A Woman of Substance* by Barbara Taylor Bradford and vowed to one day be such a woman. Sibana and I unwittingly predicted that we, like the two friends in the book, were going to be separated, and by the time we came back together, we would have accomplished great things. That's exactly what happened. Well, not exactly. Life is never that simple. Sibana left for England during our second year of college, and I did not see her for almost a decade. By the time we saw each other again, she was a very accomplished woman of means, and I was barely managing to remember my own name. Though we still cared deeply for each other, we had both changed. Things never got back to the way they were before. In a way, I lost her, too.

Writing down my thoughts was not something I planned to do. It happened by chance. Reading came first. I needed a place to escape, something to make my small, lonely world tolerable. In the beginning, books provided a sanctuary for me. Later, the words found a way to me, twinning themselves around me like clinging vines, refusing to let go. I would read a book, and a line would stick in my head. I would find myself repeating it to myself over and over again. It was like music that I could not get enough of. The words on the pages drummed out other ones and left me drunk and happy and wanting more. Keats "Beauty is truth, truth beauty." Thomas Hastings' "Rock of Ages, cleft for me, let me hide myself in thee." Khalil Gibran's "and forget not that the earth delights to feel your bare feet and the winds long to play with your hair." These were among my favorites in those early years.

I loved the way the words danced and moved and changed meaning just by the way they were strung together or placed in a certain order. I loved the fact that as long as the words came from my books, those in my ear disappeared. So, I kept reading. I discovered that words had power. They could create worlds, give reprieves, and birth new realities. They could make one forget and hope and dream. Perhaps if I found mine, I could have power, too. I wanted power, but where was I going to find it? I waited, read, waited, and read some more. Then one day, I knew where the words were. They were hiding in my feelings. If I could find my feelings, then I could find the words. It was not hard to do. My feelings were close by .The words came rushing like a raging river and swept me away. It did not take long for them to become so much a part of me that I cannot now remember myself without them. Words have saved my life and given me magic.

Given my extroverted behavior, most people would be shocked to discover that I am very shy and easily embarrassed. Having perfected the art of masquerade during my early years, I often did not know who my real self was. I was a series of fragments strung together by the love of strangers and held in place by grace. I was the many lies and stories and characters I lived and played—and still, I was none of those.

At the same time, sex was not simple for me. I could not create an alternate reality or run away from some cold facts. I was not complete as a woman. When I was around 15, I realized that I had much to learn about sex after a significant event occurred that would forever define me as a woman.

I had many conversations about sex with older, married women—my mentors and friends—most of whom were also very lonely and unfulfilled sexually and otherwise. From that, I realized that since books allowed me to discover other realities, I might also discover things about sex that these women did not know. Fear and inadequacy powered my need to study the topic. If the pleasure part would be forever lost to me, I thought, I could at least gain understanding. Perhaps if I understood sexuality, I could compete with other normal women. I had too much going against me already. Even at that early age, I understood that sex and money ruled the world, and I wanted access to both.

I searched for books on psychology and sexuality. At night, while my mother, stepfather and two brothers slept, I read the books I had snuck in and hidden under the blankets, eating up the pages long after the lights were turned off and the silence of the night settled me into rest. It was my favorite time; I was alone. I would hold a torchlight to the pages or sometimes light a candle and read until it was morning or until the flame got smaller and smaller, and I could no longer make out the words on the pages.

I read about ancient cultures and their approach to sex. I read about geishas in Japan and the gods and goddesses of India's Kamasutra. I was fascinated to learn about kundalini and tantric sex. I was drawn to the importance of seduction and wanted to be versed in the art of it. I also discovered there were other worlds, like the ones in *Fifty Shades of Grey*, where pleasure and pain combined. But they frightened me, and I did not spend a lot of time reading about them. I learned anatomy and studied physiology. I made discoveries about mind-body connections. I learned that the roots of pleasure were buried deep. I learned about people who were asexual and those who could not get enough of sex. I read about promiscuity, perversion, and the sacredness of sex. Sometimes I would practice what I had read as best as I could. Growing up in Africa, most girls get introduced to some sort of same-sex experience. A girl would have a "girlfriend" or "fejeh" in those days. Someone who was your girl crush. You would kiss and perhaps touch lightly or just know that they were your "special friend." They were still mostly innocent explorations. I remember never ever wanting anyone to touch me, but I was happy to indulge someone and use the opportunity to investigate what I had learned.

If you touch here, this happens. If you gently blow air on these areas of exposed flesh, tiny bumps suddenly appear and cover the skin like soldiers at attention. If you whisper in someone's ear too closely, there would be giggles of joy and sometimes small moans of pleasure. It was scary and empowering to see that my actions could change outcomes. The most important discovery I made from those explorations was learning that pleasure was more a mental activity than a physical one. If you could train your mind, your body would follow. I was elated. I wanted more than anything else to not be inadequate as a lover when the time came.

I was happy to learn that all had not been lost, that if I worked hard at training my mind, I could master one of the things that run the world. Making money was going to be next on my list. Papa was gone, and I was a bastard with no claim to his property. The way things were looking with my mother—and the situation with her new husband who drank too much and scared me—I knew I was going to have to secure a future for myself. No one was going to take care of me.

I started to develop an obsession. I wanted to be perfect, yet I was tainted and undefined. Having no name and with parts of me gone, I was always trying to overcompensate. I told myself I needed a little leverage to survive life; but sadly no amount of trying and succeeding would ever be enough. The more I tried, the less I felt enough. It was a race that never seemed to end.

But love was easy for me. I fell in love with whoever smiled long enough at me. I remember the first time I met Miss Marian. I was at boarding school.

I had been taken from the only people I had known—Papa, my grandmother, and Bollywood Aunty Emmah—and forced to move in with two strangers. One was my mother. The other was the new husband she had brought with her from Freetown, along with her shorthand certificate from the school she had left me to attend. Then my stepfather decided that I was too attached to my mother and needed to be taught a lesson. I did not understand the logic since my mother had been away for most of the first few years of my life.

Everywhere my mother took me, people remarked on her beauty and how much I resembled her. I loved hearing about a connection between us—if only in looks. I could not get enough of her; I was in a constant state of wonder. Was this woman truly my mother? Perhaps it was this perpetual hunger for my mother, hunger to absorb her, to make her see and want me, that got me sent away. Perhaps my undisguised longing was something too ugly of a spectacle for my new father.

"You're going away. Far. You're too spoiled," he said.

I did not understand how I was spoiled, but I made no attempt to explain myself or defend my need for my mother. How could I begin to tell him that although I had enjoyed going to the cinema with my aunt, I had been counting the years for my mother to finish school and come back for me? Or that no amount of roast beef had been able to replace the scent of her? My stepfather worked for the mines, and his job took him to different towns. He was the one who would take me to my new school—the one he had suggested. I had to spend a weekend alone with him before we drove to the boarding home which was hundreds of miles away .

I never spoke of that weekend until years later, but it had left a mark. When I got to school, I prayed the mark was invisible even though I felt that everyone could see it. I would be quiet and smile and do well in class and behave. I would not call attention to myself. I thought that if I became invisible just enough, no one would see me or the mark. I knew I could not tell my mother or anyone. It was the first of many masks I created.

Miss Marian was my first love. She was our boarding school mistress, a young woman in her early twenties who could have been on a dark and lovely ad for hair straightener with her strikingly beautiful face and very white teeth. She always smiled at me and made me feel special. She never raised her voice at me as she gave instructions. "Make your beds please and form a line," she said each morning to rouse tired sleepy pubescent and teenage girls. Others like me were still between the ages of eight and 11. Her gentle tone was a welcome one from the harsh and scary one at home and gave my nerves a very welcome rest. After making the beds, it was prayer time, and then it was time to wash up and get dressed for school. Next was breakfast in the dining hall with the boys. The few times the boys and girls were permitted to be together were for mealtimes and classroom time. Miss Marian would smile at me while reminding me of something or the other I needed to complete or had forgotten to do. I never heard a word she said. I was completely wrapped up in the warmth of her smile.

I would go about my day thinking about her smile. She likes me, I told myself. It was a wonderful feeling. Sometimes after Compline and the one hour of reading allowed just before the lights were turned off for bedtime, she would gesture to me to follow her. Her quarters were just a few feet away from the dormitory; she could always hear the girls and be very near in the event of an emergency. She told me stories, asked how my day was, and gave me candy. She told me to do well because I was smart and would make my parents proud if I did well. I felt at rest with her. There, my mask came off. It was as if I needed her to be able to breathe easy in my new home, with the weight of my secret and the pain of being separated yet again from my mother. She must have sensed something abnormal about me but never asked me any questions. She did not seem to mind my need for her.

Even after all these years, I think of Miss Marian with gratitude. I wonder if she ever knew how important she was to me, how impactful her gentle care would become on my confused, hurt, child's heart. She gave me the first glimpse of simple, pure love. She will never know how I felt when every hope of her finding my secret and making it go away so I wouldn't have to hide any more faded. Miss Marian will never know she saved my life those first few months when my heart was frozen with terror, and my belief in grown-ups shattered.

I met Patrick, my second love, a few months later. He was tall for his age, which I estimated to be 11. He was bronze-colored and spoke in a lazy drawl that sounded pleasing even to my young ears. Something in his voice made me want to be pretty. He was soft-spoken and always got the answers right when the teacher called on him to answer a question in class. I was drawn to Patrick in a way I could not explain. I knew a lot of the other girls liked him—girls who were not like me and didn't have secrets.

Patrick's father and my stepfather worked for the same company, so we ran into each other frequently at social events and parties during the holidays when we were home from school. I steered clear of him. I suspected even then that liking a boy and showing them so led to trouble. Besides, I had developed very confusing feelings about the opposite sex and did not know how to be around them. Patrick courted me like a gentleman, even when he was merely a boy, and he grew up to become one. He never pushed me to try something, to play "house", or play Mom and Dad, or play doctor-patient or tried "you show me this, and I'll show you that." The games children devise and play to explore their sexuality. At boarding school, I would spend a little time with him between classes, but I was too shy and too afraid to get too close. But I knew I loved him, and he seemed to feel the same. He usually left all the other girls at lunchtime and came to sit with me.

Then, one day, he planted an awkward kiss on my lips. It was my first. We never did anything more than that, but I know that if I had let myself—if I had let him when we got older—he would have loved me even with my brokenness. He was that kind of soul.

Years later, my supposition was confirmed. Patrick and I met at Christmas parties year after year as I flowered into young womanhood, went to middle school, high school, then college. Still, I kept him at a distance. Then, in my second year at college, I had my first profound experience of depression and a deep, deep longing to die. I wrote something in my journal, titled, "What it takes to be alive?" I do not know how Patrick got to read it, but he wrote to me on a yellow piece of paper. "It takes desire and determination," he said. Simple, uncomplicated, and wise—just like him. He was kind to me.

But Patrick must have been too good for me. I seemed to attract boys who would bruise my spirit and bring out every insecurity I ever had. The ones who would ravage my psyche and heart with no mercy. I felt at home with that kind of boy. Pain, disrespect, abandonment, and competition were familiar places for me. I would love the men who were dating multiple young women or the men who had wives and were therefore unavailable. I would make them want me. I would make them see that I was more, that I had more to offer.

I behaved wildly in college. I was not promiscuous, but I made it seem like I was. Some people thought I was the college slut. I flirted outrageously, danced provocatively at parties, yet inside I was scared and did not want anything to do with sex. Though I felt sullied, I wanted to save what was left of me for marriage. I wanted to give myself willingly to one man and one man alone. Every day, I prayed to God to make me everything some man desires so that he will love me and never want to leave me. Make me the perfect wife to make up for everything imperfect about me. While everyone in college thought I was busy sexing my way through school, I was trying to perfect myself for love. Real grown-up love.

I remember my first bad boy, Roy. Though not handsome, he had a certain animal magnetism that was irresistible. Dark, tall, and very masculine, he oozed sex as he walked, and he knew it. I knew he was trouble when we met at a fraternity party. His six-foot-plus hunky frame moved into the room with such deliberate ease that I was completely seduced before he even walked over and asked me to dance. It was unforgettable. I have only danced like that one other time—when it felt like there was no one else in the room but my dance partner and me. That night, Roy and I danced and practically made love on the dance floor. Move for move, we matched each other. I felt suffused with heat and was shocked by my desire for him.

It was the first time I had ever experienced lust. It felt good yet scary, and it made me feel womanly and somehow whole. I was drunk with the joy of being admired, and I wanted more. It was as though I had been ushered out into the sun after being in a cold, dark room: I could feel the heat warming up parts of me that had been frozen for a long time. I never wanted to not be in the sun again. We spent most of the night dancing, eyes locked with an unspoken understanding that there was no going back.

It was the beginning of a tumultuous love affair. He was a couple of years older than me, and I eventually found out that he had a girlfriend. Once I knew that, it was on. I would make him want me. I would take him away from her. He would be mine and mine alone. We danced around the edges of our lust for each other, get close, but not consummate our relationship for a long time.

Violence was common practice for Roy, and, in the beginning, I had loved it. It was thrilling to me to be roughly pulled out of a bus or slapped in front of a group of other students because I had been "bad" for talking to another boy. To me, it was a sign we had a "real" relationship. I enjoyed hearing him say, "You're mine." No one had ever claimed me before.

I would not have sex with him for many reasons. I wanted him to think I was easy and show him how far from true that I was. I was trying to prove something. I'll never forget the look on his face almost two years later when I finally said "Yes," and he understood he would be the first man I'd go all the way with. He had believed some of the rumors about me. Now, he told me he had a whole new level of respect for me. He gave me a card for Valentine's Day that read, "To a wildcat, You were worth the wait."

Inevitably, though, he broke my heart as I knew he would. After too many nights of feeling the same old feelings of loss and not being really wanted or important, I finally worked up the courage to leave him. He stayed with his girlfriend and later married her. I heard they moved to Switzerland and had kids but later divorced. He is now with a young woman almost half his age, and I am not surprised. Women always loved him.

While Roy had the kind of animal magnetism that made my blood boil, Adonis, my half-Russian boyfriend after Roy, had the sensuality of soul that eased my spirit and calmed my nerves. I had no competition for Adonis—I was queen of his heart, and he let the whole world know it. He was sweet, sexy, and good, not to mention beautiful. Cropped curly hair on a perfectly molded head, a dashing smile that lit up his green-gold eyes—the color that most mixed-race African children possess—and a strapping frame he was already building at the gym in preparation for joining the military. He had full lips that begged for kissing each time I looked at them. He was a dream. The childlike adoration that he lavished on me after my affair with Roy was a balm on my being. He never slapped me to show me I was his "woman" like Roy did, and I never had to worry which one of my friends he would sleep with next.

Adonis had to woo both my heart and psyche to make me put Roy in the past, and he succeeded. Everything was perfect except that his Russian mother hated me and threatened to kill me if I did not leave her son alone. She had married a Sierra Leonean on a scholarship in her country. She followed him to Africa after she had been disowned by her Russian family for dating a Black man. She told me she had gone to a juju man, and he had told her that I was an enchantress. She wanted me out of her son's life. She would stand at the bus stop for students going to the university and ask them, "Do you know that girl?" after saying my name. "That whore?" she would add.

I do not know what it is about me that makes people want to call me that. Adonis' mother harassed me to no end. She told him that she would never accept me even though she was married to Adonis's father, a Sierra Leonean. But as much as she tried to break us up, she could not. She gave up. Her son loved me too much.

It was a beautiful love and would have lasted if Adonis had not had to leave for Turkey soon after we fell in love. He joined the army and got a scholarship to study in exchange for some years in service. We never reconnected once he left. He stayed in touch that first year and sent me beautiful postcards and wrote long letters professing his love and naming the children we would have someday. He even bought me a promise ring made of gold with tiny diamonds. Then the letters got more infrequent and eventually stopped coming. In one letter, he warned me that the man I had fallen in love with no longer existed. It would be wrong to cheat me of him. It would be best if I forgot him.

His was the kind of love that made me want to believe in fairy tales. He was my prince. I had felt a deep connection to him and a freedom with him I had felt with no one to that point. I did not have to pretend to be a sex-pot or play my "bad girl" persona that I had developed in an effort to make men love me. His loving was good and easy, and, for the first time, I wanted "good and easy" in a man. The bad boy desire had lost its appeal.

One afternoon when we were still together, I knew he was going to come to see me after lectures, so I straightened up the small room I shared with a roommate. The students at the college shared an understanding of certain cues to indicate when a room-mate needed privacy. The other roommate would disappear or gave an excuse for leaving and wouldn't show up until the next day. So, I had the room to myself that day, and I wanted to surprise Adonis.

I took a risk and did not lock the door, praying no one would barge in as I prepared for Operation Shock and Seduce. In Africa, there is no word for privacy. People show up at your door when-ever, however they want, with no notice and no explanation. When they show up, you let them in, offer food or drink, and they can stay as long as they want. It is the African way. For that reason, I am sure there are many millions of coituses interruptus as a result of this tradition. I was lucky that day because my surprise would have been ruined if someone other than the person for whom the surprise was intended walked in.

A firm knock on the door interrupted my reverie.

"Is it you?" I asked in a low, deliberate voice, knowing full well who it was. His knock was very distinctive. Besides, I was expecting him.

"Yes, it's me, my love."

"Come in," I said, my voice liquid as warmed honey.

He opened the door to find me lying on the narrow bed with a wicked smile on my lips, smelling good from my Palmolive shower, and shining like a new penny from being oiled with shea butter in all the right places. No ashiness for me that day—a condition common to black skin when it gets dry. I had also powdered other places that needed powdering to avoid sweating in the hot afternoon heat and ruining my look. I forced my mind to believe I looked like a Nubian queen so I could pull the whole thing off.

My eyes never left his as he walked slowly, as in a trance, toward the bed.

"Lock the door," I told him urgently. "Lock it before someone comes."

He bolted the door hurriedly and came to me. He could not take his eyes off the picture between my legs.

There were hibiscus bushes of the most glorious shades of pinks and reds growing about campus. I had been walking back to my room from class earlier that afternoon and happened to pass a spectacular display of them. I plucked one. It had not adorned my hair.

Hours later, after wild and passionate sex, he held my face in his hands and asked me, "Do you know why I love you so much?"

"Why?" I asked, basking in the afterglow of our loving.

"There is no one like you in the world," he said, smiling, his tender gaze melted my heart. "Who besides you would have thought to beautify a flower?"

Not long after that, he left to travel abroad. Once again, I was left behind, feeling I can never hold on to anyone I love for long. They always leave.

CHAPTER 3

The Many Faces of War

WHAT IS IT ABOUT ME AND LOVE AND BETRAYAL? I love my mother, and she betrayed me. I had loved Salone, as Sierra Leoneans affectionately call Sierra Leone, but she, too, betrayed me. I loved her welcoming, friendly people, white sand beaches, freshwater fish, and breathtaking sunsets. I had been grateful for her many natural resources—gold, bauxite, iron ore, and her magnificent diamonds, both world-known and world-class. I admired her coffee plantations and tropical climate. I had been grateful that I was born there—until her jewels became conflict diamonds that had paid for the slaughter of her own citizens. I loved her until her once-peaceful people became strangers capable of the unthinkable.

Sierra Leone, a country in West Africa, was discovered in 1462 by Portuguese explorer Pedro de Sintra, who named it Serra Lyoa, "Lion Mountains," for the shape of the hills that surround it.

Sierra Leone has special significance in the history of the transatlantic slave trade because it is both blessed with and cursed with sitting on the Atlantic. It served as the departure point for thousands of Western Africans captured and loaded onto the slave ships that took off for Britain and the Americas. Ironically, in 1787, the capital, Freetown, was founded as a home for repatriated former slaves.

When I was born, Sierra Leone was a peaceful, small country with a population of four million. With neighbors like Liberia, Senegal, and Guinea, there was a *joie de vivre*, a peacefulness that gave Sierra Leone its allure as a destination to foreign investors and tourists alike. Gambians, Ghanaians, Nigerians, and other countries in Africa sent their students to Sierra Leone since it boasted the best university in West Africa, Fourah Bay College, my alma mater. Founded in 1827, and touted as the "Athens of West Africa," it was the oldest university in West Africa.

Like most parts of Africa, Sierra Leone is loaded with minerals and a wealth of other natural resources, all of which corrupt politicians use to enrich themselves. Most of them have fancy homes all over Europe, send their children to expensive schools abroad, and boast of huge offshore bank accounts, while most people barely have 20 cents a day to live on. When I was little, Sierra Leone was beautiful and had never known war until it opened its arms and welcomed the refugees fleeing the civil war in Liberia in 1996. Some people regret this act of generosity and blame Liberians for the war that ensued in Sierra Leone. Once the fighting spilled over the borders into Sierra Leone, it didn't take long for Sierra Leoneans to get stirred up to fight against the increasing gap between rich and poor. But how did they go from rebelling against their government to turning against each other?

How did we become monsters who chopped off limbs of toddlers and cut babies out of their mother's bellies while they were still alive? How did we become "them"—Rwanda, Somalia, Auschwitz? Why did we have to join the group of countries that would be remembered for their cruelty and crimes against humanity? How desperately wicked the heart is. I met Ishmael Beah, author of *Memoir of a Boy Soldier,* when he came to San Francisco on a book tour. He is a Sierra Leonean who had been captured and forced into a life of horrors when just a little boy. We talked and cried and laughed a little. I could not believe young boys nine years of age, some even younger, were given guns and asked to shoot their own parents. I could not believe that some were told to perform sexual acts with a parent while the other watched. There were many accounts of unimaginable acts of savagery. Where was the Salone I knew and loved?

I was born here. Part of me has died here, too.

I remember one day, years before the war. My best friend, Sibana, had gone to the beach after class and came back full of excitement, telling me that she had tasted heaven on the beach. Lumley Beach was the primary beach area at the time. There were restaurants and clubs spread all along the shore with its white sand and ocean vistas, attracting rich white men who came to enjoy the scene and its young women. On some weekends, Sibana and I would take the bus down to the beach to relax or go clubbing after a hard week of studies. It was heaven to kick off our shoes and run barefoot along the beach in the cool sand on balmy nights as the happy laughter of people drinking and having fun made us feel a part of something wonderful.

You could see the prostitutes with their short skirts, painful heels, and hungry eyes waiting for a prospect. We stayed as far away from them as we could. Some college students were said to get some of their college fees from the men who came to buy pleasure. We were careful not to give off that vibe.

For some reason, Sibana had gone without me that day, the day she told me about her experience on the beach. It was unusual since we spent almost all of our time together except during lectures. We did not have the same classes; I doubt we would have been able to focus much. We were always talking or giggling or exchanging books. Sibana was in the science department, and I was in arts and political science.

"Girl, I had the most extraordinary experience," she said.

"Tell me," I said. I was dying to know because Sibana was not easily moved. Even in the days when we were still young and impressionable, she was reserved and did not exhibit emotions like I am wont to do. She was careful while I could be gullible and naive.

"I had ice cream and popcorn together," she whispered. I frowned in amazement. Before I could ask, *are you kidding? Ice cream and popcorn is what is making you crazy like this?* she continued in a dreamy voice.

"The popcorn was hot and salty and, as I was chewing, I absent-mindedly licked some ice cream. The most incredible feeling of pleasure covered my mouth. I did not expect it. The crunch and saltiness of the corn mixed with the sweet creaminess of the ice cream were out of this world. Never have I tasted anything so delicious!"

My mouth watered as I listened. I was both jealous and happy and could not wait to go to Lumley Beach to have my own ice cream and popcorn experience. But it was not to be. I did not have it until later, here in America, and it was not the same. By the time

I got back to Lumley Beach years later, when it was again possible to fly home, there were noticeably clear signs that life as we Sierra Leoneans had known it was gone. There were no more beachfront restaurants and clubs—some had been destroyed by rebels, and others had simply been abandoned by their owners, who had fled the war. No people were playing on the beach or fishermen casting their nets, no sound of music blaring from boomboxes, no happy tourists. No children were running barefoot or selling gum and cigarettes from their mini stores, with expertly balanced trays they carried on their heads. There were no signs of life along the now debris-covered shores.

In the early 90s, Sierra Leone was named the poorest country in the world—with all of her diamonds and mineral resources, not to mention her coffee plantations and her wealth of seafood. If she had been named the poorest country before the war, how much further back had the complete devastation of the ten-year civil war taken it? With her buildings burned down, government structures destroyed, with her army of limbless orphans parading the streets, Sierra Leone was a sorrowful sight to behold.

That once-beautiful place the actor Djimon Hounsou had described as "paradise" in the movie *Blood Diamond* was no longer that. It was a hellhole with the tell-tale signs that the devil had visited and played hard there.

CHAPTER 4

Real Women Don't Cry

ONE SUMMER, WHEN I WAS 10, my grandmother told me that my cousins and I would be going away for a while to the village where she was born. I asked her why. I was always asking questions back then—before I learned that some questions are better left unasked, and some answers cannot be survived.

"You are going to become a woman."

"Am I not a woman?" I said flippantly, referring to our shared female- hood.

"No. You're a girl. After you come back, you will be a woman like me."

"How so?"

"You are going to be initiated into the Sande society."

"What is that?"

"You will see," she said, smiling, and I knew she wasn't going to say more.

I went to my friend Miriam's house. She was a slight, half-Lebanese, mulatto girl whose house was a ten-minute walk from my grandmother's. Miriam was one of those girls whom everyone wanted to be like. Her parents were rich. They had servants and air-conditioning and TV. They sometimes showed movies in the evenings, and most of the neighborhood street kids were permitted to sit on the floor of their veranda and watch. It was a treat since most of them would never step foot in a movie theatre in their lifetime. Miriam was lucky. She had curly, reddish-brown, almost-white-people hair. Silky. Not nappy. We sometimes played after school, and her family liked me a lot. They thought I was smart, so they approved of our friendship.

Most African parents will compare you to their neighbors' or relatives' children. "Look at Mama Bintu's children! They always have high marks in school. Very clever girls. One day those girls will do great things for her." Sometimes it was: "I don't want your friend coming here. She's not serious—her eyes are on her forehead, and her family has a bad name." A girl whose "eyes are on her forehead" was one who was already zeroing in on boys. Friendships were approved of or discouraged based on potential or foresight that a girl who talks back and wears lipstick will most likely end up pregnant at 15 and was therefore not welcome.

Miriam and I walked to the street corner and bought freshly roasted groundnuts that were still hot enough to burn our fingers when we tried to peel them.

I told her I was going away and that by the time I saw her again, I would be a woman.

"What do you mean by that?" she teased. "Do you have a banana and two oranges between your legs?" We both burst out in high girlish laughter.

"I am going to the Sande bush."

A look of alarm came over her face, and she abruptly stopped laughing.

"Oh, no! You can't go there!"

I wondered why not. The Sande bush was known as a special place where an important rite of passage was performed.

"You can't go," she repeated almost in tears. "Please don't go? Promise you won't go!"

I listened in disbelief. My friend was pleading with me to not participate in something that was clearly going to change things for me for the better.

"Why?" I asked, my tone superior and not in the least bit curious. I knew she was jealous because I was going somewhere that would permit me to sit with the grown-ups and have grown women's conversations after I came back. It was a position that would give me entrance into the world of women. I had seen the way girls were treated after they came back from the bush. They were in a separate class from the rest of us. It was as if a new secret code had been established. All of a sudden, they no longer wanted to play with us. Their haughty looks made us feel small and irrelevant, and they found every excuse to tell us, "You're still only a child. What do you know?" when we attempted to have any kind of conversation with them.

They all went to the river to bathe or fetch water together. We were not included, and, sometimes as soon as we approached, they would stop talking or giggling and signal quiet to each other, and we were left feeling humiliated and excluded.

"Why, Miriam?" I asked again. "Aren't you my friend? Why don't you want me to go?" She beckoned me to come closer and whispered something in my ear. I scoffed.

"That's not true. You are just making that up because you're jealous. Because you are still going to be a girl after I come back. And I will be a woman," I said, no longer able to keep my suspicions to myself.

Stung by my words, she started to cry. I turned and walked away. How cruel children can be. I was no exception.

Weeks later, after we had traveled the 200-plus miles in chartered buses to a remote part of the village where the ceremony took place, I would be the one crying and wishing that I had listened to her. But even if I had listened to her, what could I have done to avoid what followed? What power does a child have in a grown up's world?

We were taken to the outskirts of the village to a secluded area, deep in the forest, to the Sande house. It looked menacing. It was the largest hut I had ever seen, with browning palm fronds for a roof. It made me think how clever the people who made the roof must have been as they could weave leaves together so tightly that rain could not pass through them. We were led into the house, which only had one massive room and a dirt floor. There was no furniture and no electricity. It was clear that all 30 of us children and the many adults who had accompanied us would be sharing this space. *It's going to be a long couple of weeks,* I thought to myself. The only source of comfort was the fact that my mother, grandmother, and aunts were all there.

Initiation is an essential rite of passage into womanhood for most African girls in Sierra Leone and other parts of Africa, while the ceremony itself varies from tribe to tribe and country to country. Families spend years preparing for the event. The wealthier the family, or the older the name of the family, the bigger the prepa-rations. Traditional woven cloths, passed down from generation to generation, are taken out of their hiding places—old trunks reeking of camphor and opened only on special occasions like marriages, deaths, and initiation ceremonies. Beautiful, elaborate gowns and dresses are made for each girl. Fine gold and silver jewelry were specially designed by the goldsmith for the initiates. We somehow got glimpses of the fineries while we helped them pack for the trip to the bush. Looking back, I can see that they were used as a kind of bribe to get us excited. What young girl did not want new clothes and fine jewelry?

In anticipation of the large crowds expected to greet us when we returned, to be ushered back into society as women after weeks of seclusion in the Sande bush, huge quantities of bushmeat were purchased, palm wine, beer, and all kinds of special occasion deli-cacies were set aside for the festivities. It is not uncommon to have a few "relatives" you could not place show up since most Africans would be loath to miss a party. A suspicious family member would say to the unknown relative, "Tell me again—You are...?" And the questionable guest would respond, "Oh, I am your grandfather's cousin's brother's daughter. Don't you remember me? You used to be a very handsome boy when you were little." There would be a quick frown at the blatant lie, but since there was always plenty of food, the family member played along and welcomed the party crasher. "Ah, yes. Of course, I remember you. Thank you for coming. There is plenty of palm wine and food. Help yourself!"

The day of the Sande ceremony could not come more quickly for me. We had been in the bush for about a week, getting familiar with the different rituals. But staying in a hut and sleeping on a mat on the hard dirt floor with 30 other children and all those women and no electricity was not exactly my cup of tea. We learned traditional Sande songs and danced wildly around evening fires that we had helped build. We listened closely to stories about women we were told to emulate and were given lessons in feminine hygiene. We were told what to expect during childbirth and given lessons on sisterhood and the importance of family. The last night before the initiation ceremony, we had the usual evening ritual of listening to stories, but this time, we were told to be brave because real women don't cry. We were told that, after the following morning, we would no longer be children, and we would be expected to act accordingly from then on. I was exhausted.

Early the next morning, when it was still dusky, and the forest was teeming with morning noises, we were roused from sleep. It had been an uneasy night for me since my friend's words had come came back to me that evening, and I had spent most of the night wondering if she might have been telling the truth. My thoughts were interrupted when a few relatives and ceremonial women walked into the hut and gathered my cousins and me together and told us to stand in order of seniority. We ranged in age from nine to 14. I was ten. I heard singing in the background, but we were still secluded in the hut, so the sounds were faint. I was unperturbed, though—even a little curious.

One by one, the girls in line in front of me disappeared. I wondered where they had been taken. Then it was my turn. I was led out of the hut into an open area, where I was greeted by the sight of hundreds of women. Some were partially dressed, wearing raffia skirts and nothing else but white clay on their faces, giving them a frightening mask-like appearance that was reminiscent of voodoo priests. Others were in loose colorful caftans. One of the women took my hand and walked me towards a smaller group of about six women.

I started to pull away. I did not know her. Then I caught a brief glimpse of my mother before she got quickly swallowed up in the dancing crowd. I tried to shout to her through the noise, but it was too loud, and I could not see her. I started feeling very uneasy and wanted to take off running. Something told me I should run. The woman sensed my fear and grabbed my arm more tightly.

"We are only going to check you to make sure you are still pure."

I was familiar with this "checking." Most traditional African matriarchs practice the random examination of their young women's private parts all through their adolescence and right up to marriage to make sure their children are not sexually active and that the hymen is intact for her husband at the time of marriage. I told her I was not bad, that I did not need to be "checked." She ignored me and told me to take off the little shift dress I was wearing so they could "look at me."

"No ah noh dae pull me closs," I said clearly in Krio, the Sierra Leonean Creole. She had been speaking to me in Mende, my mother tongue. I could tell she understood what I said because her mouth opened in shock, and her eyes questioned: "You had the effrontery to tell me no?" I went into full-blown panic. I had never been surrounded by so many strange women and did not understand what was happening. Suddenly, I became aware of the many different loud sounds filling the air. The incessant pounding on ancient Djembes, the thump-thump of my heart, and other noises I couldn't place. But it was the yodeling that unnerved me the most, and I tried to cover my ears to block out the voices. I remembered that we had been told not to cry, but I started crying anyway, scanning the faces for a familiar one.

I had somehow progressed to the small group of women who then quickly circled me like vultures their prey. After refusing to take off my dress a second time, they just ripped it off me. I do not remember how I got to the ground, but I found myself on a small bed of banana leaves and was instructed to open my legs. I kept my legs together and tried to sit up. I felt hands forcing me back down into the red dirt. I was terrified beyond words. Because I was strong and kept fighting, the women had to struggle to position me the way they needed me. The next thing I felt was someone sitting on my left inner thigh while other hands pinned the other leg down. I could feel the muscles of my left leg straining under the weight and was sure the woman had broken my leg as she tried to ensure I was pried completely open. I screamed. I tried to get up to push the sweaty determined women off. I saw my grandmother standing above me in the group that was circled around me. Before I could call out to her, I felt a quick rub of something dry like rice flour or powder between my legs. Then there was a tug at the nub down there before pain sliced through. The powder had been used for a better grip. I screamed so loud a rag was stuffed in my mouth and down my throat. I tasted the salt of sweat and snot mingled together as I sobbed through the singing and drumming, which had become loud and frenzied to drown out my screams. The women could not risk the other children hearing my blood-curdling screams. "Someone help me," I begged through the rag. I was gasping for air and trying to breathe. I looked up at the faces hovering over me, hoping I could see my mother, hoping she would make the women disappear, hoping she would make the pain stop. I did not see her. If she had been there, I would not have been able to recognize her. All the faces had become one—a giant, dark cloud obscuring the sun.

My grandmother made her way to me, bent over, and whispered in my ear.

"Stop screaming, Hajah. Say 'sande.'" She kept repeating that: "Say 'sande,'" almost like a chant. I tried to, but the sounds came out muffled and unintelligible. My throat had gone dry, and I no longer had the strength to cry. All the fight in me was gone.

The weight was finally lifted from my leg. It was done; I had become a "woman." I lay there, long after my aunt gave me a tetanus injection to prevent infection, long after the cleansing alcohol had dried off, and the healing herbal paste had been applied to the wound between my legs. I lay there long after my sobs subsided, and the numbness in my leg had gone, and long after the realization that more than parts of my flesh had been taken from me that day.

Two days later, my mind still foggy and trying to process what had happened, I watched from my straw bed as the old Sowe, the mistress of the ceremony, rinsed caked black blood from the rusty old knife that had been used to remove clitorises, labia minora, and labia majora to usher us into womanhood. I could not tell whose blood. There had been 30 of us.

My friend Miriam had told me the truth.

African and Middle Eastern circumcision has a very complex face. It is a ritual marking a young woman's entrance into womanhood, and it is crucial to her being accepted by her community as a "full-grown" woman. Girls who are not initiated are often mocked and shunned and considered children even when they are fully adult. The ceremony and rituals are intended to prepare young girls for life as future wives, mothers, and matriarchs. They learn the skills of cooking, cleaning, personal hygiene, dancing, and, in some cases, traditional healing methods. There is also the consideration of tradition. Some African mothers, even educated ones, will tell you that they may not agree with the part of the ritual that hurts their daughters, but "it is our tradition."

But it cannot be ignored that most tribes practice female circumcision to control a woman's sexuality. Because virginity and purity before marriage are prized to ensure the honor of the young woman's family, people go to any lengths to protect a young woman's maidenhood. Circumcision is just one tool. Another is the periodic examination of the hymen to make sure a girl has not strayed. Knowing that a girl can be inspected at any time or any day by the old matriarchs can be a powerful deterrent to the desire for sexual intercourse before marriage.

And so, on the night of the wedding, it is customary for the family of both bride and groom to wait outside of the room as the marriage is being consummated, so that afterward, they can gather the stained white sheets from a torn hymen and proudly display them, confirming the purity of the bride. Many chickens have given their blood to stain the sheets of an unsuspecting new husband whose wife had not kept herself until marriage. The mother or other older women will sneak in and splatter the blood on the bed prior to that first encounter between husband and wife. These deceptions tell of the deeply entrenched reasons given for the continuation of excisions. Practiced in more than 29 countries in Africa and the Middle East, it is estimated that more than 200 million women and young girls alive today have undergone female genital mutilation. It has also been discovered recently that female genital mutilation is now being practiced in the United States.

Long before "fake news," there was "fake life"—a term we used in college to describe students whose parents were poor but acted as though they were rich. The students, especially female ones, would flash cash or ride around campus in their rich sugar daddy's cars and wear expensive designer clothes. The young men often borrowed a wealthy relative's car and drive to lectures and pretend it was his or his father's. Yet, everyone knew that it was all borrowed stuff and that they were simply trying to put themselves in a class they did not belong to.

As much as Sibana and I did not want to be caught living fake, we also did not want to be left behind. We had Rooster; a restaurant owned by a Lebanese family. It was the best fried chicken in town, and only well-to-do people could afford it. We also dreamed of eating at Shuper Burger, the only hamburger joint in town, but the cost was usually beyond our reach. But one day, Sibana and I had a little money and decided to live it up. We went to Shuper Burger and ordered everything on the menu we had been salivating over for months. We ate and were drunk with joy from enjoyment. Then the bill came. We had nowhere near the amount we owed. Sibana and I looked at each other, thinking that they were going to call the police on us and didn't know what to do. Then, I realized my mother's office was only a couple of streets away. I could go to her and ask for money. The only thing was, what was I going to say the money was for? I told Sibana that we had no choice. We had to split up. I would leave her at the restaurant to pretend we were not done eating and run to my mother's job and come back as quickly as I could. She reluctantly agreed because I teased her that I might just go and not come back, and they would arrest her.

She did not think it was funny. I do not remember what story I concocted to my mother, but she gave me the money. Sibana and I never ventured out like that again unless someone was treating us.

Sibana and I would sometimes go to "Congo," an experience similar to going to second-hand stores in the U.S. Except the clothes were spread on the ground in large open markets, and the sellers would heckle and call out: "Cam buy from me ah get de best close from oversea, from Amerika. Two for wan. una cam buy oh me padi dem ah go gee una good prize." We found treasures there, unique things that had the distinct look of having come from "overseas." We were careful not to spend too much time there; you never knew which one of your college mates were watching. We were not the only students tight on money. We would catch the bus back to campus happy and spend hours carefully washing and rewashing, in some cases bleaching, to get rid of the unmistakable smell of second-hand clothes. We were a hit each time we showed up at parties with our finds.

Sometimes we sewed identical outfits just for fun when we had a little extra cash. One that still stands out for me consisted of Alibaba pants—hers black, mine purple—complete with long slits along the sides. She loved black. We looked like we had just stepped out of the pages of "Arabian Nights." It was one of my most memorable nights at college. Everyone remarked on how good we looked. The best part was we did not feel we had to be fake to look great, just a little extra creative.

I do not ever remember talking about the hard parts of our lives with Sibana; I knew we both had secrets. I knew she had parts of her heart that had deep wounds, but she never exposed those. 'Her mother was abroad and was not well' was as far as we got whenever I tried. We did not speak of her mom's illness and how much Sibana must have felt afraid and alone. I knew she must have missed her mother when she was around me and mine, but she never let on.

Sibana was witty and always had a wicked glint in her slanted Asian eyes and a booming laugh that made you want to laugh along. I always felt less alone and less misunderstood around her. We were happy in each other's company. It was as if we had each been given a piece of the sun to warm each other's cold spaces— spaces we never ventured in.

Sadly, Sibana was an exception in my life, which, for the most part, had been full of experiences I wish on no child.

I would only get a full understanding of my history of violence later when my mind finally broke, and the doctors that were trying to piece it back together helped me trace it. I had never made connections between things and often had little understanding of the impact of certain events. My grandmother had told my girl cousins and me never to let a boy touch us "down there." If we did, we would be peppered. Literally. Cayenne was a powerful threat and deterrent. If you stole—same thing. But how was I to tell my grandmother, or any grown-up, that it was not a boy but my mother's new husband that had? She already loved him too much. Even my pleas for her to leave after he'd hit me had been met with: "If you don't want to be here, you can leave. You can go to your papa." Her husband asked that I be sent away to boarding school, and soon after, I was. I kept my mouth shut from then on. I learned that speaking of things that hurt and happen in secret results in banishment.

I was in the sixth form getting ready for college when my hymen was broken, and my trust was shattered—whatever little of it I had left. His name was Kazim. His family was prominent in the mining world, and his father had of course known Papa. He had always liked me, but I had never shared his feelings. I knew his sisters since we attended the same high school. I was 16; he was a couple of years older. Though fat, Kazim was very charming with a chipped front tooth and the enviable confidence of the wealthy. Always impeccably dressed, he liked to play Scrabble with Sibana and some of our other friends s. At that time, Sibana was living with my mom and me in Freetown. I had finally almost pushed the circumcision out of my mind. The physical wounds had long healed, and life had gone back to nearly normal. It was great not to be in boarding school and living back with my mother after all those years of separation. Those days, my house was full of high school friends who stayed long after school just to hang out because we had a fun crowd. I watched them play and brought them food and small snacks from time to time, and we would all eat and talk and laugh. I was content.

My mother welcomed all my friends and never complained about the amount of food they ate or the many hours they stayed. I took special pride in this. Not many mothers were as generous. Sometimes I read novels while they played since I wasn't much interested in Scrabble. I preferred Monopoly. One day, they played until it was very late. Everyone called it a night except for one person, and I suddenly found myself alone with Kazim. We started talking about this and that, and he asked me why I was always pushing him away. I told him I wasn't, that I was always around. He said that was exactly what he meant, that I was always playing with words. Would I come close?

"Sure," I said. I pulled my chair close to his.

"Closer."

I inched my chair slowly forward until our knees were touching. Then he started kissing me. I did not mind. He told me to sit on his lap. I almost said, "No," but thought, *Ok. You don't have to be always so afraid of men. He is your friend. You know him.*

"Just this once," I said.

We continued kissing until I felt his hand inching his way up my skirt. I thought, *Enough*. I did not like his kisses that much.

"Hey, what are you doing?" Alarm bells went off in my head.

"Nothing. Just playing."

"No, I can't play like that," remembering both my grandmother's warnings and waking up in the middle of the night to find my stepfather's hand in my underwear. I was eight.

"I don't want to play like that. Don't do that."

"I am not doing anything. Just touching your leg," he said, smiling. By that time, his syrupy voice and devil-may-care attitude were starting to annoy me, so I made a move to get up. He hardened his grip around my waist, and he told me to relax. I struggled to get out of it, but he was determined, and I was scared. I broke into a cold sweat as I tried to wriggle out of his hold, but I couldn't. I felt his fingers prying my legs open and digging into my secret place.

"Stop!" I screamed, grabbing his wrist, but he was too strong, and it was too late.

I felt something like a knife tearing through me, then warm liquid coursing down my leg. I didn't have to look to know it was blood. I could smell it. I collapsed on the floor and buried my head in my hands and wept quietly. I did not look up as he moved his chair back, got up, and walked out. He never said a word. I heard the front door close quietly behind him.

Finally, when my legs could move, I found an old towel and mopped my blood off the floor, took off my stained skirt, and went out into the backyard and buried it. It was my school uniform.

I have come to believe that trauma and grief are companions. One doesn't and cannot exist without the other. One of the things I have been proud to share about my culture is its ability to honor grief and grieving, trauma's best friend. This is evidenced by the long, elaborate, heartfelt African mourning rituals around grief. You are never alone with your pain when a loved one dies in Africa. In Sierra Leone, family, the community, and friends all mourn with you. From aunts, uncles, neighbors, relatives who come from far-off places and the village to mere passers-by who stop to pay their respects in a house of mourning, you're enveloped-wrapped in a deep cultural blanket of community. This unwavering sense of being part of the tribe of those who are bereaved sets the tone for the healing process.

Mourning rituals vary from tribe to tribe, but many are similar. The women take off their shoes and remove their head ties and throw them on the ground or tie them around their hips and sit down. One thing is universal: sitting on the floor as a symbol of being humbled by life. "I have come to help you cry," they tell you. So, we sit on the floor and pull our hair and wail and lament. Sometimes in song. Never are you alone. While some members of the community are busy helping the bereaved family with burial arrangements, others put huge pots on the fire to cook bags of rice and palm oil stews or greens and beans for the never-ending stream of mourners. Others set out trays for donations, which they empty once full, to help collect money to help with burial costs or other support for the bereaved family. This goes on for days. Weeks. Sometimes until the fortieth day.

I explained this mourning process to some of my friends when they told me about the loneliness of grieving in the West, where you are expected to "have closure," "move forward," or "move on"—and very quickly—when there is a death. I sat with them and held them and cried with them when their hearts were mourning, not only for one who was gone, but for their own hearts that were imprisoned in grief by a society that doesn't give them the freedom to grieve as long as they need to.

Conversely, the culture that holds grief so tenderly—Africa's—doesn't do so well with trauma. America has the edge there.

The callous and almost inhumane treatment of women who can't bear children is still shocking to me from a society that also creates such a wide berth for grief. In African society, no matter how educated or how accomplished a woman is, if she doesn't bear a child, she's nothing. She is ridiculed, shunned, and called a witch. Her persecution is endless.

If you have a disability, Africans minimize it or make up reasons for the handicap. They say that the parents must have done something bad and are being punished for it. "There is a curse on that family" is the trite and cruel response to the child. In the old days, disabled children were left to die in the forest. No one wanted them.

Mental illness is treated in the same way, and as a result, there are no treatment options for trauma. If you are traumatized, you are crazy. If you display any signs of internal conflict or pain, you are crazy. Since classical psychotherapy is almost non-existent in most African countries and is not practiced much, you are doomed to a life of shame, stigma, and isolation. In Africa, if you have a problem, you talk about it with your friends, families, the elderly, matriarchs, or patriarchs who are never short of words of wisdom and good counsel. That is your therapy. Though it may be true on some level—since sharing feelings and telling your troubles does provide some relief—it is a dangerous, narrow, and limited approach to the many different scenarios of mental illness. As a result of the perception that family and friends provide therapy, there are almost no provisions made for mental healthcare in Africa.

Very few if any practicing psychotherapists and psychiatrists are available. When I lived at home, there was only one that we knew of in the whole country, and his practice never saw patients. There are very few asylums, as most of the mad in Africa are left free to roam the streets. Some are periodically taken in by family members. So, there is no room for those of us in-between.

Africa has a long way to go. During my loneliest and darkest times, I could not talk about things with even some of my closest educated friends, many who hold doctorates and master's degrees, because even they had not evolved beyond the idea of a traumatized "normal" person needing help to work through their challenges. All my symptoms would have forever labeled me as full-blown psychotic crazy. Never again would I be taken seriously as a rational, intelligent, educated person. Never again would I be looked at without the label of madwoman or crazy person.

When I finally found enough courage to explain the gaps in my resume to a few friends and told them that I had been depressed for a while, they started calling me "sick." "Oh, you know, you're sick. Don't stress yourself." The implication was obvious. We all know what "sick" means—crazy. The humiliation and cruel minimization can be as bad on the psyche as any other traumatic experience and can exacerbate the anxiety and other symptoms. For being the cradle of civilization, we are bushmen when it comes to the treatment of our vulnerable in terms of mental health .

I would have to find my own well of sanity.

CHAPTER 5

Taboo

THERE ARE MANY KINDS OF BETRAYALS IN LIFE. Some leave scars that heal with time, like a loved one cheating and breaking your heart, friends turning on you, getting passed up for a well-earned promotion because your boss hates the color of your skin or is enjoying the charms of a junior coworker. Then there are others, those that cut you below the knees so that nothing can hold you up again. A mother's betrayal is such.

It is ironic to see America's cavalier approach to certain aspects of sex, given its reputation abroad as a country of puritans. I was shocked to see brothers sleeping with their sisters and mothers sleeping with their daughter's husbands or boyfriends and thinking nothing of it on the Jerry Springer show. Some even took pride in what they were doing. This was confusing me. Perhaps Jerry simply had the courage to go where no one else would go in exposing these Shocking situations not to flaunt them.

In my culture, while we know of fathers who rape their children or uncles who have molested their little nieces, it is not accepted or even spoken of. Even a friend caught having an affair with their friend's lover is not looked upon kindly. You would never hear of a woman sleeping with her daughter's boyfriend or husband. It is considered taboo.

Yet, I was cursed with this. My mother was and is married to a man I have lain with. It was not of my own volition; he was not my man. He took me against my will. I have asked God countless times: Of all the things in the world, why this? Why me? I have not had to die to be sentenced to hell.

It started when I was in college, when my mother was trying to recover from the heartbreak of her husband leaving her for another woman—the same husband who used to beat us both. She was miserable in a way I had never known her to be. My "we're going to be fine" speeches were not working anymore.

I have been trying to make things right in my mother's life for a long time. When I was a child, I had at least succeeded in getting him to stop hitting her when he came home drunk. I could take him beating me, and I could take his calling me those awful names, but I could not bear him beating my mother. One night, as he was hitting her, I ran into the kitchen and grabbed a knife and threatened to kill him if he hit my mother again. I was eight or nine, a scrawny and anxious thing. The weight of my mother's marriage to this man and the abrupt end to my regular weekend visits to Papa had robbed me of any desire for food or play. Adapting to my new father and his many rules—including that I could not go to see my papa again—made me unafraid to tell him I would kill him for hitting my mother one more time.

He could have ignored me, but he didn't. Perhaps he saw something in my eyes that told him I meant it. He never hit her again, but he made me pay. Not too long after this incident, he made sure I was sent away to boarding school—but not before he did something that would mar me for life.

When I was in college, after months of unsuccessfully trying to console my mother after he left her, her friend who had been in America for many years, thought it might be a good idea if my mother left Africa for a while and came for a visit in America. She asked me what I thought about it, and I told her to go, we would be fine, I would take care of my brothers. Waking up each day to my mother's sobs had become too much to bear. By that time, her mother, my biological grandmother, was living with us. She had been forced to flee her home in Kailahun when the rebels came and did terrible things. Whenever I found myself alone with her, I tried to avoid looking her in the eyes. They hinted of a darkness I knew I was not ready to be swallowed in. I had heard stories. One of her children was said to have been butchered right in front of her by the rebels. In a brutal revolt, they had not only gone after the country's diamonds, but its citizens. My mother was worried about leaving her children, but I told her that I would rather have her alive and away than to have her near but not there.

For so many years, she had put up with his cheating and abuse; his leaving her was the final straw. I feared that if something was not done or something did not change, I would lose her. The sadness was beginning to consume her, and I had no one but her.

We took her to the airport and watched her board the plane for America. I fought back tears as I tried to tell the boys that everything was going to be ok. What else could I have said? That I was scared and heartbroken and wasn't sure how we were going to survive?

After she left, I got busy trying to raise two boys, ages six and nine. I was 18 and had just started college. My days consisted of attending lectures, leaving campus to run to the market shop for food, coming home to cook, washing their school uniforms uniforms by hand, and then getting them ready for school the next day. I also had my own work to do. University classes were harder than the high school work I had mostly breezed through. They were busy times for me.

My mother sent us money. She worked hard, but the pay was low. She did the odd jobs that immigrants usually do when they first come to America, no matter how educated they are. Cleaning shit in nursing homes, answering phones, clerking in convenience stores, driving taxis. She did some kind of in-home care; it was a far cry from the banking job she had been doing in Africa. And I managed the best I could, but the money was not enough. I was responsible for Granny, my two brothers, and other extended family that my mother had always supported.

I missed my mother. And I cursed the fact that, just when I had begun to settle back with her after so many years away at boarding schools, she had to leave yet again. I understood the reasons, but still, I missed her. I did not have time to dwell on such things, however. I had much to do.

Each week, my mother called to check on us and get an update on how we were holding up. I never complained. "The boys are doing great. Granny, too," was my response every time she asked how we were. I never wanted her to worry or feel bad for leaving. From time to time, she told me that things were not easy in

America and that she and her friend were having some problems. She did not say much more about it. The long-distance calls were incredibly expensive, so we spent just a couple of minutes on the phone for the two most important things—to get a quick update on us and to give me the code to pick up the money she sent for our care at Western Union. Then she mentioned she had run into him—the man who would change my life forever.

I remembered him. We were related—although not by blood. His uncle was married to my mother's older sister, and he and his brothers lived with my aunt and uncle. I had met him a couple of times when I was around 13 and visiting my aunt. He was a few years older than me. My mother told me she had run into him and what a blessing it was because things had not ended well between her and her friend. She had been asked to leave her friend's house. Thankfully, he offered to come to get her; she had nowhere else to go. After all, she was "Aunty" as he used to call my mother. I was happy and grateful that my mother had found a place where she could feel welcome, and I was relieved because she sounded happy again. The high note of worry that I had detected in her voice over the past few calls was gone.

Once she moved in with him, she continued her weekly calls to check on us. But our routine telephone calls changed: she would call, hand him the phone, and he would say hello to me and then give the phone back to my mother. The first few times I spoke to him, I thanked him very much for taking my mother in, but after a few more times of it, I asked my mother why he continued talking to me even though we really had nothing more to talk about. She mumbled some sort of response, but never directly answer me until one day, finally, I told her I would no longer speak to him if she did not tell me the truth about what was going on.

She told me he had seen my picture with her and expressed interest in me. I was a young woman then, not the 13-year-old he had briefly met at my aunt and uncle's home. I told her No. I was not interested. And I had a boyfriend. She seemed to drop the subject and did not say anything more about him for a while.

When I was in my final year of college, my mother told me that he was coming to Freetown. "For what?" I asked, suspicious and slightly annoyed. "Oh, nothing. He will come, and you guys can talk." I told her I had nothing to say to him and hoped he had reasons other than me for making a whole trip to Africa.

A few weeks later, I got a call from her that he had indeed come home. I was indifferent.

He visited me on campus once, briefly, yet soon afterward, rumors started going around that a man had come from America to marry me. It was not true, of course, but Africans like to gossip and make up stories from kernels of truth and create a whole new reality. I remember that he seemed nice and friendly, although he was quiet and shy. Right away, I told him that I could not go out with him since I had a boyfriend. He did not seem perturbed at all and said he understood. We left it at that.

I went to seek the counsel of my mother's best friend, whom I had grown up calling "Aunty."

"This man is here, and I don't want him," I told her. "What am I going to do? I have refused him, and I feel bad because he has helped my mother."

"Be nice to him," she said without hesitation.

"What does 'be nice to him' mean exactly?" I asked, uncomfortable. One usually has to ask these questions when having certain conversations with elders who are often taciturn and sometimes speak in parables, leaving you with the responsibility of gleaning their meaning from what they tell you. I have never liked this roundabout way of communicating; it has always felt somewhat deceptive.

"While he's in town, go around the city with him, spend some time with him." She suggested I go with him to deliver the packages he had brought with him. When Africans travel home from America, many people send packages of rarities to deliver to their loved ones. Jeans, perfumes, and Nike tennis shoes are coveted gifts. So, I went to the house where he was staying to help him pick up the packages we were to take to the expectant recipients whose relatives had remembered them. I walked into the house and followed him into the room where he was living.

He told me to sit down. The only place to sit was a mid-sized bed in the cramped room, so I sat on the edge of it. Next thing I know, he is pushing me on the bed and pulling my skirt down.

"No! Stop!" I said to him. "Please!" I whispered, trying to keep my voice quiet enough so it would not be heard by the people who were sitting just a few feet outside the door.

He did not listen, nor did he stop. I tried to push him off a few times and then stopped when I realized he had no intention of stopping. I lay there sobbing, quietly resigning myself to the thought that perhaps he was forcing himself on me because I owed him. *Let him take his pound of flesh,* I thought. *We would be even.* He had helped my mother, and he had helped himself to me. We owed him nothing anymore.

When he was done, I scrambled up from the bed and ran into the bathroom to scrub him off of me. I never mentioned him or that day to my mother. I told myself it was just one more thing I needed to bury, along with all the other ugly things I had hidden deep inside of me.

About a year after this, my mother told me she had something important to tell me. Since our phone cards only gave us a few minutes before an announcer came on to let us know we had only one minute left, I went to a relative's office to make the overseas call so we would not be interrupted. They had gotten married, she told me. "Only for papers," she added hastily. The marriage would allow her to get her permanent resident card. As I listened, some primal alarm went off inside me, and my hands went clammy around the phone. Blood pounded in my head, I felt sick and dizzy, and an uncontrollable shaking came over me. I leaned against the mustard-colored wall to steady myself. I did not want anyone to notice that something was wrong.

Immigrants, trying to stay in America and pursue their own version of the American dream, have resorted to many things—some unsavory, some even criminal. They do whatever they need to do to stay in America. So, it was not so unusual to hear my mother say she had married him for that reason. But one's gut is never wrong. I could not ignore what I felt the moment she told me they were married.

Some temporary madness had come over me, and I asked her if she had been intimate with him. I cannot think of a scenario where an African child would ask her mother a question like that. She did not answer, so I thought perhaps she had not understood what I meant.

"Have you consummated the marriage?" I asked. "Have you slept with him? Have you had sex with him? Have you had intercourse with him?"

The words, rushed and panicked, somehow came out from a throat that had suddenly gone dry. The deafening silence on the other end told me all I needed to know. My life as I knew it was over and would never be the same. My mother and I had lost each other for good. We had crossed a line and ended up in a place from which there was no coming back.

I held the phone a long time after she had hung up, pretending she was still on the other end. I knew that once I put the phone down, I would be launched into the new reality of being a person who had shared a man with her own mother—a reality I could not bear to face.

It was my relative who finally got my attention. "It must be a very important call. You have been on the phone a long time!"— hinting that I should get off the phone before he got in trouble with his boss.

I hung up as shame, disgust, panic, and unspeakable sorrow washed over me. I managed a small 'Thank you' to my relative for letting me use his phone. He remarked that I looked like I had seen a ghost. He asked if everything was ok. I told him Yes. But I knew nothing was ever going to be ok again.

It would take years of therapy for me to be able to call what he had done to me "rape." I had always believed that I had said No, and I had tried to push him off, but hadn't done enough. I could have screamed and kicked him. Maybe I could have tried harder, but since I didn't do any of those things, I believed I had consented. But the truth is, I had been forced against my will. That is rape.

CHAPTER 6

The Price of a Green Card

I CONSIDERED MYSELF ON THE LIST OF THE SHAMED in our community—like the untouchables in India—and I would often imagine I had my own scarlet letter printed on my forehead as I walked through life. But I still loved my mother. And I believed her when she told me that I should go to America and that as soon as I got there, we would leave the city in which they lived. We would start a life somewhere else where no one knew us, and no one knew our secret. She told me they had filed paperwork for green cards for my brothers and me, and I should consider coming.

By that time, the war in Liberia had crept into Sierra Leone. My mother was afraid for us. She was also worried about my health and wanted me to see some doctors in the U.S.

I was sure that I was the unluckiest person in the world. God had forgotten me; how was I going to survive this latest assault on my being? The first assault was when her husband, my stepfather, touched me when I was eight. He had not broken flesh—but had stolen innocence. The second assault had broken flesh and stolen peace.

Symptoms of every other trauma in my life resurfaced. I suffered a persistent unidentified fever. Sleep eluded me, and I was in a daze. I broke out in strange sores. Food tasted like dust; I could not eat; I became emaciated. No doctor could figure out what was wrong with me. They tested me for HIV and AIDS. In those days, it took a whole agonizing week to get the results back. I was negative. I was even told I might have leprosy, so parts of my ear were skinned off for testing. That test came back negative, too, but by that time, I no longer cared. I had a life sentence of my own.

My mother persisted. Finally, I gave in like I have done so many times before with her. I would go to America.

I finished college, graduating first in my class with a bachelor's in International Relations and a minor in French Literature. I was offered an assistant-lecturer position at the University, but I had wanted to go to France to study for a doctorate in International Law. I chose America instead. I chose my mother.

My mother and her new husband picked me up at JFK Airport in New York. You could have cut the tension in the car with a knife. It was the first time we were all in the same space, and I wanted to throw up. My mother seemed nervous and talkative all at once. When we arrived at their home, I hurriedly got out of the car and let out a long breath. I hadn't realized I had been holding my breath the whole time. There were pictures of them on their wedding day plastered all over the walls. I saw a photo of my baby brother and me that I had taken in college after I won the award for Best Actress for a play I had written and starred in. Turning away, I vowed to take the photo off their wall the next day.

He did not live alone. His sister and his sister's daughter, then ten years old, also lived with him. Later, when I saw pictures of me that had been taken during those first few days with my mother and her husband in America, my rapist, I looked like a ghost. That first night, I was shown to my room and watched as my mother walked off to go lay in the next room with a man that had been with her child. How could she? How did she do it night after night? How could she not see my pain and discomfort? How could she not know that this was all wrong?

The questions plagued me until I could not bear pretending things were normal any longer. I felt sick to my stomach all the time and wanted to leave. It was hell. I felt trapped like an animal with nowhere to run. I went through the motions, adjusting to life in a house with someone who had hurt me but was also the reason I had come to America to see mother after seven years of being away from her. Hate, then gratitude, then hate again.

I was not the only one feeling on edge. It was no secret that his whole family despised my mother. They could not get over the fact that she had gone from being his "Aunty" to now being his Mrs. They were disgusted by the situation, and they wanted her out of his home and their lives. They were not happy to have me around, either. It became clear to me that our secret was no secret at all.

What had he told them? That I had been a willing participant? Anger burned in my chest. Finally, one night, things erupted as they were bound to since we were all ticking timebombs. I do not know who said what to whom, but I found myself in a fight with his sister, his sister's ten-year-old daughter, and my mother. It was brutal, loud, and ugly. His sister, Aileen, went after my mother first, pulling out her braids and hitting her again and again as if she wasn't going to stop until she felt satisfied she had done enough damage. At the same time, the girl, Aileen's child, screamed obscenities that would have put a sailor to shame. Aileen came at me, too, and ripped my sweater and dug into my back with her long artificial nails like Freddie Kruger, ripping my flesh and leaving a long thin line down my back that is still visible to this day. When he managed to pull Aileen away and lock her in the guest room, I went outside the room and yelled at my mother.

"Let's go! You told me that once I got here, we would leave. This is sick. These people are sick. How can we live in an environment like this?" I half asked, half pleaded.

"I'm not going anywhere," she said. "I'm not going to let them win." She was going to stay with him. I ran outside in the snow. It was the coldest winter the city had experienced in 30 years, but I didn't care. It didn't matter that, in all of my life in Africa, I had never been in snow or felt so cold. I ran and kept running until I collapsed, wanting to be buried under the white ice that resembled my life.

My mother pulled up beside me in her maroon Toyota Camry. I was fast, trying desperately to outrun my pain. I looked at her and then looked away, unnerved by the resolve on her face. I knew I had lost.

We didn't say much after that.

I told my mother to send me back to Africa. I was not going to return to that house with him, with her, with all of them. She drove me to a friend's house instead, someone I had never met. I stayed there for two weeks, crying my life out. I think I began my descent into the darkest depression of my life that night, but I was in too much shock to know it at the time. It hurt that my mother had chosen a man over me yet again. I could no longer deny I had a stranger for a mother, someone who barely knew me and apparently had no deep connection to me. I had been away from her for seven years, and we could not even be together for a week. How was this happening? I had been counting the days until I was with her again, but it was clear that having me as far away from her as possible was the only way for her to have me in her life at all. Why else would she have sent me away to boarding school after she got married when I was only eight? Had she not left me before then with aunty and my grandparents to go to the city to continue her schooling after she had me? Had she not left me to come to America? I could no longer deny the undeniable. *Perhaps I have always been an inconvenience,* I thought. I could not stop crying. My mother's friend, a gentle and kind lady, would knock gently on the door of the guest bedroom and coax me to come out and eat something "before you get sick." Her kindness almost unraveled me.

After a couple of weeks, I realized crying was not going to help me. It was clear my mother had no interest in what became of me. I had to quickly figure out what I was going to do. I had left my brothers back home with a trusted friend, but the blood diamond war had already begun, so I could not go back—as much as I wanted to. Besides, I did not have $2,000—the cost of a ticket back to Freetown.

My back was against the wall.

I had no choice but to stay in a country that was foreign to me, having no family except the mother who had essentially abandoned me. I called one of my childhood friends who had left Sierra Leone years before. Thankfully, we had stayed in contact over the years. She was in Washington state with her husband. I told her I had come from Africa, but I was in a bad situation and begged her to get me out of there before something really bad happened to me. I was grateful she didn't ask too many questions and got me a one-way ticket to Seattle. I boarded the plane and left the East Coast, not knowing what lay ahead.

My mother stayed with her husband. It was a bitter pill for me to swallow.

In Seattle, I took a job as a nanny to my friend's husband's ex-wife's two sons, J. and S. In exchange for taking care of the kids, doing some housework, and cooking, I got paid a $140 a month, plus my board and keep. I sent the money to the friend back home who was taking care of my brothers for me. The two boys saved me from completely losing my mind those first six months of being in America. They were four and six and adored me. I loved them in turn because they filled the hole in my heart for my brothers. Taking care of them left me too exhausted at the end of the day to think too much.

But I could not stay in Washington forever. My friend and her husband were both going to school. He was working on his doctorate; she, her nursing degree. They were kind to me, but I was dependent on them, and I did not want to be. As much as I loved the boys, I knew life had more in store for me than being a nanny in America.

I got word that the Liberian rebel war had descended fully on Sierra Leone, and the news of devastation was impossible to grasp. I had no idea what was going to become of me now that I had no home to go back to and a mother who had no room for me in her life.

I tried to remember all the people I knew in America and Europe. I made a list and discovered one person on my list that I should at least try to contact. Miss G. had been my math teacher as well as a Peace Corps volunteer in Salone, and she had married a Sierra Leonean. They had settled in San Francisco and had two children. I had not done well in her classes, but she'd always liked me. She would often tell me, "You just don't want to do this" when I failed her courses. "You're smart, and you do well in English. How can you not know math?" She would shake her cropped blonde head in disbelief and amusement, and I would smile into her sea-blue eyes and promise I would do better next time. She never stopped being nice to me.

We stayed in touch after she left the Peace Corps and returned to her home in the United States. When we spoke by phone, she was very excited that I had made my way to America. I told her I was in Seattle, exploring America and being a nanny in the interim. She laughed and seemed as amused as she had been when I was her student trying to give her an excuse for something she knew I could do if only I had wanted to.

"You're a city girl, and San Francisco would be good for you with your personality and your background in French," she said.

I didn't to ask her what personality she was referring to. I wanted to tell her the bubbly troublemaker she had known a decade earlier in her classroom had been replaced by a woman who was broken beyond repair.

"It is a very cosmopolitan city, and you would fit right in."

I knew I was being offered a rare opportunity, and I would be a fool not to grab it. She and her husband would help me until I got on my feet. They had an extra room in their home and offered it to me.

I got on a plane for the second time in America, heading to another strange city where I only knew two people from a very distant past. On the flight to San Francisco, I knew I was leaving behind not only my friend who had given me my first start in America but my mother and the naive young woman who had left Africa believing she could still find her way to her mother's heart in America.

The moment I drove down Dolores Street in San Francisco and saw the palm-lined roads, I felt I was going to be ok. This city—with its foggy mornings; with thousands of Chinese restaurants and tourists from every corner of the globe; and where it is not unusual to see two men in nothing but pieces of leather covering their privates kissing in the middle of the street—was going to be my new home. It was going to be my hiding place in America. No one here knew me. And for the first couple of years, I was, in fact, okay, in part because my heart had gone numb, and in part, because I did not speak to my mother during that time. I told myself she was dead to me. I was also in survival mode; I pushed my grief to the side and got a job. It did not pay much, but I was on my own and was able to pay for my room and support my brothers with the little I could send home to Africa each month. Sometimes I styled tiny braids for young African women, for between $150 to $300, to earn a little extra money to ensure my brothers did not go hungry and could still have little treats even though I wasn't there.

But it was hard work and took 12 hours or more to do. And my back and shoulders hurt for days afterward. I also charged only half the price because I wasn't really a professional hairstylist and did not have a salon. But I was happy to have the extra cash.

I missed my brothers terribly. I worried incessantly about their safety from all the news reports of the horrors of the war back home. Many nights, I wept and cursed myself for ever having agreed to come to America. We had never been separated, and I had always taken care of them—even when our mother was still in Africa and even over the seven years she left them with me to come to America. I was ten when the first boy was born and 13 when the second arrived. All of their care had rested upon me from the time they were born, as is often the case for older siblings in the African culture. But it was even more so in our case—having a mother who was never fully committed to any of us. I was not only an older sister, I was also their mom, and, in some ways, still continue to be. I felt guilty for leaving them, and even though I had taught them to be independent and strong and given them the love I never had as a child, I was afraid that, like our mother, I, too, had abandoned them.

I slowly learned to live in America. It was not easy. People did not look you in the eye when you spoke to them and would sometimes not even acknowledge you when you greeted them. One of the hardest things I had to adjust to was the pace. Everything and everyone moved fast there. The lazy African approach to time—like arriving three hours after the designated time—was not going to work there. It was also scary in a way that made me more anxious each passing day. People disappeared, especially children and women, and when they were found, they had been murdered. I could not get the face of the little beauty queen,

JonBenet Ramsey, out of my head. She was in the news every time I turned on the TV. Her circumstances disturbed me deeply, and more than a few times, I had to run out of the room when I saw her mother's stricken face. I eventually stopped watching the news completely—even CNN, which sometimes referred to the war back home.

I also noticed that Black people were different, and they were treated differently in America. I did not pay too much attention to it at first—a mistake I would come to regret. But I discovered some good things, too—pizza, round-the-clock electricity, and something called "the American dream," which seemed to have rubbed off on almost everyone I met. They had that look, the look of a promise of going somewhere and ending up there. It was infectious, their optimism. Over time, I, too, started to believe that anything was possible for me in America.

My former teacher, Miss G., and her family had been very kind to me and had helped me just as she had promised. Once I got a job and moved out, though, I did not see them very much anymore. Everyone was always busy. I missed home, I missed my friends, I missed the sun. I was lonely and sad. It was hard, but I survived.

We immigrants are caught between two worlds and have to live with the loss of the old and the promise of the new. Loss of familiar smells, foods, friends, and family, some of whom will die before we ever make our way back to them again.

We leave our homes or are chased out of them, and, through the process of settling down and doing whatever it takes to get that green card, we lose the ties and connections back home. With the loss of the taste of fish fried in palm oil, the smoky sweetness of corn roasted over charcoal, and the introduction to new American experiences like the taste of cheese on dough, we immigrants morph into something new, losing essential parts of ourselves for which there are no replacements. We adopt new ways of seeing, tasting, and being. We are no longer completely who we were before, nor are we fully who we have become because the longings of the old still echo in our new American selves.

A few years after I had settled into my new life, two things happened that set in motion a whole new series of events. The first was that I met someone—someone who was kind to me. He would become the father of my son.

The other was that my mother had every relative and friend with my telephone number calling me nearly every day to impress upon me the importance of family and how bad it was for me to be living so far away from my mother. "What would people say? How would it look if my mother was on the East Coast and I was on the West Coast?" they would ask me. "It is like taking a plane and going to Africa. It is so far." "How can you go and live by yourself?" one distant cousin accused. "Have you forgotten who you are? Why are you behaving like a white person, going so far away from your mother?" "Our people stick together," someone else admonished me.

My mother had somehow convinced all of them that she was concerned that it was too difficult for me to survive in America without community or family to support me. There were thousands of Sierra Leoneans where she lived; the only Sierra Leonean I knew in San Francisco was my teacher's husband. The calls and pleas for me to go back to my mother were incessant. "Go back to your mother," they said.

African children are taught never to force grown-ups to beg for anything. You always say Yes to everything they ask of you. So, I decided I would go back to be with my mother. It was partly from all the pressure I got and partly because, as much as I hated to admit it to myself, I missed my mother. I resigned from my job, gave up the apartment I had rented, said goodbye to my boyfriend who was crushed by my decision, said goodbye to the city that had somehow become home, and flew back to my mother.

She had found a good school for me, she said. I would go to law school as planned, and we would wait for my brothers to get their visas and join us. And then, she promised, we would all move from California to another state.

This time, I stayed at my mother's cousin's house. I asked my mother to come over one evening so we could discuss plans once I had been in town for a couple of days. She arrived, and as soon as my eyes met hers, my heart sank. Her eyes were empty.

She wanted to talk outside, so we walked towards the street and stopped about half a block from the house. I wondered why we needed to go out at night in the cold to talk. We both stopped under a streetlamp, and I got straight to the point. Now that I was there as she'd asked, I wanted to know what the plans were. But it did not take long to realize there were none, and if there were, they did not include my brothers or me. She turned the conversation to other things to avoid answering my question and then became angry because I said we should move to another state, as she had promised we would.

I could not bear the thought of my brothers finding out our secret or living in the shadow of our sin. She snapped.

"I know all about you," she screamed. "You can't tell me anything."

She went on to tell me how much of a whore I was and that she'd heard about all my affairs while I was in college and did not care what I thought of her. I wondered how my plea to save my brothers untold pain and shame had gotten us here. There was no convincing myself that my mother still felt something for her children on some level. I could no longer deny the cold truth that she did not care about me or my brothers or what became of us in America. She had once again left it up to me to pick up the pieces of our lives. I told her that I no longer had a mother and turned and headed back toward the house.

No longer able to mask her hatred, she railed at me. "You always have problems with my men. The first one you said you did not like. This one, too, you want me to leave. I am not going to leave him, you hear? Never!" She was almost foaming at the mouth with rage. A searing pain went through me. Both her men had hurt me, and that fact seemed to be lost on her.

I slowly made my way back to her cousin's house and fell into her outstretched arms and sobbed. She had been watching us through the window and had heard everything. She held me and cried with me and told me how sorry she was that my mother had done this to her own child. She expressed her disgust at how much shame my mother had brought to the family and how their pleas with her to leave him had fallen on deaf ears.

"If anything, she is more determined than ever," she said. While I was still trying to digest the fact that the whole family and possibly the whole Sierra Leonean community knew my mother and I had shared the same man, my mother's cousin then told me something I wish she hadn't. My mother had been going to fertility clinics to try to get pregnant while I had been away. She wanted his child. It nearly broke me. She was in her late forties with three children and wanted to bear a child with a man who had raped her daughter. Was there no end to my mother's cruelty?

The next day, I took the train from New York to San Francisco. I don't recall much from the four days of that train ride except that a group of Mormons got on in Chicago and asked me to join them in their Bible study and evening prayers. I said ok and thanked them. It was the first time I had spoken in three days. Perhaps they had seen something on my face that told them I needed God.

I was heading back to San Francisco, the only place I knew and could go, but now had nothing to go back to. I had given away my furniture and left my job, said goodbye to the few friends I had made, said goodbye to the fragile sanctuary I had created in the years after I had fled my mother and the scandal of our lives. I was coming back—but to nothing. This time I had bitten off more than I could chew. This was my punishment for believing her after she had lied to me so many times before. This was my punishment for refusing to let go of the idea that if I tried hard enough, she would give in and love me. This was my punishment for holding on to a mother who had long let go of me.

Once I got off the train, I made up my mind that my mother will never have access to my heart to break it again. It is the reason I was able to survive her walking out on me in the ICU years later as I lay fighting for my life.

CHAPTER 7

Even the Fat Old Men Stop Looking

I COULD NOT GO BACK TO MY OLD JOB AT SAKS. I was too embarrassed. I had said I was going to go to law school on the East Coast, and there I was, just two weeks later.

I stayed with my African friend who had told me I was too soft, the one who said that, if it were her, she would never give her mother as many chances as I had given mine. She had told me I was making a mistake by going. She had been right.

I came back with my tail between my legs like a whipped dog and stayed with her because I had nowhere else to go. I kept her house, washed her dirty underwear, and babysat her child—whom

I loved and still do—in exchange for a place to sleep and a couple of meals a day. I also started braiding hair again so I could earn a little money to send back home to support my brothers until I found another job. I prayed for my brothers to join me in America. The news of the war each day left me fearful for their lives. They were all I had.

Slowly, I started to settle back into life in San Francisco, but things were different. The city was still the same, but something had changed. It was me.

A few months after I started living with her, my friend started acting funny. She had come home from work looking sullen and withdrawn for no discernable reason. I tried to stay out of her way; I did not want to risk being put out. Where would I go? One day, I was leaving to run an errand and asked her if she was going to be home when I got back since I had no keys to get in. She said she was going to a party, but she'd be back by the time I got home. I ran my errand, came home, and she was not there. I sat in the car, thinking perhaps she was caught in traffic. Four hours later, there was still no sign of her. By that time, I needed to use the bathroom very badly, and there were no public bathrooms anywhere near the house. It was after midnight, and it was foggy, cold, and dark, and I did not want to risk getting out of the car and going to the overgrown bushes beside her house to relieve myself. So, I peed in a plastic bag, tied a knot around it, and used it to warm my hands and keep them from freezing. When she finally showed up, she opened her door and held it open for me without a word of apology. It was 5:00 a.m. I knew it was time to pack my bags. Thankfully, things had gotten a little more serious between my boyfriend and me, and we decided to move in together.

Not long after that, I had my first panic attack. It started with worsened sleep patterns and fatigue that would not go away. I hadn't been speaking to my mother, and, after a while, the family members who she'd told I wasn't talking to her, started calling. They wore me down. Each would tell me how bad it was of me not to speak to my mother. What was wrong with me? Did I not know that we only have one mother in this world? And on and on. So, I started to call.

If he picked up when I dialed, and if I heard his voice, I would break into a sweat, and my heart would start racing and for hours afterward. I would feel unsettled and out of sorts. But it was the recording on their answering machine with her personal greeting that unraveled me. It was the pride in her voice, the settled joy in her tone, that did me in. Then the other voices came, too, the voices of his sister and niece who had attacked us that night. I couldn't get them out of my head.

"My brother fucked both you and your mama."

"I will never leave him."

"You're nothing but—"

Then came the flashes of images of my mother in bed with him. I willed my mind to stop, pleaded with my eyes not to show me things I couldn't bear to see. I prayed. I cried. I could not push the Stop button in my mind. It was as if my brain, my heart, and my mind had all conspired against me.

The torment was constant. I lived in my own private hell—a hell I could share with no one until—one night. I called my mother, and *he* answered the phone. His voice gripped me, and I could feel it choking me and squeezing the life out of me. I slammed the phone down and felt an urgent need to run. I felt as though the walls in the apartment were closing in on me, and I couldn't breathe. I ran out the door into the courtyard as if a hundred demons were chasing me. Something terrible was happening to me, and I could not stop it. It felt as though my heart was beating its way out of my chest, the world was spinning around me in dazzling speed, and I was falling and falling into a bottomless hole. I screamed one word: *Jesus*. I was going out of my mind; I could feel it. I remember feeling terror, unlike anything I had ever felt before. I started a cry/prayer: *"Jesus, please help me. Jesus, please help me."* By the time Alexei drove me to the emergency room, something in my mind had snapped. I remember pleading with the doctor to make it stop. I heard words like "panic attack," "psychiatrist," "nervous breakdown," "medication," sleep.

It was the beginning of my battle for sanity and wholeness. My mother was called and told to come, so she flew in a few days later. She was told her daughter was suffering from post-traumatic stress due to many, many factors. The main issue that compounded things was her marriage, which, she was told, posed an ongoing source of trauma and anxiety. She listened, quiet. Her rage, tightly suppressed, seeped out of her, darkening the brightly colored room, leaving me scared and hopeless.

Joint therapy was suggested, but she refused and, once we got home to the apartment Alexei and I shared, she expressed some of her anger at me for telling our "business to the world." She left me with complete strangers and flew back to their home without participating in anything that would even remotely help me not lose my mind completely. I knew then that my mother no longer loved me, that she no longer cared.

It was my Slavic boyfriend Alexei who helped me bathe, who fed me small bites of toast to create a cushion for the pills that had begun to burn holes in my stomach. When I became catatonic and numb, it was he who spread blankets on the small patch of grass in front of our apartment, so I could lay in the sun and absorb some life. It was he who lined up all the doctor's medicines on the dining table like little pieces of a child's board game and put them in Monday to Sunday pillboxes to make it easier to take. I no longer had the capacity to be responsible for even the small basics of my life. It was he who drove me to the therapist, who talked me into believing I will survive and smile again—someday. My mother had left my care in the hands of people who had no obligation to me, no reason to be saddled with me. They cared for me simply because they were good.

The only reason I know I did not go completely stark-raving, public-disrobing, mad was because God still had a plan, and the plan did not include me running naked through the streets, kicking trees, and singing to myself. After six months, I gained 80 pounds from Zoloft and Coca-Cola; I would eventually balloon up to 240 pounds. I gained 100 pounds in less than a year. *How could it be? How had this happened?* I had stopped traffic many times and had men jump out of their Ferraris to ask for my number. I—who had been drawn, painted, admired? I, whose "arresting looks" had driven an admirer to have a figure of me made so he could have a replica of me because my physical beauty brought him so much joy? I, who had been told by a writer I met in America, in the hundreds of pages he wrote about my physical appeal, who had called me, "every man's dream," was now just a sorry idea that once was. The one thing that had always given me a little edge was now gone. I was fat and sad and looked ugly and un-me. I did not recognize the person in the mirror with the big head and dead eyes staring back at me. I never knew that heads and fingers and feet get fat, too. My belly was round like an African drum—not unlike the belly of exulting village chiefs, who sit under the shade of the trees in their compounds, drinking palm-wine and eyeing young virgins coming back from fetching water from the river. I knew I was in trouble when even the fat old men stopped looking, and I had to put my feet up on a chair to tie my shoes. They had been the only ones looking for a long time now.

I had become someone who had lost her way. Sometimes I wondered if I ever even got the chance to find it. Blow after blow, disappointment after disappointment, as I struggled to hold on to my optimism, which was on the verge of being replaced by brutal anxiety. How much cortisol from fight-or-flight can flood your system before you eventually drown in it?

I became a creature living in the shadows. Being in African community crowds terrified me, so I stopped going to parties, weddings, and other functions that bring people together. On the rare occasion I ventured out, I was reminded why it's best not to. The anxiety and shame, two constant companions that accompanied me, were never far behind, and the anguish of feeling so exposed was unbearable. Who knew my secret? Who didn't? The drumming I heard in my head was the sound of my heart beating from panic, not the funky dance number blaring out from the DJ booth at some event. *They know. Are they looking at me with pity or disgust?* While the questions I asked myself were many, one thing remained the same. I knew that as long as I lived, the freedom to wander among my people, my friends, and my colleagues in ease was something I would never again know. All my relations are colored by the one thing I would give anything to undo.

Whatever choices may have been mine to make in my life, I have been robbed of. I will never take a potential husband and introduce him to my parents in the traditional way—another rite of passage in Sierra Leonean culture. How can I ask my fiancé to put the calabash, filled with my bride price, in the hands of someone who had lain with his wife to be? How would he ever relate to his future mother-in-law, who is married to her child's abuser? How will I navigate the murky waters of incest the rest of my life?

I pray that my son does not learn of it. I hope, at least—not while I am alive. I know what being clothed in shame has done to my life. I know how much smaller and lonelier my life has become. I do not want my son to be hurt directly by any of this. He has done nothing to deserve the burdens of my past.

I hid my secret from my non-African friends. I knew their behavior would change towards me if they knew. It is human nature. Questions they would never ask would hover over us like a threatening cloud. The African friends who knew, I told myself, saw me outside of my shame. It was as though I had a birthmark on my face. They knew it was there because it was visible, but they were not bothered by it because they loved me. Still, I couldn't help feeling dirty and uncomfortable around anyone who knew.

It was hard enough to live knowing that some people knew. How could I survive if the whole world knew? I could not live with being pitied. When my friends on occasion told me, "to know you is to love you," I wanted to hug them and feel good that they thought of me that way. Instead, I was left confused and wanting to cry. How could they love me when my own mother didn't,?

Survival would require somehow embracing all that I am and all that I have been. It would take some time to get there.

CHAPTER 8

Give Me Sadness Any Day

SADNESS IS THE OPPOSITE OF HAPPINESS. It is not depression. Depression is its much uglier cousin. Depression is a darkness so all-consuming, a sorrow so wretched, a despair so unrelenting, that those of us who suffer from it see no visible end in sight.

I have wrestled with the demon of depression for as long as I have known myself. While much is known about the disease, still more is a mystery. An undeniable and irrefutable psychological component of depression—despite its extraordinarily complex nature and symptomatology—is loss. The most devastating of these is loss experienced in childhood.

I have often wondered which one of my own losses triggered my sickness. Was it the loss of innocence, my papa, my parts, or my body and soul? Was it the constant abandonment? Had I already been born with the curse and blessing of depression? I know that there have been no simple answers to my struggle, yet somehow, I have survived the horror of journeying through the hell of it.

"The pain of severe depression is quite unimaginable to those who have not suffered it, and it kills in many instances because its anguish can no longer be borne." William Styron, in his award-winning book *Darkness Visible*, could not have put it better. For most people looking in from the outside, depression is something indulgent. You hear the trite: "snap out of it when you show signs of distress" or "just take your medication and you'll be fine," but what they do not know is that depression, like a body, has limbs, and loneliness is its brain. In the event you make the mistake of sharing with people you consider close to you that you just want to end it all, to stop the pain, you open yourself up to such a barrage of negativity that leaves you feeling even worse. You are also left with the painful fact that you're alone in your pain, and you should never again make the mistake of asking for help.

Suicide is often considered the greatest act of cowardice. In some spheres, it is a clear sign of lack of faith. As a depressed person, I also have to deal with the shame attached to the illness and the fear of judgment. Sadly, as in almost every area of life, poor people get the short end of the stick. While both rich and poor suffer the same devastating symptoms of mental illness, rich people are not judged with the same harshness. When a celebrity has problems and goes to rehab or a mental health facility to get help, he is admired and, in some cases, becomes even more appealing as a public figure. For a poor person, coming out of the mental illness closet is a kiss of death. Of all the horrible facets of this disease, the loneliness is the hardest.

I recently went through the pages of the journals I kept 20 years ago and was shocked to read entry after entry describing one agonizing day after another and my prayers and pleas to God to make it stop. I wept as I read about the agony of unnamed fears, the deep black endless sorrow, the tremors, the nausea, the panic, the bone-weary fatigue that makes taking a breath a labor, and the prospect of getting out of bed an impossible challenge. The torment of the night when sleep remains only a dream, trying to make it all go away using whatever tools are at hand—prayer, people, meditation, medication, exercise, rest. How had I survived this for two decades?

Those of us who suffer this wretched melancholia are called "crazy." But what if "crazy" is to know the horror of living the one thousand four hundred and forty excruciating minutes of each day—and to still try to face the next one? "Crazy" is such a harsh word. I have been called it many times, and each time it cuts deep. I flinch when I hear it, and no matter how many times I do, its effect is still unnerving and leaves me wishing I was anyone but me.

My first therapist, Dr. G., had recommended Kay Redfield Jamison's *An Unquiet Mind*. My mind was certainly very far from quiet. I could relate. The author was a brilliant scientist and lecturer, reading the book was the beginning of my understanding that people can be smart, accomplished, educated, and mad.

Perhaps others like me have wounds that are invisible to the world. Perhaps they too take flight in another world to survive the pain. Perhaps madness as we know it is simply a wound of the soul.

There are no pills to heal the wounds of the soul. I tried. Pills for anxiety, some for panic attacks, others for bipolar disorder, depression, post-traumatic stress disorder—the list goes on. Perhaps all these are symptoms of a broken heart and wounded psyche. Some medicines have helped me manage for a little while, at different points in time, but they never did cure me. Some created more problems for me, like the 100 pounds I gained from Zoloft in six months, and the tics and tremors of anxiety symptoms I suffered for years—and still sometimes do. The fogginess in my brain that left me sleepwalking through life most days and the subsequent memory loss that I now struggle with. I was even given lithium, though in low doses. Lithium was used in the '60s and '70s to treat schizophrenia, and my doctor was quick to reassure me that they have since found other uses for the drug. She believed I would benefit from one of its other uses, like the debilitating insomnia I struggle with.

I do not blame those doctors. They were trying to help, and I think they might have even saved my life.

While I exhibited some of the symptoms of some of their diagnoses during my worst times, I could not be categorically classified. My situation was not a classic textbook case, they said. After years of therapy, kind Dr. G. once told me that she felt going back home to Africa would heal me. Going back home to whoever loved me might very well be the key, she thought. How could I tell her I had no one but my grandmother, and she is old?

Dr. G. explained to me that sometimes plants that are moved from their natural soil do not do well when transplanted, and sometimes, although they manage to survive, they do not thrive and are never the same. I believed some of that. The coldness of the people here in the U.S., the isolation, the often-superficial assessment of people, the constantly trying to reach the American dream, whatever that is, were all the ways in which Africa made me forget her faults and long for it. But I also knew I had left Africa with deep scars. I had also run away from the war. What ground would be kind enough to nourish me back to life? The one soaked with the blood of friends, family, and my fellow Sierra Leoneans who had been butchered like pigs? It would not be an easy transplant for me. So I stayed here, wandering America.

A big executive in San Francisco who had over 500 employees fell for me before I got fat and, for a while, helped me be numb to the discomfort of waking up in my skin every pain-filled day. We dated briefly before I met and fell in love with my son's father. He showed me the America I had always wanted to live in but only saw on television or read in books. He drove us in his Porsche to the Russian River, where we dined at restaurants that had no prices on their menus and where I was the only person of color in the room. He took me shopping at Saks and bought me a pair of crimson-colored Jimmy Choo's that would feed a family of four for a whole year in Africa. We'd take spa trips to Osmosis and other luxury hideouts in the Bay Area. These are experiences I will cherish forever. For a moment, I lived the idea of the American dream with my designer clothes, expensive handbags, fancy gifts, and custom-made perfumes and became the envy of a few friends. He adored my brothers, who had come to America four years after me, and gave them a glimpse of that world, too. He was impressed with how they had turned out in spite of the ravages of the blood diamond war that had brought them to a new world. He thought they were intelligent and had promise and would succeed in America with a sister as driven as he believed I was. He often said to them, "You guys have access to all the opportunities America has to offer." They got their Armani suits and fine watches and English silver shaving sets, even though they were barely old enough to shave. He enjoyed seeing the look of awe on their faces with each new extravagant gift. He was amused that, although I enjoyed the luxuries, I wasn't carried away by them. And he was shocked to hear me casually mention I gave a $5,000 handbag away he had given me for a birthday present.

"I will have you know my papa was not a poor man," I reminded him from time to time. He would smile and tell me he knew—there was something about the way I carried myself.

But he never knew the real me. I hid her well. He saw the well-educated, smart, sophisticated, sexy, smiling image I presented to the world. Though I enjoyed the luxuries, I was especially happy that my brothers got a chance to live a little. I have always wanted to give them the world. Since he was a fashion executive, I learned about haute couture and the importance of fashion in American culture. I learned from him that a well-cut blazer and the look of affluence got you admittance in certain worlds that might otherwise be closed to you. I learned that looks matter. People judge you by appearance here in the U.S.

I had always had a sense of style, but this man helped me refine it. Years later, when the pennies in my son's piggy bank were all I had to count, I remembered what I learned from my time with him and was able to feed my son through my work as a personal shopper, shopping at the same stores I had frequented, able to get whatever I wanted. Sooner or later, things end. Even paradise is not forever.

He remains a great friend—long after the love notes and failed dreams. Though I no longer go on those shopping sprees—he resigned from his job after a series of health scares and lives mostly on retirement now—I have a deep and meaningful relationship with someone whose impact on my life has gone far beyond Manolo Blahnik and Jimmy Choo.

CHAPTER 9

The Tin Foil Thieves

I CAN BE IMPULSIVE AND PRONE TO RECKLESSNESS. Given my luck, this astonishes me. Courting trouble should be the last thing I allow myself to indulge in. But I did, over and over. But crime? When people are drunk or high, they act stupid, yet I was neither high nor drunk. I was enjoying a rare time of happiness and was in a somewhat relaxed state of mind. This was due, in no small part, to the fact that I was dating a very shy, good-looking young Tom Cruise look-alike who had accepted my emotional baggage and was treating me as though I was somebody other than me. Even though I had told him things I never wanted anyone to know.

I was also still basking in the aftermath of my wonderful introduction to the good life by my now ex-executive. I was working, and my brothers were doing fine. I had just taken the LSAT and scored very high marks. It was going to happen—my dreams were taking shape. I was headed to law school.

I always wanted to work where I could be a part of making decisions and setting policies that would change things for a lot of people. Especially children. I knew only too well the plight of children and how, without mothers being whole themselves, the chances of them making it to become healthy, happy, productive members of their communities were slim—or even downright impossible. I was beginning to believe that happiness was possible for me and that the next bad thing was not about to happen. And I was in this frame of mind when I made the very wise decision to commit a crime. I did not know how to be when life felt calm. Having been in fight-or-flight for most of my life, experiences of nurturing and stability were too uncomfortable for me. I decided to become a thief. Even for me, it was pushing the envelope.

It was some time in the late 90s, and my boyfriend at the time, Alexei, was an engineer. He had heard at work that if you wrap foil around a store sensor, the alarm would somehow be disarmed and would not go off. The kind of sensors they had on merchandise back then would start beeping loudly as soon as you came within a certain radius of the exit in stores. When he told me about it, I said, "Let's prove it! Let's see if it actually works!" He hesitated, but then I pleaded, then cajoled, unable to contain my excitement. I thought it might be fun to prove something like that. Alexei could never have imagined or suggested such a thing. He was too steady, too solid. With two parents still together after decades, he was an only child and had been doted on and sent to the best schools in Russia to prepare him for a good life. He was skilled in the language of computers. He was someone who had a future. We met because he had just been hired as an expatriate from Europe and, like me, was new to America. He had no reason to want to live on the edge.

It was this sense of normalcy about him that had drawn me to him. He had everything I never had and always wanted.

We headed to Macy's, my store of choice. We were prepared. I had come with a roll of foil and a heart that was pumping enough adrenaline to wake up ten dead men. We went up the escalator to the first floor, looking for their women's department. I didn't want to ask the overly made-up, bored-looking, 20-something sales associate behind the counter. She did not seem like she cared one way or another to make a sale.

These days sensors are sleek, almost pretty, and, in most cases, fairly unnoticeable. Back then, they were the Neanderthals of security devices—big, ugly, and very visible. We went up and down the escalators, from one department to the next, down many aisles until we found the women's sweater department. I would take a sweater. How exhilarating the feeling of being bad. A sense of confidence I had never known came over me. And I was with someone who loved me; I was not alone. Plus, an adrenalin rush that came from knowing that I was making something happen for a change. I grabbed three sweaters and walked close to the fitting room area. I took the roll of foil out of my purse, and we started wrapping the sensors in it. Poor Alexei looked a little nervous. His cheeks were suffused with color, and his hands were shaking slightly. I'm sure he was having second thoughts but went along with it because I seemed so carefree and sure—characteristics he would never have associated with me just a few months before. Then I decided I only needed one sweater, but the sweater we settled on didn't quite fit in my purse. I was confident that even though it was sticking out of my purse somewhat, as long as the alarm didn't go off, I would be ok. And why would it? It was wrapped in foil.

"Ready?" I asked. He nodded silently. We went down the escalators and headed towards the large glass exit doors. The next thing I knew, the sensors were going off louder than I'd ever heard them before. The high-pitched sound was slightly off-key and sounded different—as if the sensor had developed a super high ring, especially for me. The security guards were upon us.

"We got you," said one of the two security guards, and my heart sank. "Put your arms behind your back." No. Please, God. No. I was shaking as I looked around, hoping no one I knew had seen me being cuffed and led away. After all, my job was only a block away, and my coworkers and I went there sometimes to browse or have lunch in the basement where there was a cafe. The sound of my heart was pounding in my head. I could kick myself. *Look what you have gone and done? You want to bring trouble on yourself—that's your business. Why include someone else? Someone who had been nothing but kind to you?* Thoughts raced through my head, and I felt terrible as we were led down the stairs and into their loss prevention room. I hated myself.

Being handcuffed is not pleasant; it's uncomfortable and painful. My high from earlier had completely disappeared, and panic gripped me when I heard the guard say, mockingly, "We were watching you the whole time. You did not even try to hide. You're going to jail."

This wasn't happening. I hadn't heard right, I told myself. *This was a dream. I wasn't going to jail—could not go to jail!* The look on his face told me it was no dream. Shit shit shit! I wanted to vomit. I was sweating and tried to explain about the foil and sensor. That we were not really thieves even if we had stolen. He wasn't buying it. Apparently, I had taken a very expensive sweater, and, when the amount of whatever you steal exceeds a certain dollar amount, it is a crime. In this case, a felony. I had neither looked at the label nor the price of the sweater I was going to jail for.

After what seemed like hours, I asked the guard who had been doing all the talking while we were still sitting in his office. He told me we were waiting for the van.

"What van?" I asked, still thinking he had been joking about us going to jail.

"Transport," he said, with a look of glee on his face.

I couldn't help thinking: *A good day's work. Another criminal thwarted.* Perhaps a bonus or commission. I was in complete shock. I was going to be locked up in jail in America.

Papa god sorry for me. I reverted to my native Krio tongue and started to pray silently, fighting to hold back the tears. How long will I be in jail? Who was going to tell my brothers that the sister they'd looked up to all their lives was a criminal, a common thief? The one whose example they had been told to follow? Shame and sorrow washed over me. The van arrived, and we were helped inside. *Am I dreaming? I must be.* We made a stop somewhere. There was a divider between the driver and us, and we could not really see where we were being taken. The great divide between the good and the bad, the upright and the unrighteous. We stopped somewhere. A man in handcuffs climbed in. Or, rather, was "helped" in. Another criminal. He barely glanced at us and gazed in the distance.

We soon arrived at the jail because the van stopped. It was not a long drive. We were led up some stairs, and I heard sounds but could not understand what was being said until I heard a mocking voice say, "Say goodbye to your boyfriend." That got my attention. I had been able to keep some level of control up until then because I was not alone. But then I was going to be separated from Alexei. Terror gripped me, and I started freaking out.

"Please, please let me go with him," I begged. "I need to be near him. Please don't take me away from him. I have no one here."

They ignored me as I cried openly. Alexei was led away in a different direction. All my fears around abandonment surfaced. I half said and half yelled at Alexei, "Please don't leave me here! I am scared." He gazed briefly at me with a look of profound apology and managed to say, "Everything will be ok. Ok? Don't worry," as the door shut behind him. In a daze, I followed the female officer I had been handed over to. I heard something about booking. A language I do not understand was being spoken. Prison language. Suspect, case, processing. What does processing mean here? It sounds scary.

Things moved quickly. I soon found myself in line with other women, and we are told to form another line. Each woman is signaled to a box-like contraption just wide enough to accommodate spread-eagled legs. I was next, and I stood frozen until the stocky black guard with tight braids that looked like they hurt shouted, "Pull your panties down!"

"Why?" I stammered.

"Bend over," she barked, ignoring my question. There is something in her tone that brooks no further questions, and I obeyed. I saw something that looked like a glint of mockery, of something superior in her manner, as if to say, "Gotcha."

"You Africans come to our country, go to school here, take our jobs, befriend those white devils, and think you're better than us. I had heard these complaints from many African Americans since I had been in America. *You people, think you're better than us, but look whose ass is spread before me now,* her eyes said with barely disguised hatred. Her gloved hands poked around secret places to make sure I was not hiding anything. She told me to cough. I did—and farted. One of those fear-farts that precede diarrhea and stink like rotten eggs. Humiliated beyond words and asking all African people to forgive me, I pulled up my underwear and limped like a whipped dog to where I was told to go next. For what will officially label me as a criminal—my mugshot and fingerprints. "Move it," somebody said, pointing in my direction. I am moving too slowly and holding up the line. My legs, still shaking, managed to get me to the front of the line where my purse was emptied, its contents documented and sealed. I was led into a cell. I was told my purse would be returned to me on my release. The words sounded ominous, and another wave of panic hit me. How long was I going to be there? There were about a dozen women in my jail cell, most of whom looked like ladies of the night with high heels, short skirts, visible cleavages, bare midriffs, and neon-colored eyeshadow.

Cold eyes swept me up and down and dismissed me. *Pussy. Look at her whimpering in the corner,* their eyes said. I was struck by their hard and calm gaze. It seemed like they could have been there about the same time the day before. I quickly lowered my eyes. I had received enough bad looks for one night. The rest of them mostly ignored me and talked to each other.

A few were stretched out on the cold concrete slab, fast asleep. How can anyone fall asleep here? Across from me was the men's cell. It was twice as crowded. Perhaps men commit more crimes. I could not look at them too long; they looked like they'd never smiled a day in their life. Most of them were Black, some were Latino, and a few were white. The women were mostly white, with the exception of just one other Black woman who stared straight past me as if I did not exist when I attempted a weak smile of comradeship. Hey, we are the only two here—the thing minorities often do to feel less alone, less exposed.

It looked like it was going to be a long night. I was terrified and did not know what was going to happen. I could not help wondering about the people behind bars like caged animals. Did they have mothers who prayed for them each night and wanted a good life for them? Had some had a good beginning and squandered it for a life on the streets? Had some lost their way because they had no one in those crucial formative years to set an example for them and teach them about life? Had others been driven by circumstances to become criminals? I did not know what group I fell into. I realized at that moment in jail that we were no different from one another: the educated versus the uneducated, the abused versus the cared-for, the poor versus the privileged. We were all just people whose freedom now lay in the hands of others.

I tried to make up stories about each person to pass the time. I needed to keep my mind from thinking about a life in jail. I imagined them with families. I imagined them having hopes and dreams. I imagined them away from there. There was no excuse for what I had done. I had brought this on myself and deserved to be punished.

After what seemed like forever, I saw Alexei escorted out by a guard. Soon after, I heard my name called out. Bail had been posted for me, and I was free to go.

It felt like I had been there for days, but it had only been nine hours. I floated out of that jail and never looked back, vowing never to be that casual about my freedom again.

The whole nightmare was not over. We were to appear before a judge. We were going to trial. What if the judge did not like me? What if the judge was one of those who hated Black people and considered all of them criminals just because they were Black? What if I came across the wrong way? What could that wrong way be? I was a nervous wreck. I could be behind bars in America while my friends and college mates were already getting ready to graduate medical school or were mid-way through their doctoral programs. I could be in an American jail when they were thinking I was in law school or doing an internship somewhere—not wearing an orange jumpsuit and being the woman of some prison baddie whose advances I would have nowhere to run from.

I know without a doubt that being an African born in Africa played a role in the judge's decision. I have always felt rage when I have been told: "You're different from them—the Blacks here." I have made some snide comments and given not-so-friendly responses in retaliation, refusing to be assuaged by the "You're nicer, not aggressive" differentiation. "The Blacks here are lazy, not like you guys from Africa" has been the message, as if the Blacks here are not from Africa. As if their ancestors had not been brought here as slaves. I have always believed that belittling any Black person is belittling all Black people. I hate this divide imposed yet again on Black people. It is exhausting and depressing making a case for Blackness, whether it is African Blackness or African American Blackness.

But this was the one time I was happy about the "you're not one of them" stereotype. I could not go back to jail. Not even in defense of my Black heritage.

I had prayed long and hard a few days before our court appearance, trying to come up with reasons and explanations for what I had done. I had told the security guard at Macy's the story about trying to prove if science worked, but he had not believed me and had taken us to jail. What if the judge did not either?

That morning, I walked into the courtroom and was given the Bible to swear on. In that moment, I knew what I had to do. I had no choice. I told her everything. The truth, exactly like it had happened. A strange calm had taken over me as I explained that the whole thing was my idea. I told her my boyfriend was a good person and had only been pulled into this by stupidity and perhaps love. I told her I did not know what had gotten into me to do such a thing.

I was getting ready to start school and was not a criminal. I told her I knew I had done a very bad thing and was very ashamed.

The judge listened intently, all the while looking directly into my eyes. For a few seconds after I finished talking, she was quiet. Finally, she said that she thought I had simply made a silly mistake, and everyone makes them sometime in their life.

"Learn from this. I don't think I will see you back in my courtroom."

She dismissed all the charges. No criminal record.

She had believed me. I smiled a relieved *Thank You* to God and walked out of the courtroom like someone who clearly understood they had just dodged a bullet. The hard-nosed women in that jail were a cold reminder that I could not survive a life of crime. Lucky for me, I had not ended up in jail for my stupidity as the "Orange Is the New Black" star Piper Kerr did. Unlike her, I would not have survived.

Some days, when I look back on that day in court, I feel pretty certain that had I sounded unpolished, had I not had my distinctly African features, if my fancy Stuart Weitzman designer pumps, peeking discreetly from the leg of my well-cut suit, and if an accomplished, white engineer beside me had not all sold me as a productive citizen, the outcome would have been very different. Other days, I believe I had simply been given a reprieve.

Perhaps one day, my son will forgive me for being a person who went to jail—if only for a few hours.

CHAPTER 10

House of Horrors

IT WAS JUST A COUPLE OF MONTHS AFTER I had been in the hospital for a life-threatening illness that my son was conceived in a five-minute quickie. I had been home for two months when Alexei surprised me and flew my brothers in to see me since he knew it was the only thing that would make me feel better. I was in too much pain for much else, and I figured he had made me happy—why not make him happy, too?

Three weeks later, I started feeling sick and having some crazy symptoms, so we rushed to the emergency room thinking I might be having another embolism. When the blood tests and urine results came back saying that I was pregnant, I almost collapsed from shock. It couldn't be. I was not supposed to have children!

When I was in my teens, I had surgery to remove ovarian cysts, and the surgeon told my mother that he thought I would never be able to conceive.

By the time my son was born, I had few words left to describe the most beautiful yet painful experience of my existence. For the week I was in the hospital, I endured multiple surgeries, including a C-section and a tubal ligation to stop me from ever getting pregnant again. Then I was sent home. I was to continue on blood thinners for a considerably long time. The doctors warned me I could have another blood clot with no warning. One more thing for my crazed mind to latch onto.

I had worked hard to survive an orgasm-less life, but I was not to escape unscathed the other ravages of my circumcision. My troubles resurfaced after we left the hospital.

At home, things were not easy. I was bruised everywhere, and the surgery sites hurt badly. Then I noticed something else. A painful kind of pulsing sensation down there. I thought it would go away in a few days, but it didn't. It got worse. By the second week, I could not sit on a chair. My vagina was on fire. How was it possible? I did not have a vaginal delivery. I went to the hospital and was told I had pelvic floor dysfunction. The weight of the pregnancy had put a lot of strain on my reproductive organs, and all the scarring from the circumcision had finally gotten on my vagina's nerves, literally, and, boy, was she angry. I could not sit and could not stand upright. Between the pain, a baby who cried every waking moment, and my incessant sleep problems, I was a time bomb waiting to explode. My preterm baby, who had no visible problems except reflux because his intestines were not wholly developed before he was born, was inconsolable while he was awake. He only stopped crying when he fell into an exhausted sleep, which lasted only a few hours. After which, he would wake up, and the cycle would begin all over again.

I held on in excruciating pain for four months. The only time I got relief was after my weekly shot at U.C.S.F. At the clinic, the doctor would put a gloved hand inside of me to feel for where the spasms were originating from, and then, with a six-inch needle, inject the numbing medicine into the offending site. Blessed relief for a few hours, until the medicine wore off, and I was back in hell. I was weary beyond words, and the pain left me too drained to bask in the magic of my son.

Still, I insisted on giving my baby the best care, no matter what. I did his laundry, including his palm-sized cloth diapers. I washed and sterilized all his bottles. I could not breastfeed. My doctors had asked me if I could live with myself if my son started showing signs of being "slow" at five years because my breast milk had been "poisoned" from all the medication I had been given while I was pregnant. It was the first time I finally broke down and cried throughout my whole pregnancy ordeal. I could not nurse my child. Could not feed him the thing that would have been the most ideal for him. I started my child on formula the very afternoon the doctors posed the question to me. My feelings of inadequacy could not compare to my fear of risking his sanity by insisting on standing on ceremony and breastfeeding him.

By the fourth month after his birth, I was crazed with pain, exhaustion, and sadness. Most days, I was on my knees, crawling to pick up my baby since standing hurt too much and sitting was impossible. I would lie on my side to feed him.

It was on one such evening my mother called. It was the first time I had spoken to her after I found out she had left me in critical care in the hospital to marry him a second time. I must have said something to the effect of, "Now I understand why people kill themselves" or something along those lines. I did tell her that I had taken the pain medicine the doctor had given me for the pelvic floor pain. They were muscle relaxers. She must have heard something in my voice during that conversation. She called an ambulance for me and called Alexei and told him he should come home—that I had sounded strange on the phone. The next thing I remember was opening my eyes in an ambulance and being driven somewhere.

When I woke up hours later, I found myself in a strange, hospital-like environment, and I immediately asked for my baby. I was told he was at home. I told the staff I was going home—I needed to be home to take care of him. The nurses looked at each other with a look that sent a chill down my spine. I knew then that something was very wrong, that I was in trouble.

"You can't go home."

"What? Why?" I was shaking so badly I could barely get the words out.

"You tried to kill yourself. We have to keep you here until we are sure you are not going to harm yourself or anyone else, including the baby."

This could not be happening. This was not real; it was one of my nightmares. I had seen the movie *Girl Interrupted,* about a young woman locked up in an asylum and the terrors she lives through. Please, God, let this be unreal.

"Me? Hurt my baby? I would never hurt my baby. I love him more than my own life." I said this, looking right into the nurse's eyes, hoping she would see I was telling the truth, trying not to laugh at the absurdity of what I was hearing.

I continued trying to explain to her that I did not want to kill myself, that all I wanted was to sleep. A long sleep—a "make up for four months"-kind of sleep.

They looked at me with tired eyes that said, "we've heard it all before."

It began to sink in that this was no cruel joke. I was not going home. I finally broke down. Great, wracking sobs came from somewhere deep inside me. I was crying for the child that had grown up too fast in a world she'd had to navigate all by herself. I was crying for my papa, who had died and left me defenseless against all the people who had preyed on my innocence. I was crying for the mother who would leave me again and again. I was worth nothing, was nothing, meant nothing. I was crying for my brothers who were far away from me now, they, who had been my first reasons to try and survive my life. I was crying for Alexei, the father of my child, who had been the only family I had had these past few years. I was crying for the loss of the only thing that had finally made life worth living—my son. I was crying so hard; I could not stop.

The nurses did not respond to anything I said. I pleaded to something human in them. Please, let me go home. Please, let me go to my child. He needs me; I could never hurt him. Please. My voice, hoarse and weak with defeat, came out small and barely recognizable. The more I pleaded with them, the less approachable they became.

I felt someone take me by the elbow and heard her say, "I will take her to her room." I recognized her as African by her accent. Confused and trembling, I let her lead me away. I was cold. My bones felt chilled, and it felt as though I would never feel warm again, even if I were lying in the belly of the sun.

As soon as we were out of earshot, she whispered, "Do you want to stay here forever? Stop crying. Right now."

"Wipe your eyes," she commanded. I turned to look at her. A simple face with clear, gentle eyes. Never had an ordinary face taken on the magnificence that African nurse's face had. With her unremarkable features and ordinary look, hers was the most beautiful face I had ever seen.

"I can't stay for long—but listen to me. You are in the house of crazy people. Everyone who is brought here is mad."

I started to protest. "I am not, at least not 'this place' kind of crazy," I said quickly. I briefly explained the circumstances around which I had been brought here. She took my hand in hers.

"I believe you. Now make them believe you. Wipe your eyes." By then, they were almost swollen shut and burning like hell. "Smile," she continued. But not too much. Act normal."

What does normal mean for someone like me? I have never known normal. She must have seen the confusion on my face.

"Act friendly," she insisted. "I have to go now."

I thanked her and watched her walk quietly out of the room. I knew without a doubt that she had been placed there for me. Someone was looking out for me.

Saint Helena Behavioral Rehabilitation. My new home. The bell rang, and I noticed people coming out of open hallways leading to a big room. It was the first time I really looked around me. There were no doors. The windows were unreachable and sealed; the walls were painted some nondescript color. The faces that weren't blank had the expression of "forgotten," "dead," "hell." No one spoke. My heart started racing, and I felt panic setting in all over again. I couldn't stay there. I could not survive a day there left alone—oh no. *Don't let your crazy mind carry you away, silly girl. Focus and stop that sniffling. Focus and stop imagining worst-case scenarios. This is not the time for that.*

I had begun crying again after seeing the looks of the lost souls shuffling alongside me towards the dining room. *Remember what the nurse told you? You want to get back to the baby? Then toughen up and do what you must do to get out of here.*

The tall white nurse gives instructions, hands out medications with a small cup of water, and waits until each patient dutifully swallows them. I remembered one more thing my African angel-nurse had told me: "Do not drink the medicine. Whatever you do, don't drink any medicine they give you." I knew I had to somehow hide the pills in my mouth. *Now you're thinking. Concentrate on the plan. Follow the instructions the angel-nurse gave you. Do not focus on the sights and sounds around you or even the terror now gripping you.* I managed to maneuver the pills under my tongue as the nurse watched, never taking her eyes off me even once. I waited until she had her back to me before going quickly to the bathroom and flushing them down the toilet. After that, I went to the nurse's station and smiled a small, friendly-but-apologetic smile.

"May I say something?" I asked. "I am sorry I was loud earlier. I just panicked when I was told I was not going home to my baby." Blank faces. "You see, I am not from here. I am from Africa, and I have no family here to help me with the baby. His father works, and until I came here, I was the only one caring for him. He is only four months. It is why I was so upset. That is no excuse for making so much noise and disturbing others. Thank you for understanding, and I promise you it won't happen again."

Another apologetic smile and I walked to the communal fenced-in "outdoor" space, my legs shaking uncontrollably. What is it about this place that strikes such terror in me? Is it because they can make a case that I am dangerous and have my child kept from me? Is it because they have the power to take my freedom away permanently? My apology was barely acknowledged, but I could see the muscles in the back of the tall white nurse easing slightly. She'd had her back to me the whole time.

Except for the occasional sounds of sorrow and whimpers, it was quiet in the "outdoor" space. No one talked much there. What was left to say?

Later that afternoon, I went back to the nurses' station, hoping they would not hold it against me for stopping by a second time. I needed to know what came next. I was told I was going to be seen by the doctor soon and get an evaluation.

"When will I get to go home?" I asked, trying to fight fresh panic.

"Well," the tall nurse's condescending tone both rankled and scared me. "The doctor will see you, and then he gets to decide what happens next." I had a thousand questions, but she had already turned away. I could feel the almost-familiar coldness emanating from her. *Does she ever smile?* I wondered.

I looked for my friend to ask her about the "evaluation." Somehow the word sat heavy in my head. But I could not find her, my angel-nurse; perhaps she was off or never coming back. My heart sank. Just like that, some strange doctor who did not know me or my history would have my fate in his hands. In the meantime, I was informed I had one phone call I could make. I called my little brother. My first baby.

As soon as I heard his voice, I started crying again. I couldn't help it. What if I never saw him again? What if I would never get to leave this place? I told him I was scared. He managed to reassure me somehow. As painful as it was, the phone call with him gave me a new determination to fight to come home for him, too—and his brother.

I was told it was time for bed, so I went to my assigned room. I had a roommate. She was white and middle-aged, but she looked eternally old and did not speak, even after I said hello. I knew it was going to be a long night. Earlier I had noticed something peculiar. All the patients wore tennis shoes that had no shoelaces on them. It was a time before lace less sports shoes were fashionable as they are now. I wondered why. I was relieved to find my African angel and then almost lost my cool and grabbed her, trying to hold onto the only good in this place, my one source of light. But then I gathered myself quickly when I saw the quick flash of warning in her eyes. I asked her about the laces.

"No laces are allowed so that people don't strangle themselves," she told me. She did not say "and others," but I heard that too in her voice.

I sat up all night. It was easy for me, thinking that even without shoelaces, people could still do really bad things if they wanted to, badly enough. I managed to keep my mind busy with thoughts of my child and the wonder of becoming a mother. Then it was morning, and I was relieved to get into the shower. I let the water run over me a long time as though I was cleansing myself from the sheets I'd lain in, cleansing myself from the nurses with their soulless eyes. The water was not hot enough. I was sure it was purposeful.

I knew I had to do exactly what my angel had told me, so after breakfast, I went to talk to the nurse who scared me. I was trying to act normal. Not eating would have called attention to myself. I managed to do almost all the things the others did and participated in all the required activities. I do not remember seeing another Black person there—patient or employee. What was an African doing working in a place like this? I had asked the nurses when the doctor was coming, and I was told the next day. I would be evaluated first by one doctor then would have to appear before a board to have my case discussed.

CHAPTER 11

A Case for Baby

I WAS NERVOUS AND EXCITED that I would finally get to see the doctor. I was also scared out of my mind. That evening, just before she left, my new friend managed to find a few minutes to talk to me and give me pointers.

"You are going to be asked why you should go home. What will you tell them? Are you going to say you have had issues with your mother and that's why you ended up here? Tell them the truth. The one you told me. Tell them the truth in the way they would understand. This is important. Make them understand."

I have always loved debating and acting. In college, I wrote and starred in a play called *The Revelation*, a watered-down version of the story about my life, for which I won the Best Actress award. I didn't think it was fair since I hadn't acted much, I had just been myself. I remembered being in kindergarten, one of the three "beautiful ladies" in a school play, and my line had been "Beauty of beauties, am I not the most beautiful one of them all?" The crowd had shouted, "You are!" But my friend's line struck something in me: "Beauty does not count, but character." The crowd had erupted. Something told me that I wanted that thing called character. Whatever was so powerful that could render beauty countless I wanted.

I have always been ambitious. Throughout high school and college, I was in every debating team that would have me, and I vowed that, regardless of the position we took, I would make sure I made my point even if we ended up losing. We never lost. That morning I was to appear before the board, I told myself that if I have ever needed my persuasive abilities to work for me, this was the time. I would be making the most important presentation, the most important argument, the most important plea of my life. I was going to be making a case for my baby. He was the only reason I wanted to live another day in my miserable existence.

I had sat up all night trying to plan out my defense for why I had taken those muscle relaxants. I could not decide what to say first and how to say it, so I prayed. I asked God to give me the right words. To let the right words, lead to the right outcome, which would be to get out of there and go home to baby.

My palms were sweating. I had never experienced that particular symptom of anxiety before. My heart was pounding in my head. I told myself. "Trust God. You have done nothing wrong. God gave you that child. He will bring you back to him."

I had tried not to focus on the baby those two days. I would have come undone had I thought about how I missed feeding him and hearing his endless cries, how I missed the feeling of holding him close and inhaling his sweet baby scent, how I missed looking at this extension of me, knowing that he was mine—the one, beautiful, pure thing in my life. I missed the feeling of gratitude that filled me every time I looked at this little person who had done so much for me already. I had felt completely bereft that first day I had found myself in that place, and I knew that had I focused on the possibility of being physically separated from him, I would have lost all hope and never would have been able to do what I needed to do to return to him.

As I walked into the room, I told myself, *Whatever you do, you have to get back home to the baby. He needs you. He needs you to survive this world.*

There were three people waiting for me: one man and two women. I said, "Hi." They said hello in return, and, after some clinical questions, they started their questions.

"How long have you been depressed? How often do you think of harming yourself? Do you have a plan?" And on and on. Then it was time. I knew it the moment I heard this.

"Why do I think we should take the risk of sending you home when you have not even been here long enough?" the man asked. He seemed to be the person in charge.

"Long enough for what?" I asked.

"Long enough to get well," was the answer.

I told them that wellness was my child. Wellness was in that little bundle of a second chance that God had been merciful enough to give me. I told them the story of my life and how I had ended up in America and this place. I did not talk long, but I told them enough to give them a sense of who I was other than the case they had on file. I told them about the child who had grown up in Africa and managed to live through her early years and make it to America. I told them how hard it had been, but I had always managed to survive. I told them about how my child had been conceived and the circumstances around his birth. I told them I had made a promise to my son that all he had to do was make it to the world, and I would take care of him. I told them that if they thought I was too "crazy" or too dangerous to be sent back to my child and society after everything I had told them, then let them decide.

The male doctor looked at me.

"I've heard a lot of things in my profession, and I've seen a lot of things in my life, but I have yet to see a woman who wanted her child more. I cannot imagine how it must have been for you to have endured such a pregnancy and the circumstances that followed.

"You could never hurt your child. You are one of the bravest people I have ever met, and I hope you know when you leave here that your life is worth something, and that not even your mother is worth dying for. She is living her life. Go live yours with your son. I wish you the very best."

The other two people had been crying halfway through my story, and by the time I got to the part about going without sleep for four months, one of them had excused herself. She never joined the panel again. I was overcome with so many emotions from the doctor's response and was so drained from the past 48 hours that I just sat in the chair without moving until the doctor's voice brought me back to myself.

"You are free to go home. I am going to write your discharge papers. One more thing I want to say to you: please ask for help. You've done a remarkable job of surviving, but no one can make it alone. Try to find people who care about you and let them be there for you and your son. You need the support. You and your son deserve a chance. You are going home today."

I jumped up and wanted so desperately to run and give that doctor a hug, but I knew such displays were not permitted, and I did not want to tempt fate.

"Thank you, doctor," I said, my eyes brimming with tears and my heart overflowing with gratitude. I could finally breathe. I rushed out of the conference room, straight to the nurses' station, and shouted: "I am going home!"

One of them permitted herself a hint of a smile. The tall one just raised an eyebrow and said, "We are well aware. You can go get yourself packed."

I did not need to be told twice. I had done it. I had won the biggest case of my life. I felt a new surge of energy from the thought of seeing the baby again. I didn't have much to pack. I changed from the "prison" gown into my own clothes, gathered my papers, and waited for the guard to take me through the gates to Freedom.

I vowed that day that nothing will ever make me want to not live again. I begged God to take back all the prayers I had prayed to Him to let me die so I would not have to live in skin that I had never felt whole in. I asked Him to give me life so that I can watch my son grow up. I asked Him to keep me here so that I would be here to hold his hand when the world was hard and broke his heart.

Nowadays, when my friends jokingly say, "You're crazy," I smile—though not comfortably. I have, after all, been locked up. And I have the papers to prove it.

Two months before I got pregnant, I had a massive bilateral pulmonary embolism and had been on life support in intensive care for a week. I was put on blood thinners, possibly for the rest of my life since no one understood why I had developed clots in my lungs without any warning.

It was strange how it happened. I had felt unwell most of the day and could not really put a finger on what was wrong. By evening I felt a small tightness in my chest, but no pain. I must have looked grey or some other scary hue—Black people turning grey is not a pretty picture—but it must have been bad enough for Alexei to say we should go to the Emergency Room. I told him I was okay. I had had migraines that made me feel worse. He threatened to call the ambulance if I did not let him take me to the hospital. I capitulated and said okay.

Since I hate loud noises and can't stand the sirens of ambulances, he drove me there. We got to the hospital just in time. The doctor suspected something but could not be sure. She sent me in for a CT scan even after the initial tests all showed I was okay. She later told me that something made her push for the scan even though, based on my preliminary results, everything seemed okay except my heart rate, which was over 280 beats per minute. I passed out just as the contrast dye was injected into my arm. I woke up in the ICU and would spend the rest of the week there, including my 32nd birthday, coughing up blood the size of large grapes. I told God that if he let me get out of that hospital bed and let me breathe again on my own without the pain that felt as if a million daggers had been plunged into my heart, I would never ask him for anything else as long as I live.

My mother was told to come since I was critically ill. She did, but she did not stay. My therapist, Dr. G., knowing the tumultuous nature of our relationship, advised my pulmonologist and primary care doctors that she did not believe I could survive an "episode" with my mother in the condition I was in. They explained the situation to my mother and told her to leave.

She came to my bedside. I was barely conscious through all the medicines and machines breathing for me, but I knew enough to know I wanted my mother there. I was scared and wanted my mother with me.

"Mama, noh go yaa. Please, noh go?"

She calmly told me the doctors had told her to go, so she was leaving. I pleaded with her not to leave. I could feel the burning in my chest as I watched her walk out the door. I cried for I do not know how long, moaning like a wounded animal. I curled into a fetal position, my back facing the world the rest of the day, too ashamed to show my defeat and pain to the nurses and my friends who had come to visit. How could she leave me?

I turned 33 the next day. I asked Alexei, then still just my boyfriend, and my friend D. Francois to celebrate my birthday with me. I wanted to remind myself that I was still alive even though I felt dead inside. They brought a cake from Emporio Rulli, my favorite Italian Bakery in Larkspur. I cut it and gave it to the nurses. I did not taste it. I have a picture of me that day sitting on the toilet with the gold wrapping paper of my cake sticking out of the wastebasket. I wonder who took it.

I am a mother now. Placed in my own mother's position, what choice would I have made? I know it would not have included leaving my child. When we had a conversation about that incident a while later, she insisted she had wanted me to be okay, and that was why she didn't stay. The doctors had told her to leave, and they knew best she claimed.

I was told that after she left me in the hospital on life support, she traveled straight to Africa and organized a big traditional wedding for the family to participate in. She married the man who raped me. Again. The civil ceremony performed in a court in America was not enough for her. She wanted our people back home to know she was his Mrs. I wish I had never been told. It was the biggest blow and left the deepest wound.

I was not supposed to get pregnant. The doctor in Africa had said so. I had not been on birth control for the nine years I had been with Alexei and had never gotten pregnant. How could I be pregnant now? The emergency room doctor who had run the tests, including another CT scan to rule out blood clots, repeated, "Your pregnancy tests are all positive."

Before the reality of it could sink in, she went on.

"You're pregnant—but you can't keep the baby. You are on blood thinners—and could very likely be for the rest of your life since we can't determine what caused you to have your pulmonary embolism in the first place. I am sending you to a high-risk specialist."

My new doctor was a bright and confidence-inspiring practitioner from Korea. I felt I was in good hands from the very beginning. She took her time explaining to me that since it was not a normal pregnancy, I should expect some challenges. A slew of tests followed, including an ultrasound that showed a yolk sac that was empty. There was no heartbeat—no way to determine if it was a viable uterine pregnancy or an ectopic one.

"You're a tough one, dear," she said after I had spent the week being poked, prodded, and questioned incessantly about anything unusual I may have noticed. All the while, I insisted I was okay with doing as many tests as required until we had an answer.

The second blood test showed a doubling in the blood hormone of the fetus after a week but still no conclusion on anything. I was pregnant—but not really? I would I have to go back for another blood test in a few days.

We lived in limbo for weeks. I was miserable. Why does even this have to be so complicated? Why couldn't I just be happy for the miraculous? I had actually gotten pregnant! Still, Alexei and I went for a walk one evening and decided on names. I chose a name from the Bible. The baby's name would translate as "God is with us." I knew God needed to be with us every step of the way in order for this child to be. I named a child that had not been confirmed to be officially existent. Perhaps I was daring God to give him to me by choosing a name; perhaps I was psyching myself to believe. In the meantime, I continued to have moments of God's grace and words of encouragement from my most wonderful OB-GYN. I look back now and see how strong my faith was then. I see how much easier it was for me to surrender and say: *God, let Thy will be done.*

I lived like this throughout the months I carried the baby—in faith and terror. When the pregnancy was finally confirmed weeks later, I was told I could not keep it and would need to have a planned abortion. Pregnancies, blood clots, and blood thinners don't go together. Keeping the pregnancy would be tantamount to committing suicide. I was taking Coumadin, a blood thinner, and could potentially have a miscarriage and bleed to death if it happened while I was alone and out of the reach of immediate medical help. I told the doctors that was a chance I was willing to take. I was not going to have an abortion to "save my life."

Once I had signed all the papers relieving them of any liability, my faith journey began. The doctor switched me to a different medication that did not cross the placenta but was still a blood thinner, but there would still be a possibility of a miscarriage. The new medication, Lovenox, was given by injection. I would have to administer the shots myself into the fattiest part of the lower belly every 12 hours until the child was born. I believed my child had been sent to me for a reason. I had no hesitation in saying Yes to carrying him. Yet, there were the hard facts that I was taking enough medication that could not only potentially result in a miscarriage but could also cause him to be born with many defects—neurological and physical. The doctors were very clear. There were days I wondered if I was playing God by deciding to have the baby in spite of every warning I had been given. But I could not not have him.

Some claim that you cannot have both faith and fear at the same time, but I lived both—my faith just a little was larger than the fear. Living in the moment—a concept that was very foreign to me before the pregnancy—became the only way I survived during that time. My days were almost predictable. Wake up. Pray. Give myself the shot. Run to the bathroom every few minutes for the next few hours after I had injected the blood thinner to check and see if I was hemorrhaging. Each time I walked in the bathroom, my heart would be in my mouth, praying there was no red coloring my underwear to match the Victorian red I had painted the walls of my bathroom months before—a color choice that now haunted me. I would look between my legs. Nothing. Then breathe. Deep breath, a quick prayer thanking God that we—baby and I—had survived one more moment. No blood, breathe, no blood, breathe. I would repeat this cycle hundreds of times until eight months, two surgeries, and one thousand seven hundred and thirty self-administered blood thinning injections later, my son was placed in my arms.

There will never be words to describe that first holding of him. Have I not kissed his nose a thousand times—each time sweeter than the last? Have I not clasped him close, holding this extension of me in reverence? There is no way to describe the fierce need to just hold him to me. Never will I give my heart so completely and so freely without wanting anything in return. My favorite nickname for him is "mama's heart." Because of him, I have come to know the sweetest love. Through him, I have come to love myself for the first time in my life. He is my breath outside of me.

I look at the wonder that is my son, and I know I will never know love like this again. The love I have for my son, this holiest of loves, humbles me into gratitude.

As much as I have wanted my son more than anything in life, I have also been in constant fear since he was born. A few months ago, I was going through important documents, journals, and photos, which I had to sort through because they had become wet and molded from being in boxes under the stairway of the small apartment we now live in. We have moved five times since my son was born. He's twelve now. The notebooks I had kept in my teen years in Africa and the journals I had kept my first few years in America had gotten damaged. I salvaged what I could. I cleaned them with eucalyptus and tea tree oils to kill fungus and dried them out in the sun for days. The ones I couldn't save, I threw away. I couldn't help but wonder how much of my life had gone to waste because of circumstances beyond my control. I found menus, lists, receipts, and notes to myself preparing for his birth and birthdays.

My son was helping me go through the boxes. His gloved hands were eager to toss away what he thought I no longer needed to try and save. I made sure I removed anything labeled "private" and asked him to read everything before throwing anything away or put them in a pile for me to go through. He was excited to get glimpses of certain parts of my life. He found the papers and notes labeled "my heart" and untied the ribbon I had tied around them. He knew those were about him. He read that, from my hospital bed, I had requested to have everything in the apartment all white on the day I brought him home—from curtains to flowers. He read my menu for his first birthday, with a guest list of a hundred and a menu with food from every part of the world. He read my notes to the caterer for his first cake and the five types of ice cream I ordered. He learned that I had been up for three days straight, preparing and cooking 30 dishes all by myself, in addition to roasting a whole lamb for both his first and second birthdays. Mania has some benefits.

He saw samples of the handwritten labels describing each food and the region it was from. He saw my lists for baby clothes and toys and gasped at how much one organic baby towel cost 12 years ago. He saw a stained picture of Angelina Jolie and Brad Pitt pushing the stroller they had bought their first child, and I explained that he had ridden in the same kind of stroller. It was a gift from my old friend, the fashion executive who had dubbed my son, "the little prince." A prince, he said, needed to be riding in the finest baby carriage. My son saw my detailed descriptions of to-do lists to prepare his first Halloween and first Christmas. He learned that for the first year of his life, we celebrated each 21st—the day he was born—with cake and wine and hors d'oeuvres because it was his first September, his first October, his first November—all the way up to him turning one.

He remarked on the fact that at the top of all my to-do lists was "Pray." He saw photos of the living room walls I had painted purple and orange to match his orange and purple cake, complete with a little crown. He marveled at the photo of himself looking like a little maharaja in the traditional handmade outfit princes wear in India, complete with little bells on the edges that jangled every time he took a step, I told him. With great big tears in his eyes, he looked at me and said, "You loved me so much?" I smiled; tears welled in my own eyes. I was too overcome with feeling to speak. How could I tell him I loved him in ways I will never be able to put in words? I love him, but not without my own reasons. I love him for who he is but also for what he has made me become.

I was so happy and terrified after he was placed in my arms. How I had wanted a child! I was told it was never going to happen—and here he was. My grandest gift. How was I going to take care of him, broken as I was? What was I going to give him, poor as I was? How was I going to raise him when no one had raised me?

CHAPTER 12

Recycling Diva

I AM SOMETIMES AMAZED at the degree of disconnect people have when they make certain decisions and their lack of awareness that each choice they make comes with consequences. I am no exception.

I think back on the times my mother chose to leave her children at one time or another for one reason or another. Had she been away from us too long to have the roots of her children sink deep into her? Is that the reason she has been able to put us so casually behind her and live like we do not exist? Over the years, when she has been angry with us or dissatisfied with her life, she has lamented the fact that she had my brothers and me, and she has told us her life would have been very different had she not had us.

We have had conversations in which she repeatedly asked me, "Why don't you consider leaving your son with me or with his father?" Hadn't life become so bad and hard and living in San Francisco, so expensive?

Some of my friends asked me , "What happened to you? You were smarter than us in college"-referring to the smallness of my life. Sometimes they'd say it behind my back. They were happy and rubbing it in my face.

My friend and her family in Seattle —the friend who had bought my ticket to Seattle when I ran away from my mother my first week in America— told me the same thing. "Just leave the child with his father. He will take care of him, and you can come here and get yourself back together. We will help you. When you get back on your feet, you can go get him, or he will come looking for you when he is older. You are his mother. He will not forget you."

I listened in disbelief, sorrow, and rage. What kind of help included leaving my child? "Does she think she's the only one who ever had a child?" "Does she think her child is somehow better than other children?" I heard it all.

"Look at you," my mother said, her meaning not lost on me. She told me her friends lamented my life because "your daughter had so much promise," but was now destitute and "roaming from one place to the next like a homeless person—divorced, jobless, and sick." There is nothing worse for an African mother. My state of affairs clearly meant she was not to look forward to having her child take care of her in her old age, as most African parents expect their children to. I had not only failed myself, I had failed her.

I heard it all. I understood some of their reasons. I wanted to believe they meant well, but my heart could not hear of leaving my child.

How could I survive without my heart? How could I leave him when I had been left and know well what that did to me—what that does to a child? How could I begin to make them understand that leaving a child carves a hole in them that your coming back will never be able to fill, no matter how much you try? Why would they ask me to do the impossible?

I stayed. No one helped. I stayed in San Francisco, where I had joint custody of my child with his father, where the price of a tiny studio could get you a whole house in other parts of America. It was not easy. Sometimes all we had were the pennies in my son's piggy bank. Coinstar would give us $20 or $30 when we cashed in our coins—enough to buy a couple of gallons of gas, some food, plus one or two other necessities like toilet paper and soap. Once, we even got close to $70, our highest payout, and treated ourselves to sundaes. We cried, but together. Laughed. Danced to "Fever" and Miriam Makeba's "Malaika" on the streets of San Francisco. I would stop the car, turn up the volume on the music, and twirl him around and around, oblivious to the world around us. People stopped and stared. I could never leave him. We were bound by our need for each other. His for his mother—a need every child is born with—mine, as a mother doing whatever she must to spare her child the anguish of growing up without their mother. I took any job I could that allowed me to manage the custody schedule with Alexei. As a single mother, I had to pick up my son after school since I had no family here, and the few friends I had were busy with their own work and lives and could not pick him up for me. I refused to take him to strangers. The concept of taking my son to childcare was foreign to me even if I could have afforded it.

It is not part of the African culture. We do not have daycare centers or preschools for babies and toddlers. Grandparents, aunts, uncles, relatives all took care of you until you were old enough for school. More importantly, I know what can happen to children who are left with strange people. Sometimes even family. Most times family. Most child abuse cases reported are perpetrated by a family member, relative, or friend of the family. I would take no such chance with my child. I also had another motivation. I wanted to take care of my child until he was old enough to go to school and catch the bus by himself, until he was old enough for me to explain things to him that had never been explained to me. I wanted to teach him self-awareness and self-care, self-respect, and respect for others. I would teach him to be careful but not close-hearted. What was giving up a few years of my life to give my child a good start?

I believed his formative years were fundamental and would shape him for life, and I made the choice to spend that time with him, away from the full-time commitment of work. I wanted him to know my love and be grounded by it and have it be the one thing he could always count on, apart from God's love.

For a couple of years, I was able to do this easily. But then, his father and I separated when he was two, and I suddenly found myself with a small child, no money, no family, no career, and nowhere to go. Alexei and I had carved out a life together and, while it was not perfect, I never imagined myself without him. He was all I had known, and, for many years, I ignored the signs that there was trouble in the relationship. So, we bought an apartment together and made plans for the future. I was going to take him to Africa to meet my granny; we were going to travel the world together. There was no thought of ever leaving him because I did not see how I could survive without the one person who had become the center of my world. Codependency can be very blinding.

Before my son was born, I had resigned myself to being with someone I realized I barely knew, someone who did not have it as "together" as I had thought he did, someone who clearly needed to face his own demons. Something shifted in me, though, after he was born. Suddenly, I wanted him to see a mother who was strong and capable and whole, and I knew that as long as I continued looking to Alexei as my savior, the mother my son would grow up with would be one he did not deserve. I made the choice to do one of the hardest things I have ever done: leave the safety of a relationship that provided physical comforts and stability for my son to "find" a self my son would be proud of. It was a huge price to pay.

Having never envisioned my life without Alexei, I did not know where to begin. I had no savings of my own, knew no one who had a place for a 35-year-old woman with a baby just shy of being two, and had no job prospects. I had been home with the baby and had planned on staying home until he was at least in Kindergarten.

I couldn't do the nine-to-five. I tried a few. After asking a couple of times if I could leave early to go pick my son up from school, they always politely told me, "You really should find a part-time job. This is not the place for you." In 2005, when my son was born, there were very few jobs available that allowed one to work from home. Especially women. You had to be in tech, rich, and white. I was none of those. In college in Africa, I had seen computers, but had not used them—they were reserved for science students and a few professors. (How far we've come, and how much things have changed.)

I tried corporate work. That didn't work. I did not know how to backbite and kiss ass to get a promotion and no longer wanted to sleep with men who only had use for my flesh, so I washed stovetops and scrubbed toilets of dried menstrual blood and other unmentionables. I sold makeup and started a greeting card line, which went nowhere. It takes money to make money. I saw the lady who invented Spanx on TV being interviewed. She had started with her savings of $5000, and today she is a multi-millionaire. I did not have money to get my cards printed, so that failed, too. I modeled jewelry and wore a fake belly to sell maternity clothes. I did personal shopping for the rich-cleaning out their closets and telling them what they could or could no longer wear. It paid well until the fair-trade campaigns started after people died in the ware-house fire in India. No one wanted to be seen in public spending $4,000 on lingerie or one dress.

Those were hard times. I tried to do anything I could to earn a living. I even tried getting a job at a warehouse, packing vegeta-bles in crates for Veritable Vegetables, a company that distributes organic produce to retailers and restaurants. They did not hire me. I tried to join the people you walk by but do not see in your grocery stores—those who stack your paper towels and Pine Sol on shelves to make life easier for you. I did not get the position. Apparently, I was not even qualified to be a shelf-stacker. Finally, I decided I would start a non-profit and hoped it would help pay rent here and help some children back home. I had been especially moved by those whose mothers had been killed in the war, those who suffered the nearly impossible feat of trying to fend for them-selves with no arms.

The Recycling Diva, my non-profit, was going to help a few children, even as she tried to take care of her own son. One friend asked me, "Who is going to let you pick up their recycling look-ing like you do?" So, I traded my long braids for a crew-cut and exchanged my Prada sports shoes—remnants from my days at Saks—for thick, heavy-soled sneakers that poor people wear because avoiding having to pound the pavement can sometimes take a while. I printed business cards with a photo of me wearing a bright smile like Mma Ramotswe in *The No. 1 Ladies' Detective Agency* and handed them out.

It would not be easy. "Can you please save your bottles and cans for me after you close down for the night?" I asked businesses I had patronized when I could afford it. "I am starting a recycling business," I explained, and told them where the money would go. Recycling was just getting introduced to the public and was still mainly a matter of choice. Some of the business owners said they would do what they could but not to expect much because their particular business did not deal much in plastics or cans. Others, like Mitchell's Ice Cream, told me, "Sorry, we have someone else already." Getting Mitchell's would have meant scoring big. An entrepreneur from Senegal who had done well for himself and had the only West African restaurant/bar in San Francisco wanted to help. "I can't guarantee anything, though," he said. "You have to come early. Those people doing the recycling are very aggressive and sometimes fights break out." I understood. They were fighting for their lives. I knew what that was like.

I was competing with Mexicans and old Asian grannies. The grannies always broke my heart. What was an 80-year-old, hunched-over granny doing out in the foggy streets of San Francisco at 3:00 a.m., pulling a cart, and using a grabber to look for soda cans and empty plastic bottles? That would never happen in Africa. In moments like those, I missed home.

I learned later, after hiring a U-Haul truck to put my bags of recycling and getting only $40 for the whole truck, that aluminum was the cream of the crop, not plastic. I could not compete there for long. Having to wait each night until the restaurants closed and took out their trash began to take its toll. Though I could not sleep most nights, anyway, going through trash was hard in more ways than one. Besides, the Mexicans, with their open-back pickups, were masters at it. They had been doing it for years before anyone took notice. They knew the places with the most aluminum cans and other valuable recyclables and, in some cases, had established relationships with the bar and restaurant owners.

One night, my friend came with me to see exactly what I did and to help me. We drove around the Mission District for a while and got a few bins, then we stopped by Mitchell's, which was about a block away from where I lived. My friend Madame, as we called her, wanted to check out their recycling area, which turned out to be a lot where they had huge metal containers, not just plastic bins. I explained to her that I had already been there to ask, and they had told me I was too late.

"I don't care. Help me up. Let's see what they have here," she said.

She climbed on a little tree stump, and I pushed her up the wall of a container. She was a petite woman and not hard to lift, so almost fell over as she reached down to grab anything she could from the bin for me. My heart almost gave out in terror as I watched her lose her hold. I grabbed her feet quickly and was able to get her down before she toppled over into the huge metal receptacle. We fell on the ground and laughed and laughed until tears streamed down our faces. Then we decided to call it a night.

I continued going through trash for a while, even though I was making no money. I told myself that every business starts rocky. I should try and not give up. So, I tried, but nothing changed. The few cans I got amounted to just cents. But it was the smell that finally got to me and the fear that if I got sick, I would really be in trouble. My health insurance had just recently been canceled by my ex-husband, though I had begged him not to. I needed health insurance more than anything. He canceled it anyway.

I will never forget the stench that assaulted me when I opened the rented truck one morning to put the last of the bags I had gathered that week. It smelled of stale beer and rottenness, of sadness and desperation, of despair and hitting rock bottom.

There is a myth that there is help out there for single mothers and women who work minimum wage jobs. But the system is set up to make those who are down, stay down. I discovered this when my back was up against the wall after my best efforts at selling plastic failed. I asked friends to ask people they knew about any job opportunities, and some advised me to go to the Department of Social Services and ask for help. In the meantime, until something came through. I had resisted out of pride for a few years; I knew I was well capable of working and earning a living. I did not see the reason to take money away from people I believed needed it more than I did. But when all my attempts to manage on my own failed, and I knew I had nowhere else to go and no one to ask, I swallowed my pride and made an appointment to talk to a social worker. The failure of Recycling Diva was a big blow.

From the moment I walked into the crowded waiting area and saw the look of resignation on the faces of the mothers in the room and heard the weariness in the voice over the loudspeaker calling out the number that was next in line, I knew I had made a mistake in going there. When it was my turn, I was ushered into a large area in the back that had been divided into cubicles big enough for two chairs and a small desk on which an ancient-looking computer sat. My worker was about 23, but she had the tired eyes of a much older person who had listened to too many sad stories. She asked me what she could do for me, and I told her I had been told there was help there for someone in my situation—a single mother, working part-time, with a young son, struggling to survive in San Francisco. She told me we needed to fill some forms to get a case open, and the process started. After almost an hour of questions that left me wondering if I had asked for a $100,000,000 grant, I was told I had to bring in my proof of income, my child's birth certificate, identity card, and other documents before anything else could happen.

I left feeling drained and cursed myself for becoming a statistic—the stereotypical Black woman on welfare. I went home and gathered all the documents they had asked for and took it to them the next day. I was told I would hear from them as soon as the papers were processed. It could be up to three weeks. When I finally heard back from them, it was a letter of denial. I did not qualify for food stamps or any cash benefits. If I had any questions, it said, call the number at the top of the page. I decided to go in person. I had questions that a phone conversation was not going to satisfy.

This time, my worker was in a hurry to leave work early. She had just moved in with her boyfriend, and they were already having trouble with the landlord. She did not think they would be staying in San Francisco anyway; Oakland was a better choice. Her salary was not enough, even combined with her boyfriend's, to afford the rent. I told her I was sorry and would not keep her long. Why had my application been denied?

"You make too much money."

"What?"

"Your income exceeds the limit."

Confused, I asked again. What income? If I had enough money to live on, I wouldn't be here asking for help."

She explained that the child-support my son's father sent each month—which barely paid for the studio we lived in—was "too much income." I asked her about the living expenses form they'd had me fill out and all the information I had given her about my life to show that we were nearly destitute. She looked at me then, apologetically, and I almost felt sorry for her. I didn't envy her having that job.

"I understand. You and your child qualify for health insurance, but, unfortunately, if you make more than $400, you are not considered a candidate for food stamps or cash assistance."

In other words, there was no help for people like me who were not completely without income but who could barely survive on what they make. I asked her what would qualify me for their help. If I didn't earn any money, then I could get the $500-800 they gave some families, plus vouchers for food. What single mother is going to survive on an $8-an-hour minimum wage job after paying for childcare so that she can go to work at that same job?

"So you're telling me I would be better off not working?" I asked, in shock.

"If you want to get food stamps and cash, then, Yes. If you give up your child support, then we can fill out a new application and say your circumstances have changed."

"Even though the assistance you will give me will not be enough to cover my rent?"

"Yes," she replied.

I laughed. I thanked her and took one last look around the room, my heart going out to the mothers waiting on the hard, plastic chairs for their number to be called and walked out with a new understanding.

I called my friend Afua, who is from Ghana, to share my experience with her.

"They told me the same thing when I went there," she said.

I was stunned. Afua is a divorced mother of two who was teaching classes at one of the universities in San Francisco. She is a brilliant woman who has two master's degrees and was working on her Ph.D.

"My sister, we were deceived," she said. "We were told when we came here from Africa that, if we worked hard, we can have anything we want. We were told that the Black people on welfare here are lazy and just want to take advantage of the system." It made sense to me what some of my African American friends had told me about why a lot of mothers in low-income communities opt to stay at home. Working-while-poor only results in more poverty if the government has anything to do with it.

I agreed as we hung up the phone and prayed for our lives in America to make sense. We had exchanged stories about our colleagues and school mates who were now doctors and heads of multinationals. We talked about our girlhood friends who now owned five cars and lived in mansions with maids who addressed them as "auntie" and "madam", titles reserved for the rich and respected. What would we say to people back home- the cousins and uncles and friends who wake us from sleep 4:00 am to play the visa lottery for them to come to America? That we had come to America to beg for bread and sell trash? That for many of us, immigrants and even those born here, the American dream may remain only that- a dream?

CHAPTER 13

Fear

SOONER OR LATER, YOU GET TO CONFRONT THE DARKNESS. You either find it, or it finds you. I have always been afraid of death. Afraid of what it takes from you and what it leaves you with—loss. When my papa died, I was 11. I sang "Kama Chameleon" at his wake in front of hundreds of people, and I still don't know why I chose that song or why I broke into song. He was buried before I was brought to the wake. When Elizabeth, my best friend, died at 15, I refused to go near someone who had, just hours before, held my hand in hers. She could no longer shake off the flies sitting on the blanket, covering her, as she lay on a mat on the cold, cement floor of her widowed mother's tiny parlor. I peeked through the window at the unmoving shape under the blanket, hoping that—any minute—she would push off the grey-and-black-striped cloth off her face. She never moved, and I stayed outside. I could not bear to see her in death.

It would be the last time I would get anywhere near a dead person. Other people died over the years, but by then, just like my fear of snakes, the fear of the dead had climbed to nearly intolerable levels. I would have a panic attack just seeing a coffin. I told these things to Alexei when we talked about the 1001 reasons I hate nights and why I am afraid of lying down to sleep—they remind me of the long sleep: death.

How can one live in Africa and be afraid of snakes? I was—and they were everywhere. Sometimes they would appear in my dreams; they seemed to show up in random places whenever I was around. I could not help thinking they somehow knew I was afraid of them and that was their way of tormenting me. My phobia was so bad that even seeing a snake that had been mangled by a car's tires and no longer posed any threat disturbed me and left me in such a state. It did not matter if it was dead. My cousins and friends knew this. They deliberately tried to frighten me every chance they got. Sometimes they would take a piece of rope or fabric and twist it into a coil and, while I was unguarded, throw it at me and scream "Snake!" I would scream and jump up to try to get it off me. On more than one occasion, I peed myself.

Although I was more scared of snakes than is considered normal, it is quite common to see children crushing the head of a cobra before it had a chance to bite them. Anti-venom is not readily available in Africa.

Mango season was a time of both excitement and anxiety for me. I was always on the alert, standing close to a neighbor's mango tree, hoping for the yellow temptations that were pure joy when you bit into them. We would go in groups and find stones to throw at the mangoes to knock them off the branches. The biggest and ripest ones were always out of reach. We encouraged the kids who were the most adept at climbing without a rope to climb up the branches closest to the mangoes we wanted and shake the branches vigorously. We promised them a larger share. Then, when the mangoes came raining down, we were ecstatic. We ran out of the way, laughing, so the mangoes would not fall on our heads. Not only mangoes were shaken down. I had seen a snake or two fall down onto a child's back or head. I knew to always stand a distance away, never directly under the tree, while it was getting a shakedown by a little mango thief.

One of the few reasons I was relieved to be in America was because there were no snakes! At least not like Africa, I thought. Not in the big cities; I would have to go to the zoo to see one. Here, I only had to worry about them in my dreams. I believed all this until I walked down the street one day and saw a man casually strolling down the street with the biggest boa constrictor I had ever seen wrapped around his neck. I almost fainted. Why are such things permitted? Keep your snake at home! Somebody can have a heart attack! I almost forgot: "it's America." People are free here to do whatever they want. After that incident, my hopes that I had escaped snakes in America unless I purposefully went to the zoo were crushed.

It was only the beginning. My first therapist, Dr. G., whom I came to love, told me she loved snakes. Over time, our discussions got around to my fears, and, of course, snakes were on the list, so we talked about them. Her daughter, she said, had a few at home. Her daughter's baby snake had been so cold she put it in her bra to keep it warm. That was it. I had come all the way from Africa to meet a Russian doctor whom I saw every week who liked snakes and carries them in her bra? I could no longer run. I had started feeling paranoid when I went to see her and would peer behind the small divide separating her main office space from the little area she used to store her teas, office supplies, and printer. I had begun spending most of the 45 minutes I was with her watching the enclosed area to see if something was going to come crawling out, only answering her questions absentmindedly. A space that had been a place of solace and respite now became a source of serious anxiety.

The realization that my fear could possibly take away good things from me like Dr. G. was enough. I knew my running days were over. I told her I assumed she knew where I could find snakes if I wanted to see them. Shocked, she asked if I was sure. I told her that I knew exactly what I needed to do. She directed me to a pet store on 48th Avenue. Two days later, I woke up, got dressed in a great-looking suit, picked up my handbag, which doubled as a briefcase, and asked the father of my son, then my boyfriend, to give me a ride.

"I have an appointment with destiny," I told him.

He looked at me and smiled. "What does that mean?"

I told him I was no longer going to wait for the shock and terror of seeing a snake but was going to face one, purposefully. For the first time in my life, I recognized that the things I feared the most somehow always made their way to me. What if I chose to face them? Would they still have the power they had over me? Would I stop being afraid, would I be even more afraid? I was about to find out. Alexei told me he was happy for me if that was what I wanted to do. I assured him I had a few things I needed to do, but this was the first.

We went into the store, and I greeted the friendly owner, who thought I had come to purchase a pet. I told him I was on a medical mission, that I had a phobia and wanted to—no, needed to—see a snake up close. He was very obliging and thought it was very brave of me. If only he could see how my insides were shaking and how terrified I was! It is amazing how humans are sometimes able to fool each other so completely. I am especially good at it. My doctors have told me so. I never appeared as distressed as I should have in certain life and death situations, they marveled. I could not tell them about my having perfected wearing masks since I was a child.

The pet store owner led me up a dimly lit staircase into a room the color of smoke. The smell was earthy and unfamiliar. I was terrified. I asked him to show me the snakes since I had looked around anxiously but had not seen any. I wanted it to be over with quickly. He opened a glass case and took a small snake out. It was cream-colored. My heart leaped in my throat upon seeing it, and I stood frozen, watching him stroke the little snake gently. I realized in that moment that merely seeing it up close was not going to be enough—that, until I actually physically touched a snake, there would be a part of me that would always be enslaved by my fear of it. I held out my hand.

"Put it in my hand," I said, my slightly tremulous voice filling the small space.

"Are you sure? You don't have to do this, you know. Most people would be okay with just coming face to face with what they are afraid of."

I told him I needed to do this.

I smiled. "Please give it to me."

He placed the snake carefully in my hand, which was shaking so badly he told me to be careful not to drop it. Nothing had prepared me for the feelings that went through me upon that first contact. The immediate feeling was shock that the snake felt quite warm. I had always imagined them to be cold. Then an almost overwhelming feeling of freedom and gratitude came over me. I knew that after walking out of that room, my relationship with snakes would never be the same. I let the snake crawl all over my hand and up to my shoulder before I offered it to Alexei.

"Do you want to hold it, too?" I asked him. He nodded slightly, and I placed the snake gently in his open palms.

I felt like I was floating down the stairs as I made my way to the area where the store owner had told me I would find him. I thanked him, ran out in the middle of the street, threw my briefcase in the air, and screamed, "I did it! I did it!"

It was one of the greatest feelings of accomplishments I had ever felt in my life.

Emboldened by my snake victory, I decided it was time to face my other big fear. After running away from death so long and never quite escaping it, I realized I had to do something radical to begin the process of accepting the inevitable.

It turns out, getting to a dead body that wasn't a relative or friend was much harder than walking into a pet store and picking up a snake. Alexei and I went to a few mortuaries in the city, and they all said No except one. I explained to the kindly middle-aged Hispanic lady managing the front office our reason for being there—my fear of death and dead bodies. I told her that it would be extremely helpful and healing for me if I was confronted with a body. She smiled and said she understood. We were in luck.

They had a gentleman lying in the chapel. There was going to be a viewing in a few hours, and we could go in quickly before the family came. It was the first time I was in such close proximity to a dead body. I had not seen my father's corpse. He was buried before I was brought to the wake. I had been five or six when my grandfather died and have little recollection of the incident. We walked into that room on Valencia Street and can say nothing of what it looked like since my attention was drawn only to the man in the coffin in the center of the room. We came close and stood beside the coffin. I willed myself to really look at death up close. I was struck by how still he was, lying in his final bed. Although I had a ton of questions in my head, which he could never give me answers to, I thanked him for his gift to me—that I had been allowed to see him so I could be free—and left. I wrote a poem in honor of the nameless man in the coffin, which I titled "Paleface," so I wouldn't forget.

Over the years, since I held that snake and watched Paleface in that coffin, my relationship with fear has shifted. I cannot say I am comfortable in situations where there is a snake or a dead body, but I can say I'm no longer enslaved by paralyzing terror.

When I became pregnant nine years later and had to administer hundreds of blood thinning injections to myself, one of my attending doctors told me that if you gave her $10,000,000 to do what I was doing "just to have a baby," she would pass. She was afraid of needles.

CHAPTER 14

My Impossible Love

"IT IS NEVER A GOOD IDEA TO TELL ALL YOUR SECRETS TO A MAN; there is no room in him to house all of you," mothers in Africa warn their daughters. I did not follow this wisdom when I fell in love. When Alexei told the courts that he thought I was unfit as a mother because I've had so much trauma in my life, I was stunned and left reeling from the blow. There was more, and they all came from things I had shared with him about my past, things I had told no one else but him.

He told them about my childhood; he told them that I had had a most horrendous pregnancy and suffered post-traumatic stress after the baby was born. He told them that living with the fact that my mother was married to a man who had forced himself on me had left me broken beyond repair. He told them everything.

I looked for the man who had held me when I had sobbed my heart out on his chest—and could not find him. I looked for the man who had held me tenderly and told me I had done nothing wrong and had nothing to be ashamed of when I told him I was covered in shame and most days wanted to crawl into a hole and never show my face to the world again. I looked for the man who had told me how much he loved the depth of my soul and the person I had become because of my troubles. I could not find him.

Perhaps he had been ashamed of my history all along, but love had kept the shame at bay. Perhaps he had always hated the baggage I came with but had enough use for me to keep me around. I wondered about that and other things. I wondered if he told his parents. The uncertainty leaves me nervous in their presence even now. I know his Vietnamese girlfriend knew. The officers told me that they had drafted the court papers together. How many other people has he told? My life is now a part of the documents of the courts. Everyone who was in court that day had known what was underneath my peach-colored pencil skirt. My circumcision made it onto the trauma list he'd made to prove to the court just how damaged I was.

We had met at a café on Sutter street, a block away from my job in San Francisco. He spoke little English and had the sad eyes of the Russian poets in Dostoevsky's books. I was drawn like a moth to a flame. *I will make him smile and make him forget his sadness,* I thought to myself. I was good at taking other people's sadness away. On the surface, he was everything I wasn't and had everything I didn't and wanted. My fashion executive, D. Francois, and I parted amicably when I told him I had met someone. He understood. Ours would never be a relationship that would lead to marriage or something more permanent. He gave his blessings and even met with my poet for tea every Friday for years afterward. They became friends.

From the beginning, we both saw in each other what the other needed. I needed someone who was dependable and gentle. Someone who would not rattle my broken selves and could see me without my masks. The facade with D. Francois had begun to take its toll. Hiding so much of my life and never being able to share my struggles and my real self left me feeling like all our exchanges were somehow rehearsed. He became confused when I changed my name to assume my papa's name after three decades of carrying the name of the man who had beat me and stolen my innocence as a child. How could I share other things that were much deeper and darker than a name change? He could never understand nor relate to the many convoluted and oftentimes corrupt layers of my life. I could never picture him knowing about the unspeakable.

But I bared my soul to my poet. He was my confessional. I needed another being to hear me and see all of who I was and choose me if they wanted to. I no longer wanted the burden that came with brightness. The most vibrant flowers always call the most attention to themselves. I needed a rest from being bright and beautiful and unreal.

My poet needed my warmth and instinctual nature of finding wounded birds and helping them heal. He needed my heart and my unreserved well of affection for the people closest to me. Coming from a communist background and all the privations of the soul that go along with that made him bask in his "African sun" as he called me. He told me he wanted a child someday, and I told him I couldn't have any. My ovaries were not right, and there was the big question I always wrestled with in spite of how much I loved children: How could someone like me bring a child into this world? He wanted someone to call his wife; I told him I had never imagined marrying anyone. What did I have to offer as a wife? He most definitely did not want a woman like me, I told him. But he did, he said, and in the beginning, he showed me that he did.

He took care of me and said I was wonderful. He told me flowers grew in my cracked places. I, in turn, loved him fiercely, without limits or boundaries. Some say I had put him on a pedestal; I say it was more than that. I worshipped him. He had done more than smile at me. He had taken care of me when my mother left me, when I was losing my mind. He had saved me from being locked up in a jail in America. He could have asked anything of me, and I would have given it gladly.

When he had loved me, I had never felt more alive or more hopeful. He had loved me, damaged. He was with me, had chosen me, accepted me. In exchange, I gave him my heart and my voice. I made him God. He could do no wrong—did no wrong.

I was always making these impossible bargains then—I only discovered this fact in retrospect. It was only a matter of time before living with a god would begin to prove exhausting. He was never wrong and never apologized when I told him he was. If I expressed my feelings, I was shut out. Walls impossible to scale were immediately erected. Since I felt so insecure and worthless, being treated coldly or dismissed brought up my terror of being left, so I capitulated. Even when he was wrong, I apologized—to keep the peace so he wouldn't leave me. Never sure what he was thinking when he was silent—which was often—I started to feel like I was in prison. I started getting anxious around him and became a child all over again—the child who wanted to be good so my mother would love me.

I started devising ways to make myself whatever he wanted me to be in the moment. The only problem was, I could never tell what that was. In the end, his coldness and my need for warmth drove me into the arms of a woman. Women have always been kinder to me.

She owned a gift shop in one of the finer neighborhoods in San Francisco, and she asked me to manage it. The affair did not last long and ended badly. He was there when the person I cheated with hurt me because I could not marry her. I had only been looking for a little love, and it didn't matter where it came from. I could not marry a woman. Perhaps I deserved what I got. Perhaps I needed to be reminded of something I already knew: that no one wanted me. Alexei comforted me, but I don't think he forgave me. I would pay for the betrayal later. He would hurt me as I had hurt him. He would take the one thing I had taken from him when I left him—his heart. And he took mine: my child.

CHAPTER 15

Child Protective Services

THEY HAVE TAKEN MY CHILD. My ex-husband, the courts, and the person he paid to report me. I was at home when the phone rang. A woman introduced herself and said words that froze my blood.

"Your son is not coming back to you. He is going to be with his father. You have been accused, and we are investigating. Do not go near his school. You are to appear in court next week."

As she instructed me to, I took a pen and wrote down addresses and dates. She said something about the court providing a lawyer since I could not afford one. I heard her words from a far-off place. My heart had stopped beating. I was still holding the phone after she hung up.

I felt the lava of tears burning my cheeks. I have cried so much. I thought I had used up my lifetime supply of tears over the years and wondered where the reservoirs of tears come from. Breath escaped me, and I heard over and over again: *Calm down. Breathe.* My friends tell me my very life will depend on it. But how was I to do that when life is always at my heels? When I am never allowed to catch my breath fully before some other disaster hits? I was tired of all of it. Every time I thought it couldn't get any worse, life would deal me another blow with a smirk, as if to say, "oh yes it can. It just did." I was tired of the hopelessness of fighting myself and the world.

Where would I begin this time around? Those two days when I was at Saint Helena Behavioral, when my son was four months old, I was not accused of hurting my child. I was accused of being human. This time, I was to stand trial for possible criminal charges. I have been accused of the unthinkable.

Why had I ever been born?

I should have sensed trouble when Alexei decided that we needed a place to go to make decisions about some important issues pertaining to our son since we could never agree on anything. We had done that kind of thing before. He would find the therapists, pay for the sessions, and gives me dates, and I would go. They always sided with him. I should have known this time would be no different. One therapist lived in Berkeley, and we would both drive to her for a 45-minute session and then drive back to San Francisco. With traffic, the effort took nearly four hours each time we went. We had a couple of joint sessions, and then one day, the therapist asked if I could come alone. I went. We talked. I told her about some parts of my life and shared my biggest worry—that my son would be negatively affected somehow by all the stuff I had survived in spite of all the work I had done over the years in therapy to heal myself. She listened, amazed that I had survived the pregnancy at all. Her husband was a pulmonary doctor, she said, so she was familiar with embolisms. She thought it incredible that I had survived the war and the parts of my life she knew about. She wanted me to come to see her again after that, alone. She was intrigued by me and wanted me to see her outside of the joint sessions we had with my Alexei. I thanked her but declined because I was already working with someone.

She did not take the rejection kindly. Her tone changed after that conversation, and I knew the same pattern was going to repeat itself. She was siding with the person with the checkbook. I told her I did not think she was fair in our sessions. I explained that I drove all the way across the bridge each time to come see her because I wanted to give my son the best possible chance at coming out of this very unstable childhood somehow intact. I wasn't sacrificing that time and energy only to have my son's father have the last say in matters we needed her impartial judgment on. I told her I wasn't coming back.

A few days later, she left me a voicemail saying that it was important and in my best interest to call her. I did. She said something urgent had come up, and I needed to go see her. I drove to her office, curious, and hoping nothing was wrong with my son. She told me Alexei had shared some concerns with her. She showed me some photographs I had taken of my son with his iPad and told me she thought they were inappropriate. I didn't understand. She wouldn't explain, only told me that she was a mandated reporter, and she could report me to Child Protective Services.

I laughed. "For what?" I asked.

"Child abuse."

I looked at her in amazement and laughed. "You're really serious?"

"Yes." She said that I was in very serious trouble. I told her the whole meeting was ridiculous.

"Go ahead and report me. But don't threaten me." I was getting angry and tired of the insinuations about the photographs. I got up and politely told her that I was leaving. It was a Friday. I knew she had been angry with me after she had tried calling me a few times to schedule a one-on-one with her, and I had not responded. I could tell by the threatening tone of her voice when she left that last message asking me to come in that something was wrong, but I had not been prepared for this. It was clear that Alexei was behind it.

The following Monday, I dropped off my son at school as usual, but the principal told me that I should come back to the school at lunchtime for a meeting. I said I would be there. I got to the school office around 11:00, and as I entered the conference room, I saw one of my son's teachers leading him off to another room. A lady and a gentleman came into the room and introduced themselves as social workers with Child Protective Services. They were there to interview me. A complaint had been filed by my son's father, accusing me of child abuse. His then-girlfriend was co-complainant. Someone I didn't know. I was stunned. I managed to keep my composure and answered all the questions asked of me. When it was my turn to respond—after answering questions I never imagined I would have to answer regarding my son—I told the social worker that I have thousands of photographs of my son. I explained that I have been chronicling his life since birth, and I try to capture moments with the photos I take. I explained that even though I also keep journals about him in which I recorded his first words, his first day at kindergarten, the zoo, etc., I am especially passionate about photos of him because I have only one photo of myself as I child. I told her it was very important to me that my son knows who he was when he grows up. I did not tell the social worker that I did not want my son to have to piece himself together like I now had to since no one had taken the time or cared enough to give me definition. I did not tell him that most of what I know about my childhood comes from people who were there when my mother wasn't. The social worker listened patiently and asked me more questions. He said he had no reason to be concerned and did not believe the pictures were inappropriate.

The social worker had also spoken to my son. He looked up from the stack of papers he had been looking at and said, "Be careful. You have an extraordinarily strong bond with your son. That's my impression from talking to him and to you. Whoever wrote this complaint does not like you." He told me that the person who had "reported" on behalf of the father had called their office that morning asking Child Protective Services why they had not arrested me, and why the child was still in my custody.

It was her—the doctor Alexei had hired as a "family therapist"—who had made the call. The social worker told me in confidence. He also shared with me that they had told her that she had done her job of reporting, now let them do theirs in investigating, and she was not the one to dictate the outcome of whatever complaint she had filed.

I thanked him for believing I would never hurt my child and for his warning.

I took my son home that day after school, disturbed by the whole incident, but I did not want to spoil our afternoon together. He was going back to stay with his father the next day, so I played it cool. I asked him how his day had been and if some people had talked to him. He said, "Yes." They had asked him some questions, and he had told them, "My mama is the best. She would never hurt me." I smiled and patted his head, my heart filled with many emotions.

It was the last time I would be alone with my child for a long time. The therapist and my ex-husband made repeated calls to Child Protective Services office, asking why my son had still not been removed from my home. They were angry with the social workers who had let me take my son home after interviewing me and decided they needed to up the ante. Things were not going according to their plan. So they went up the chain of command to make sure my child was taken away. Some big shot head of some department called to tell me that my son was being placed with his father. The social worker I had spoken to had been removed from the case.

I called a few friends and told them that my son was gone. No one believed me. They knew that if my child had indeed been taken from me, there was no hope for me. After hanging up the phone with the big shot boss at CPS, I managed to get dressed, get into my car, and drive to Oakland, where my best friend lived. I don't know how I made it there without getting into an accident.

"What am I going to do?" I asked my friend.

Though not beautiful in the classic sense, Ogoni made up for her stocky frame and large nose with a warm personality and indefatigable optimism. She hugged me and told me not to worry, that everything was going to be okay. She thought we should seek the counsel of an attorney since she was from Africa, too, and had never been faced with such a situation. Immigrants have little or no knowledge about their rights in America until they get in trouble or have reason to become involved with the judicial system. Her brother knew an attorney in Gilroy who would see us. This time, Ogoni drove. The reality of what I was up against was beginning to sink in, and it showed in the way my hand shook when I handed her the keys.

I barely took in my surroundings. He was a thin and friendly, middle-aged white man who, after I described the pictures to him, reassured me that everything was going to be fine. He told me that every parent has pictures of their child in some stage of undress. He had taken some, too, of his own children. My son had been wearing a vest with no boxers and playing with his lightsaber. He had been so carefree and happy, and I wanted to freeze time so he would always be the way he was in those few seconds. Instead, I tried to capture the moment with my camera. That was what I was guilty of.

It turns out the attorney was wrong; the social worker who had warned me was right. The photographs could be used as a weapon. All someone had to do was use the word "abuse." I found this out when I went to court the following week.

I could not sleep those first three days before court. I was waiting to go tell whoever was in charge of the case that they had to give me my child back, that time was running out for me. My godmother, Mimi, had not let me be by myself for too many hours since my child had been taken, and we arrived together at the courthouse. I owe her my life. In the courtroom, I noticed that there were three groups of people. I recognized only one person from the first group: one of the social workers from my interview at the school. I looked around for the man who had told me that he knew I had done nothing wrong, but he was not there. My heart sank. I saw Alexei and two women and the parents of one of my son's friends. I was surprised. Alexei did not have any friends. All of his friends had been my friends—people that I had brought into his life when we were together. Then there was another group of people I did not know at all, one of whom approached me.

"Hello. Can we talk for a minute?" she said with a pleasant smile on her face. "My name is Jess. Jess Dearman. The courts have appointed me to represent you." My heart was pounding again. "But unfortunately, I can't help you. I am so busy at this time that I can't take your case. I am really sorry. I read over your paperwork, and you're going to need someone other than me. Someone who can put in the work you need. My colleague is very good. I will introduce you to her."

I looked at her fully for the first time. Miss Dearman was a young woman in her mid to late thirties with dark brown hair and an intelligent, serious face. She was clear-eyed and carried her not-small frame comfortably. Now, all the important decisions I have ever made that have changed my life have come from my gut, and something told me that this was the person who was going to get my child back. I knew it; I could feel it in my whole being.

I fell on my knees. "You don't know me, and you're very busy, but God has told me you're the person to help me. Please, please take my case. Don't send me to your colleague. I believe you when you say she is good, but it's you I want, you I need."

Embarrassed by my desperation, Miss Dearman asked me to get off my knees and sit down. I was trembling and prayed silently as I sat on the edge of the seat she offered me. I knew I could not let her walk out of that room without agreeing to take my case.

She looked at me with a straightforward gaze. "You don't know me. How can you be so convinced that I can help you? My colleague is very experienced and has the time. You should go with her. If I take your case, I am not going to be able to give it the attention it needs, and that would not be fair to you."

"Please," I begged. "I hear what you're saying, and I will take that chance. Just, please say Yes. I know I may not be acting reasonably by insisting you take my case since, as you rightly said, we just met, and I really don't know you. But I believe in God, and I know, I feel it in my heart, you are the attorney I need representing me."

Mimi stepped in and said, "Jess—May I call you Jess? Please help her. She has no family here. I am the only one, and I am old. All she has is her son."

After a long pause, Jess Dearman said 'Okay,' a little reluctantly, and with an I hope-you-know-what-you've-done look on her face. I got up and gave her the biggest hug with the biggest smile on my face, not caring if I was allowed to or not. It was my first smile since my child had been taken away. She told me we would meet in a couple of days so she could get some more information.

Court did not go that well for me that first day. I hadn't known what to expect, but I had definitely wanted to hear that my son was coming back to me that day. How naive, how stupid, how clueless I was then about the American justice system. By the time the allegations were read, and the judge made her preliminary statements, I realized that my son wasn't coming home that day—and God knows if ever. There was talk of supervised visits, which my attorney had to explain to me. My mind had gone blank when I heard that there was going to be another court date.

Jess explained to me that the court had decided that I would have visits with my son a couple of times a week at Alexei's discretion as he was now the custodial parent. Until the case was closed, he was in charge.

Relieved that, at last, I was going to see my child, I swallowed my disappointment. Jess and I met a few days later. We talked a lot about me, my son, his father, my family, the photographs. She told me we had an uphill battle. My ex-husband had written in his complaints things about me that had already nudged the case in his favor—my mental health challenges, my childhood, my mother. Enough for the courts to not have an unbiased opinion since they were going by what he told them.

Alexei earned a six-figure salary and appeared shiny on paper. He was happy to brag to the courts about how he and his "partner" were comfortable while I was not working and "could not even feed myself"—another reason why I was not to be given my child. No one asked me to give them some background on him, his own childhood, his character, his demons. No one asked me to tell that, born to a mother and father who had their own stories growing up in cold-war Russia, he was as broken as I was. No one asked me why I had left the person I had made a life with for ten years, even though I had no place else to go with a two-year-old baby. No one asked me about how cold, unemotional, and controlling he was or how he had sold the apartment we had bought together—for which I had provided the $30,000 down payment—but that he claimed to sell at a loss after we divorced. No one asked me about the rage buried behind his soulful eyes—a rage that erupted the day he got angry and kicked the wall so hard it broke and left a hole the size of his shoe. The hole gaped like an open wound for all the years we lived in that apartment. It was an unapologetic reminder of the hole in my soul that my poet couldn't fix because he had his own wound to tend. No one asked me to tell how incapable of empathy he was. No one asked me anything.

Jess told me I needed to find people to write character letters for me. I was going to need them. Although I had no family in San Francisco, I had cultivated some relationships over the years. I was close to the parents of my son's best friends, his teachers, and my own friends, some of whom were lawyers themselves. I told Jess I would have no problem getting those people to vouch for me. They knew me as a person and as a mother.

The first day my son was brought to see me was a day I will never forget. Jess told me that I had been allowed an hour and a half. Alexei was the one who decided how much time I was to be given. He was now the custodial parent.

They met me at the West Portal playground. Sylvia, the social worker from Child Protective Services, brought my son to me for that first visit. She was a bronze-colored woman in her fifties with reddish-gold hair who could have come from any part of South America. She was from the Fiji Islands I discovered sometime later. My son ran to me, but Sylvia immediately walked up to us before I could do anything.

"I am sorry, but because of the accusations against you, you cannot be in certain situations." She was trying to tell me that I could not hug my child.

"I am also going to be within earshot at all times so that I can hear you two talk." I must have looked up at her a certain way because she said, "It's part of my job."

I fought the tears as I looked at my son. He looked drawn, confused, and in a daze. I knew he must have been uncomfortable to be picked up and driven by someone he did not know. It was the first time he had been with someone who was not family, apart from his teachers. I knew how shy he could be, even among his friends. Prior to CPS, he only had his grandparents, who had moved here from Europe when he was born, plus his dad, me, and my dear friend Madame. I asked my son if he would like to go on the swing, and he said, "Yes."

I had chosen the swing because I knew he always seemed to like it when I made a show of pushing him on it. It also gave me a way to touch him if only indirectly. Pushing him, I could at least feel the weight of him. I asked how school was and tried to keep things light and funny. After what seemed like five minutes, I heard Sylvia say, "Time's up. We have to go now."

There was no way an hour and a half had gone by that fast. I told my son I loved him and that I will see him soon, and I watched someone, a stranger who now had more access to my child than I did, take him by the hand and lead him to the car and ask him to get in. It was only after the car was out of sight that I collapsed on the faux asphalt that covers public playgrounds and broke down. I laid there like a discarded doll on the dirty plastic floor and cried and cried and could not stop crying until a young Hispanic woman approached me and asked if I was okay. I wanted to tell her. No, I was not ok, and I was never going to be okay again, but I couldn't get the words out. Grief had struck me completely dumb.

Things went like this for a whole month. As the days passed, I became less and less aware of life around me and seemed to come alive only when it was time to visit with my son or when I would meet with Jess to get or give updates. I asked the social workers if I could bring him food. I told them that I had always cooked for him. Even on the days it was his father's turn to keep him, I would send him off with food—fried plantains and Jollof rice and stew that he could eat bowl after overflowing bowl of. They told me,

'Yes.' So I cooked everything he loved and brought it each time I was permitted to see him. I brought him clean clothes and his favorite pair of shoes that he had left at the house. Sometimes I saw him getting out of the now-familiar white car with too few clothes on and looking unkempt.

One day, he was brought to me at some public library wearing two different shoes. I wept in front of him; I could no longer restrain myself. He looked like a child someone had left to wander the streets because they no longer wanted him, and they were in a hurry to get rid of him. How had my child ended up looking like no one loved him? He was shivering in the chilly San Francisco afternoon and had no jacket on. Everyone knows you always need a jacket or sweater in San Francisco. I took mine off and helped him into it. By this time, some of the social workers permitted me certain liberties. They had started seeing me as a human being and as a mother, one who loved her child very much. They told me so.

How had his father sent him to school with his hair all knotted and matted, which is typical of black hair if you don't grease it and comb it? How had he let him go to school wearing two different shoes—one black, the other green? Was it because he knew I had prided myself on taking the best care of my son and was happy when people said he was handsome and stylish—that seeing my son like that would disturb me? Would he neglect his own child just to get to me? I knew the answers. He would hurt my child because that was the only way he knew he could break me. I feared my son would get sick, not only from the cold but from something more—something I could not soothe with soup or song. He looked pale and drawn and a little less of himself each time I saw him. It broke my heart.

While things were looking up with the social workers, a different one every few days, things were not going so well in court.

Alexei fired his attorney, and Jess called me in a panic that he had a new one. He had hired a criminal lawyer, the most expensive in the city. Jess feared her. She had a reputation for being ruthless and almost never losing a case.

"If you've ever prayed before, this is the time you're going to pray like you never have before." Jess, a non-Christian, recognized that it was going to take powers other than her own to save me. I was now looking at not only losing my child for good but possibly going to jail.

Before this new information could sink in, Jess told me, in no uncertain terms, that I was also going to need a criminal lawyer.

"Looks like the case is headed in that direction, and, as you know, I am not a criminal lawyer." Where was I going to get money to hire an attorney? Jess worked as a public defender in Juvenile Court, so I didn't have to pay her. I had no time to feel terror or any of the many emotions going through me. I had work to do.

"I need you to get all the people who know you and all the families and friends that have been around you and your son to write letters to the judge about you. Who you are and the type of mother you are. It's called a Letter of Character. Get on it now!" There was a new urgency in her tone that I hadn't heard since we began working together.

Our friends had heard that we were in court and that my son had been placed with Alexei. One or two of them sided with him and believed what he told them. The rest did not, and when I met with them to ask them to write letters vouching for me, they cried for me. Perhaps for themselves, too. They understood; many of them were mothers.

"How could this be? You love your son so much and would never hurt him!" "What kind of system is this?" "What can I do to help?" "This is wrong!" "Write," I told them. "Tell that to the judge."

They wrote, telling the judge how they knew me and their experience of me as a mother. "She has a bond with her son that we envy," one wrote. "She has done an amazing job with her son," wrote another. "That boy needs his mother. Please send him back home." Still another claimed, "She is the only one I am comfortable sending my son over to for sleepovers because she not only loves her own son, she loves and cares for other children, too. My child always comes back happy and says he wishes he could stay longer because aunty was so nice, and he had so much fun."

Jess was happy with the letters, but I could tell she was still worried. There was still the matter of the criminal attorney. A friend from Africa who was in the army knew an attorney that he felt was very good, although not cheap. Mimi went with me to see her. We climbed up an old and musty-smelling narrow stairwell in a brick building on Folsom street and walked up to the receptionist who told us the attorney was expecting us. Michelle was a slender, woman with shoulder-length brown hair who looked like she invested time in the gym. She was one of those women of indeterminate age who could have been anywhere between 28 and 40. I liked her firm handshake and friendly though reserved manner. She was bright, confident, and thorough. Michelle asked me tough questions that made me feel that if ever we were to go to trial, she would be capable of going against the shark my ex-husband had hired. She asked for a retainer fee and said she charged by the hour. I explained that I had no money and asked if she would take my case anyway, and I would find a way to pay her. I just wanted my child home. I would find the money somehow, I pleaded. She agreed. Mimi took out her checkbook and wrote a check for partial payment of the retainer fee. Relieved, I hugged my godmother tight. She had saved the day once again. I looked into her kind eyes and thanked her for all she had done for me.

Mimi would be with me every step of the way until I got my son back. She prayed with me or told me to pray when the days got too long, and I did not know if I could survive the agony of waiting. She gave me a talking-to when I had been up four days straight and looked like I would not survive a fifth. She told me that if I did not get a "hold of myself, that boy would have nothing to come home to when it was time to come home. And what would become of him?" She made rice and spoon-fed me as though I was a baby after I had lost all desire for food. I shed 20 pounds easily, like a snake sheds its old skin, the first three weeks my son was gone.

Mimi did all this and more for me—yet she was not without her own challenges. She was 77 years old and in constant pain from her multiple back surgeries and hip replacements. She walked with a cane and limped her way through all the weeks of my trial and never complained. She had used the little money she got from social security to help me retain the criminal lawyer when I was wringing my hands trying to figure out how I was going to put a down payment on my freedom. What had I done to deserve all this from a woman who knew me from nowhere?

We had met at "the Pink Store" as she had dubbed Magic Johnson's thrift store, "Out of the Closet." I had been looking through the dollar rack when I heard a warm voice say, "Hi. Would you like to try this on?" I turned around and came face to face with a well-dressed older lady with a full head of thick white hair that made me jealous. She was reminiscent of a more glamorous era and had a certain pizazz that made me want to talk to her more. She handed me a denim jacket.

"I think this will look good on you," she said, smiling. That was the beginning of my very wonderful and divinely-ordained relationship with Mimi. We had gotten remarkably close very quickly after we met and spent a good amount of time together. She introduced me as her friend to her son and daughter. Outsiders would always ask if I was her biological daughter when she introduced me any time we went anywhere together.

One day, she said, "I am just going to tell people you're my goddaughter," to avoid having to deal with lengthy explanations. That was it. That was how someone who had no blood ties with me, someone whom I had just met by accident, turned out to be my own real-life fairy godmother.

More than just cheap costume jewelry, one can sometimes find real treasures in a thrift store.

I had never known the depth of my ex-husband's hatred for me. It all came out during our time in court, and I was stunned by it. Long after the social workers had come and visited my home to see where my son and I lived; long after they had written their reports; long after the attorney appointed to my child—the attorney who had disliked me upon sight and had made comments that made Jess tell me "we're in trouble"—had come to see our living situation and interviewed my son and wrote her findings, in which she said that my son was the most articulate eight-year-old she'd ever met; long after she changed her opinion about me and concluded that there was no truth to the allegations made against me and that I, in fact, loved my son very much and we were very bonded, my ex-husband still refused to have my son stay overnight with me. While the investigation was going on and not concluded, he had all rights to my child. He got to determine how many hours a week I could be with my son and how those visits were arranged.

When Jess asked him for an overnight visit on my behalf after my son and I had been apart for nearly two weeks, he said, 'No.' He said he did not want me alone with the child. A child that, just weeks before, we had both had custody of.

Mimi stood up and appealed to the court, saying, "I can be with them, Your Honor. I can go over and stay the night at their apartment. I can act as chaperone if the father is concerned about anything." Alexei refused. He said he would have to choose who would stay with us and, since he did not have anyone at that moment, my overnight request was denied. I, who only weeks before had lived with our son, taking care of him, helping him with homework praying with him and kissing him goodnight for bed, had now become someone he said he "didn't trust to leave alone with the child."

It reminded me of an incident weeks before when I had met with my son on one of my allowed visits with a social worker at a restaurant. They varied the locations where we would meet: public parks, libraries, cafés, street corners. My son had been very excited to see me, and I had ordered food for him because he said he was starving. He told me he needed to use the bathroom before his food came, so we both got up and walked towards the bathroom when the social worker walked in front of me and blocked me.

"You cannot go in there with him," she said.

I had never wanted to. I had only wanted to stand by the door and wait for him. I took any chance I got to be close to him since somebody was always watching us and listening in on our conversations the whole time the visit lasted. Yet, all the ways in which I was humiliated and criminalized during that time did not hurt as much as hearing my ex-husband say with the coldest look on his face that he did not trust me alone with my son.

There are times when family is all you have. When my brothers learned of the CPS case against me, they told my mother, who lost no time doing what she does best—wounding me. We were not speaking at the time—one of our many periodic breaks from each other. She never once called those months that I went through what was perhaps the worst time of my life. Instead, she made comments I will never share with the few friends who asked me when my mother was flying in to attend court with me.

"So what if she goes to jail? Will her son be the only child that ever lived without a mother?" She concluded her verbal onslaught, saying that I "deserved" to have my child taken from me. What had I ever done to her?

Hurt and angry beyond belief, my brothers shared this with me. She had gone too far—even for them. They stopped talking to her for months afterward.

Nothing in this world could ever convince me otherwise—my mother hated me.

How many times has she said mean horrible things about all three of us over the years? How many times has she said we are all failures and have nothing to show for our lives- how we should be doing this and that for her and don't. How most of her troubles are because she had us. Her life would be much different had she not had children or brought those children to America and on and on. How many times have people asked to us "why does your mother hate her own children so much?" Perhaps she is justified and we are guilty. We have not yet built her the proverbial house expected from every African child whose parents had labored for them. I had promised her a villa when I was about 11. I was her firstborn and wanted her to know that although I was a girl, I could still take care of her when I grew up. My brothers have tried, and I am proud of them. We love our mother . Each of us doing what we can for her but it may never be enough. It certainly does not seem so.

My brothers knew I could not face all of it alone, and both of them could not afford to come to San Francisco, so they decided my youngest brother to fly in for the last day of the trial. My aunt, my mother's friend, the one who had invited her to come to America, offered to come with him. I will never forget her standing up in court and telling the judge how brilliant I had been in college and as a child and how proud she was of me and the accomplishments I had made. She told the judge that I loved my son very much and that she believed a mistake had been made. She told the court that this was no ordinary mother and son relationship and that, for more than the obvious reasons, I needed my son, and my son needed me. My non-biological aunt stood up for me that day like a mother would for their child.

My brother was next. He told the judge that I was the one who had raised him. I was 13 when he was born and had taken care of him as a baby and all the way through. He shared that I paid his school fees for the private schools I made sure he attended and helped support him until he graduated from one of America's finest colleges. But more than that, he said, he was grateful that I am his sister. He shared with the court that he is the man he has become because of the lessons I taught him in kindness, perseverance, hard work, and the fear of God.

People were visibly moved after my brother spoke. I looked around the courtroom at my friends, my godmother, Jess, and some church members, and I thanked God for the people who had shown up for me when I most needed support.

And I waited.

Finally, the judge looked up from her papers and gave a slight smile in my direction and said that after a very thorough investigation, the case against me was dismissed.

"You can go pick up your son."

I didn't wait to hear any more. I grabbed Jess, gave her a hard hug, and raced out of the room as my brother, aunt, godmother, and friends struggling to catch up with me. I waved them a hasty goodbye and blew them kisses as the elevator doors closed. I drove at breakneck speed to my son's school to get him. It was over. It had been two and a half months, the longest 75 days of my life.

After it was all over and we had gone back to sharing custody of our child, there were times when I screamed silently in my soul against Alexei. I wanted to look into his eyes and tell him our eight-year-old son had said, "My papa has no soul," but I wrote in my journal instead. It was much safer. There is no telling what an animal will do when their child is threatened—even a human animal. I wrote him instead:

I have become something I don't recognize, a woman fraught with worry and filled with bitterness and rage

you have taken my child and emptied me out and filled me up with your poison-hate

I will be empty again to make room for love

for this is what my child needs

I will try and go beyond perceptions and emotions to be a parent who is conscious and present

I will fight for the awe-inspiring, often scary responsibility for shaping a child's life and destiny

I will fight for peace for my child

Court was over, people went back to their lives, and life carried on, but there were times I still wanted to rage at him for taking my child. There were times I wanted bad things to happen to him after my son came back to me with wounds I knew only God could repair. There were times after hearing my son say, "My heart was on fire, Mama, every day without you" that I wanted to damn his father's soul to hell.

I prayed instead. I asked God to heal us all—my son's father, too.

Like me, my son now lives with a betrayal of a parent. Over these past few years, after CPS, and after he started having anxiety attacks, my son has slowly revealed his experience of what happened to him during that time. His father had told him that he was not going back to Mama's house. He did not understand the full implications of that; one day turned into the next and the next, and he neither saw me nor came home to me as usual. He also did not get my check-in calls—calls I make to ask how his day was and wish him goodnight or pray with him on the days he is with his father. He told me he held his cat at night and buried his head under his mattress and would sob quietly so that his father and his girlfriend in the next room would not hear him cry. His father got him a rescue cat to take his place after his new girlfriend claimed he was paying too much attention to his son and there wasn't enough for her.

A light went on in my head as I listened to him bare his heart. I understood why my son had seemed dazed and confused that first time he was brought to see me. He was seeing a ghost. He thought I had died. He had believed it for a whole week until he was brought to me at the playground in West Portal for that first supervised visit. No one, including his father, had explained about court and a case or an investigation and why he did not see Mama for a whole week. It was the first time he had ever been away from me that long. He had been left to emotionally navigate the whole process alone.

The consequences were devastating. He looks at his father and the world now with one brow raised and sometimes still asks me, "Why did he do that, Mama? Why did he hurt me so much? How can I forgive him for taking me away from my mother? How can I believe he loves me after what he did?"

It has been five years. Therapy has helped, loving has helped, prayer has helped, but I know that the experience has made a different person of my son.

I found out afterward that the photos my son's father had accused me of abuse with had been taken to the most renowned and respected child forensic psychologist who had examined them and told the courts there was nothing in them to suggest abuse. I still wonder what if someone had looked at the photos I had taken of my child and, based on her interpretation, my son was not given back to me. Someone who had never seen me or known how I am with my son, someone who did not know how much I love him. What if, for whatever reason, they had concluded wrongly, concluded I was guilty because they are human and make mistakes? What if, as a result of that mistake, my son was removed from his mother for good? When I imagine this possibility, I can't help but be angry at my son's father all over again. I am amazed that anyone can make such a reckless gamble with a child's life. I cannot help but think there have been mothers and fathers who have been wrongly accused and never got the divine break I got.

One day, many months after the Child Protective Services ordeal, I was rubbing shea butter on my body after my bath when I noticed the slightly lighter colored marks running down my thighs.

I recognized them. They resembled the cut of a baker's knife in bread dough before it is put in the oven. I realized then that the body, too, can split open under strain. It can be stretched.

God had looked out for me, once again, in the form of the judge who had presided over our CPS case. From the moment I had walked into that courtroom and felt the hostility directed at me, I sensed a warmer, almost sympathetic energy from her. The few times we looked into each other's faces; a kindness emanated from her in the smallest of smiles she gave me. A year later, after my son and I had weathered the hardest parts of that ordeal, I decided to write to her. She had been on my mind the whole time as well as my phenomenal attorney, Jess, whom I still pray for.

I wrote to the judge and gave her a quick introduction to the woman she'd only met on paper. I told her about the non-profit work I was now doing and that I had always loved the law and had started but did not finish law school. I also wrote her a poem and framed it, hoping she would accept, I dropped it in the mail. She sent me a heartwarming reply saying she knew the women I worked with were lucky to have me, and perhaps one day I will consider going back to law school. She wished me a good life.

Almost two years after CPS, I got a call from Jess telling me her boss wanted to talk to me. She had a huge favor to ask me. I could not imagine what I could possibly do for such a person, but said yes, gladly. They wanted me to speak at a town hall meeting about how important pro bono lawyers are in the juvenile courts. The governor wanted to cut off the funding from which my attorney and her colleagues get paid. I was honored and happy to speak of the fact that, without my brilliant attorney, whom I would never have been able to afford, I would have lost my child forever. I got a standing ovation when I finished. Others joined me in making a case that getting rid of attorneys like Jess was not an option, and society has a moral obligation to ensure that all children, rich or poor, are given a chance at life outside of juvenile halls and prison yards.

We won. Jess and her boss invited me to the lounge where they were having celebratory drinks a few weeks later. I was their guest of honor. They believed their victory was in no small part due to my fervent plea and sharing of my very personal experience with a pro bono attorney who would be lost to others if the money for her salary was taken away.

The judge was at the party. I walked up to say hello, and she hugged me instead. She told me how happy and grateful they all were for my participation in the campaign. She thanked me most of all for the poem I had written her. I was pleased and beamed from ear to ear as she shared that she had been having an especially bad day when she received it, and it made all the difference. She told me the poem was "exquisite" and that she has hung it in her chambers to remind her every day to give each person who appears in front of her a fair chance.

The Judge Who Refused to Judge

I sit across from you
the gulf between us wider than the Atlantic
separating my home from yours
its depth deeper than the hate-filled stares
damning me to hell

I am convicted
but you don't judge
Dead woman sitting
strange hands have reached inside
and ripped out my heart
my child has been taken
but I
am condemned
I see
you haven't judged
No trust fund to buy me justice
the brown of my skin
screaming
guilty guilty guilty
'twill take more than a village
to bring this child home
still you do not judge
All hope lost
my fate is sealed
my son my son
my son is gone
'twill take grace in the flesh
to pull me through
you were that grace
judge N-A-D
you were the judge
who refused to judge

It is ironic that the very agency that investigated me in the
CPS case ended up recommending me for a job that has direct

links with their offices and the courts. The head of the CPS department—the one who had worked with Alexie and me to arrange co-parenting once the case was closed—believed that from the reports made by the social workers who had supervised visits, coupled with her own experience of me, that I was an exemplary mother and had a lot to offer the non-profit organization. She encouraged me to put in an application and name her as a reference if they needed one. They didn't.

In the interview, I talked about roads traveled, people I met, experiences I had, obstacles encountered and overcome. Every tear shed had cleaned out a little more of the bad stuff and made room for some better thing. Like this one. How wonderful that I could feel such confidence. For the first time, I was not ashamed of who I was, of the experiences I called forth in that interview. Experiences that placed me in the perfect position for my new job, my new calling: Counselor.

For the first time, I felt okay with who I was, and I was glad I had become the person who had stunned my interviewers into even wondering if I was real. The Director of Programs got up in the middle of the interview and did a victory dance around the room because she was so happy she had found me.

How incredible the feeling that I was wanted—needed in fact—for what I could bring to the position. It was exhilarating to feel that my skills mattered, that my learning mattered, that my intelligence mattered, my open-hearted approach mattered, my intuition mattered, my instincts mattered, my ability to self-express and communicate well mattered, and that my compassion all mattered. The essence of who I am matters.

I was offered a job on the spot without trying, without giving references or proving myself some other way. It was stunning to discover that being who I am was enough, that being who I am was really the only requirement. It blew my mind. Of all the jobs I had done in America, this was the first that let me believe that I can succeed, not in spite of who I am but because of who I am.

I felt validated.

Never would I have dreamed that what Alexei had done and the events before and after were preparing me for this new phase of my life. I would be working with women with mental health challenges and their children. Some had children who had been placed in foster care. Others had just come out of prison and needed a year in a program where they would receive mental health services, get housing, attend day treatment classes designed by counselors like me to help get them ready for their new life. Part of my job would entail helping them reunify with their children. No one could have been more perfect for the position. Although I never shared my own experience with the Director who had interviewed me, still, the fervor in my heart to help these women get their children back had come through.

Ten hours after the interview, my old demons of self-doubt appeared, and I was sure I couldn't possibly take the job. I couldn't do it. It just wasn't going to work. There was my son's custody schedule, which always made it difficult to do full-time work. There were also the demands of the job. I would work 12 hours for three days, and, on the fourth day, I would do three hours in meetings, totaling a 40-hour workweek. It was also a night shift position. It was easy to put all the right reasons in place to support my decision not to take the job.

I shared all of this with my friend Ogoni, who gave me a different perspective.

"You can do this job," she said. "Don't let anyone know everything about your past work history and struggles. They don't need to know you're a single mom with no family here. Tell them you can do it. I know you can manage things. You're an African woman. You're strong and very smart.

"Do you think they hired you for no reason? Or do you think it is for your pretty face? This is America. If they give you their dollah, they will make sure they are getting something out of it," she added.

I smiled, grateful for the levity she had brought. After talking with her, I realized that I could adjust bedtimes and mornings and rearrange parts of our life—but I could do this. I could try. I needed to give my son an example to follow. You don't quit when things get hard. You find a way.

It also meant I would have my first full-time job in the United States in 18 years. I would have benefits and health care and paid sick days and vacation. I would have a chance at a certain kind of normalcy in America, not to mention a monthly paycheck. There was also the promise of meeting new people, interacting with others on a professional level, learning and growing, but most of all, contributing to the world using my gifts. The 12-hour night shifts were nothing to sniff at. Working as a single mother around my son's custody schedule left me sleeping only about 10 to 18 hours a week, given my chronic insomnia, sensitivity to noise, and my inability to sleep during the day. One can do the impossible with God's grace.

As soon as I made the decision to try the job, a certain joy took over me. I was going to be happy to do this work. It felt like a calling. My self-esteem and other things needed it. I was grateful I had spoken to my friend. I learned a big lesson—sometimes your way is not the only way and may not always be best for you. The counsel of good, trusted friends can change one's life. Navigating that situation also taught me to keep working on being flexible and open.

I settled easily into my job as a counselor. I went through the certification process, which was both intellectually challenging and very stimulating. It qualified me to work with clients in an official capacity, but it was my life experience that truly made me one. I had found the best possible job for myself—one that was rewarding emotionally, spiritually, and psychologically, if not as much financially. I loved participating in the treatment groups our program offered: anger management, nutrition, mental health, journaling and art, meditation, and mindfulness, among others. I learned as much as I taught. I could have done without the documentation aspect of the job. It was tedious, and some parts of it seemed needless and unnecessary. I liked working on the treatment plans and goals we made for each client. It left me hopeful that they were headed somewhere—perhaps to a new job, getting off or going on some medication, meeting the requirements for reunification with a child or family. Whatever it was, there was a sense of moving forward in that part of my job that made it meaningful.

Nothing made me happier than having our clients at the non-profit social rehabilitation program I worked with tell me they were glad I came in to work with them each day. No one understood them more, they said. I would often smile to myself quietly at the mysteries of this life. The depression I had suffered through all my life, the many challenges and often heartbreaking trials had all led me to a place where those very experiences were making a difference, and I was of help to others. Nothing gave me more joy than to pull from my own bag of tricks to help a woman go through the anxiety of appearing before a judge to make a plea for their child. Nothing gave me more satisfaction than to sit with someone who was having a dark day, hold their hand, and say a prayer or meditate on the ins and outs of both our breaths until they felt human again. Nothing made me happier than to do a few loads of laundry for a client who had no energy to get out of bed that day to brush their teeth or say good morning or cry. Some coworkers told me I was doing work out of the scope of my salary. Others said I was too nice and resented me for it. They said it made them look bad, as if they were not doing their "job." They had no idea I had lived through similar days our clients were experiencing—days when I did not know how I was going to survive the next agonizing minute and had only made it through because someone had shown me a little kindness. I was finally beginning to settle into what I believed was my calling.

But a year later, I made a routine visit to my doctor. And, once again, my world was turned upside down.

CHAPTER 16

Mammogram à Deux

IT'S A CURIOUS THING, this business of being a woman.

Not too long after I started my new job, my female center was "brushed" to scrape off tissue from the part of me that defines me as a woman. Especially these days, when penises can be traded for vulvas and vice-versa, my uterus remains the one thing that says: "She can nest an egg, grow a baby, continue the human species." As if I was not mortified enough as I was, propped up, trussed up like a chicken, ready to be stuffed, I had to manage the "Are you clean enough down there? Do you smell good?" thoughts racing through my head. I grabbed a sanitizing wipe in a last-minute effort to clean myself some more before the doctor got between my legs to examine me and take samples for a variety of tests. I tried to rearrange the mass of my very generous African backside on the hard, tissue-covered examination table. I hoped, from the doctor's perspective, a shapely derriere.

"I was circumcised as a child doctor," I said, very matter-of-factly, trying to prepare her for the shock of finding parts of me missing. Clitoris and labia removed during the female genital mutilation coming-of-age ceremony performed when I was ten. Mercifully, I had been spared the partial sewing of the vagina in addition —done to create a tighter pocket for a future husband's pleasure.

I remember the look of confusion and something else on the white male gynecologist's face a few years before when he had examined me and discovered this fact. I wanted to spare doctor C the same thing. She was warm and very pretty.

How do you manage to look cool and unaffected in that position? With legs up, knees bent, a metal clamp inside you, the cold device cranked up like a child's toy, to open you wider still? Its sharp edges digging into tender flesh, exposing your most private self and leaving you like a mouth forced open. The whole process is not unlike being on the dentist's table. Slightly uncomfortable, I squirmed.

"One more scrape and we're done," Dr. C. said gently. I lay there afterward, shamed and shrunken. Did the doctor find me tight and clean? Was she horrified by my thick curly bush? Did I look like I have had a fair share of men plunder their way into me? Did I smell of rain, roses, or rainbows? On and on, my mind went.

My thoughts eventually returned to Dr. C. Does she wake up in the middle of the night from a nightmare with the gaping jaws of a thousand anguished vaginas screaming in silence in her face? A tableau in a horror flick came to mind. What sights and sounds and smells she must endure, my doctor. What would possess some-one to study the care of women's vaginas?

"Since you're here, we might as well do your mammogram. You're due, you know." I was jolted out of my reverie and scrambled to cover myself with the cropped tissue gown specially designed with an open front to leave little room for dignity. I gathered the paper wrap around me as best as I could, praying it didn't tear, and revealed my already-exposed nakedness.

"Sure, doctor. You're right." Extra bright smile. Was this day ever going to end?

"If you have any problems, just come back."

"Thank you so much, doctor."

"By the way, you did great. You did really good," she said, smiling.

You have no idea. I thought back at how, just moments earlier, I had wanted to keep my legs closed so tight that no amount of trying could have pried them open. An act of rebellion. A clam. No strange eyes and hands on me or in me. I had not jumped up and run down the hallway half-naked with a clamp dangling between my legs, fleeing to the room where the sad bundle of my undergarments awaited me. Yes, I had done great.

"Hello. Dr. C. sent me to do a mammogram," I said quickly, hoping the young man in the white coat behind the computer would tell me they had closed for the day.

"ID and insurance card, please." I guess they were still open for business. "Thank you. Please sign here. Fill these out and come back to me." I did as he asked and handed him the filled-out forms.

"Someone will call your name shortly. Please take a seat."

"Miss K?"

"Yes?"

"My name is Lynn. I will be doing your exam."

I followed the chipper technologist who wasted no time telling me to "take off everything waist up" as soon as we entered the small, cramped room. I looked around for my paper cover. This time there was none. I missed my little-room-for-dignity sheet. No pretense at covering up here. I am trying to hold my very large, very heavy DDD breasts up as I listen to Lynn explain the process.

"I am going to place your breast, one at a time, on this tray and press down hard so I can get a good picture." Standing there, exposed yet again, I am not as embarrassed as I had imagined I would be. Perhaps I was getting used to being made bare and examined by white women with very different body types from mine. Cool hands lifted up my right breast and placed it gently on a plastic tray like a love offering to the machine-god.

I watched her moving it this way and that way, looking for an angle only she could determine. I am moved into silence by some unnamable feeling. My usual friendly, "Hello, how are you" is not forthcoming. Perhaps I was not as embarrassed because this experience of having my breast in a woman's hands who was neither lover nor friend, while unsettling, was not so bad as having the scarred center of me exposed to a stranger—even if she was my OB/GYN. I am curiously calm and even somewhat detached.

"I am going to press hard. Don't breathe, don't move."

One boob down. Left breast lifted, positioned, adjusted.

"Don't breathe, don't move," and then we were done.

I couldn't help but blurt out, "You must have seen a lot of breasts!"

"I have seen them all—all different shapes and sizes."

She didn't mention color.

"Your pictures look great."

I stared at the screen. *Those can't be mine*, I thought to myself. There were two perfectly-rounded globes staring at me. It was like looking at an airbrushed picture of yourself—you know it's you, but you also know it's not. I thanked her and quickly put on my one piece of clothing and walked out. I had had enough of being probed for one day.

The doctor called back a couple of days later and told me the mammogram had shown something, but they needed a biopsy to confirm anything.

They did a new test on my breast that left me with a new appreciation for cow's milk. A biopsy. Lying face down on a table high enough for a doctor's chair to fit underneath, I had one of the strangest experiences ever. Being so high up in the air and looking down at the blonde head of the doctor as she tugged at my breast sticking through a special opening carved in the table for breast biopsies, I couldn't help but think of Alice through the looking glass. I felt like a cow being milked. I thanked God that at least cows don't have to endure the excruciating pain of five-inch needles that no amount of numbing medicine can eliminate, as the doctor digs into tissue to suck up cells to confirm or disconfirm the presence of cancerous ones.

Four days after the biopsy was done, I had just picked up my son from school when the doctor called. As soon as I answered the phone, I got that special feeling that the doctor confirmed.

"I am so sorry. Your results were positive."

My son was in the back seat. I smiled politely in the phone as if she could see me, thanked the doctor, hung up, and drove home a different woman. I was now a woman who had cancer.

CHAPTER 17

The Emperor Pays a Visit

SIDDHARTHA MUKHERJEE titled his 600-page biography of cancer, *The Emperor of all Maladies,* given that no disease poses more questions, and that, despite the millions of dollars spent on research, there is no disease more controversial or more feared.

Cancer. One word that changes everything. No going back to what you knew, to what you had and didn't even understand the value of. No going back to who you were before cancer. I had been walking around complaining about my life, completely unconscious of how, in just moments, that life could change. I had been going through my days moaning about this and that—traffic, small inconveniences, petty slights from people I really cared nothing about—all trifles. I realized I had taken so much for granted, believing my life was hell, until cancer came along and brought me face to face with the terrifying face of death and the stark reminder of my mortality. Things I had believed were so important suddenly became inconsequential and ridiculous—like saving up to buy a better car or worrying I will never lose the "pouch" —the name I gave my after-baby belly.

Cancer came in like a worm and ate the center of my life. Everything now revolved around it. How I longed for it not to be true. I prayed for another outcome, another reality—anything but this. The first few days were exhausting, fighting this new normal of terror alone except for a little boy who was told a truth too big for his mind to fully comprehend. I had no peace, then sudden moments of grace. A call, my child's uninhibited laughter, an act of kindness that would jolt me back to a place of gratitude. A helpful reminder that I was still very much alive.

I had been alone with my son in the car when I had been given the news and had not allowed myself to "hear" and feel. It was after he went to his father the next day that feeling came back. I wish I could have remained frozen. Giving in to the emotions that came with feeling nearly crippled me.

A cancer diagnosis affects every part of your life. There are physical, emotional, and psychological roadblocks to navigate each day. You live with one or more of the five stages of grief every day even though there is no dead body to show that someone you love has died. Some days it is the voice of denial that is the loudest. *I can't have cancer, this is not happening, this is not true. They've made a mistake. I should seek a second opinion.* Other days, it is anger. *Why did this happen to me? What did I do to deserve this?*

On easier days, there is surrender. *It has happened. I am still alive. I will seek treatment and do whatever I can. It is what it is.* Then there are those other days, the D days. Days when your world is so black, it feels like light will never shine through again; days when the incommunicable hell that is cancer eats up every source of joy around you; days when even the presence of your child is not enough to put a smile on your face.

One D day, I ate a few spoonfuls of rice seasoned with the salt of my tears. I wasn't supposed to eat rice anymore; the cancer diet doesn't include it. I was born and raised on rice in Africa. We had it for breakfast, lunch, and dinner, and I love it. Rice is all I know as a starch. It seems simple: You have cancer you can't eat rice. Not so for me. I have been without so much for so long—people, things, happy feelings, an existence devoid of experiences that fill up a life and make it bearable, even beautiful. Giving up the one thing that tied me to myself and home was another blow that cancer dealt. I was exhausted. After days of being good -of blending kale, collard, and broccoli, I longed for something familiar, something that connected me to myself and gave me comfort. Something that made me feel still alive and human. I ate a little rice that day with guilt. I did not and could not enjoy it. I worried that I was gambling with my life and felt guilty that I was not trying hard enough to survive for my child. For the second, third, and two hundredth time, after chewing on that last spoonful of rice, which had lost all appeal and tasted like sand, I realized how much my life had changed and how long the days ahead were going to be.

The words "surgery," "radiation," "chemotherapy," and "survival" would become the most thought about. Words like "battle with cancer," "cancer-free," "remission," "mastectomy," and "lumpectomy," quickly became familiar and important. Signs on busses with "no woman should have to face cancer alone" appeared at random. Cancer, cancer, everywhere. It seemed like the world had become one giant cancer center. Cancer had taken over my life.

My fear of what cancer could do—of it taking me away from my child or my life—left me with no life at all. I had been diagnosed barely two weeks and had not even begun the journey through more tests, surgery, radiation, and God knows what else, but I was already losing my mind from worry. At the rate I was going, it was very clear that, if I did not get a handle on myself, my fear would kill me before the cancer did. I turned to prayer, asking for peace, for guidance, for courage. I asked for clarity to see the lesson in this, to welcome whatever gift it was bringing me. In my fog, I managed to take care of my son, my biggest hero. His existence reminded me of God's love for me, and I needed that reminder more than ever.

On one of my harder days after diagnosis, after crying for hours until the tears were no more, I peeked through swollen lids at his small form curled at the foot of the bed in peaceful slumber and begged God to keep me here for him.

One day, when I was not so little, but I had lived through enough to know that the world was a scary place, I sat on the cement step in front of my grandmother's house and told God to make my experiences and suffering count for something. I had not seen the decades of bad things that lay in store for me. I did not yet know that I would be cracked open and spill out. I did not yet know that the day would come when it no longer mattered if my suffering meant something, when all I would want would be for God to just make it go away.

One day, during her visit for my surgery, I was driving with my mother and having a random conversation that eventually came around to cancer. Most conversations those days invariably ended there. She told me she "understood" how I felt. A rush of emotions left me silent the rest of the 45-minute drive home. Later that night, I wrote this plea as the loneliest tears I have ever cried fell from eyes that had already cried too many cancer tears:

For My Friends and Family: I love you but you don't understand

I love you but you don't understand
You haven't felt the ground shifting beneath you
And you are falling deep in the black cancer hole
I love you but you don't understand
how the world stops
when you hear the words "have cancer"
and the "you" you're familiar with suddenly becomes a stranger
you desperately want to say goodbye to
I love you but you don't understand
the infinite whys, hows, what ifs, and what nows in this new universe
I love you but you don't understand
You don't have cancer

On New Year's Eve 2016, exactly 14 days after that fateful phone call, I sat in a small Vietnamese restaurant the color of seafoam waiting for the spring roll appetizer I had just ordered. My heart was overflowing with gratitude. Across the street was a tribe of homeless people I had just walked by. It was freezing outside. I had stayed a while in my car just watching them, debating if I should give my warm coat and hoodie to the one lady my heart had been pulled to as I drove up to park my car in front of their encampment.

"Hi. I have some things I think might be useful?" I had said to them.

As I pondered the joy and something a little more than relief she showed after putting on the thick black coat and the hoodie, I was overcome with the weight of God's goodness. Here I was, an African living in America with no family except for my boy, and although I was far from living large, I was better off than most. I was driving a Pontiac Grand Prix, which had broken down more times than I could count, and which was the same age as my son. It still looked good, and sometimes it got me where I need to go. I was staying in a tiny one-bedroom with a kitchen just big enough for one person to move around freely. In my beige, ankle-length coat, I probably looked like I had just stepped out of the pages of Vogue or some hip club, with a little cash in my pocket, and the sweet anticipation of a nourishing meal on my mind. I thought to myself, *Life has not been too unkind.*

How easily one of them could be me. I had slept in my car before, when the circumstances of my life had knocked me over, and I could no longer stand on my own two feet. All those thoughts and emotions washed over me as I watched them huddled together on the concrete pavement that chilly December night.

"Thank you," my new friend said.

"You're very welcome," I said, smiling.

"I love your shoes," she said, her voice raspy from the cold or something else.

I was wearing shiny sports shoes with glitter on them that I had found in the Salvation Army thrift store 15 minutes from where I lived. They looked fancy and expensive.

"I thought you were Spanish," she said with a puzzled look on her face.

"Really?" I asked, shocked. "As black as I am? I am from Africa."

She looked up at me fully and mumbled something about Africa, which I couldn't make out. I smiled and told her we're all from Africa. She agreed, pulling the hoodie close to her face in a gesture that melted my heart. I waved and walked toward the restaurant that I had found on "Best Cheap Eats in San Francisco."

As I sat waiting for my food, my heart thanked God for all the events of the day. I had woken up that morning and dragged myself to my appointment with my therapist, bringing things I had wanted to discuss, questions I wanted to ask, and things I hoped she would make disappear even though I knew she had no power to. The session had not gone as planned, and yet everything we talked about was what I needed to hear —food, faith, forgiveness, cancer.

"You're not going to die," she said. "You are not going to have a heart attack. Your work is not finished here," reassuring me about the strange pain in my chest that had begun ever since I got diagnosed with cancer. My therapist was an angel, combining medicine, psychotherapy, spirituality, and heart to her practice. A far cry from the detached, bored, and often-broken therapists who charge a full week's pay for a session leaving you more confused and damaged than when you came in. I have seen a few of those. I left her office laden with gifts. The best of which was the lightness of heart I felt walking back to my car.

I headed to Oakland Flea Market and got an hour and a half massage from the Chinese "doctors" who give some of the best ten-dollar massages the fancy spas charging ten times more could ever rival. I was happy to talk to my brothers while I looked through stacks of books someone had put a "free" sign on. They're hard to get on the phone sometimes.

Just as I was leaving the market after spending three hours there, I saw my amiga, Gloria. I had first met her while she was working, cleaning the smelly bathrooms at the flea market I go to every couple of months to see the large open market that reminds me of Africa. I would say Hi and Thank You each time I saw her. I had been drawn to her unlined face and marveled at the fact that she managed to keep a pleasant demeanor doing such unpleasant work. I had peeked behind the yellow-taped stall warning "Not in Use" and seen things that paled in comparison to the dirty recycle bins I had once combed through to make a few dollars.

Over time, we became friends. She hugged me tight that day, and we held each other long, then pulled apart slowly.

"I have prayed every day for you."

I had told her the week before that I had been diagnosed with breast cancer. We both teared up. She held my hand in her warm, calloused ones and smiled.

"You stay here long time. You live long time and grow old," she said.

I hugged her again, tears running down my cheeks. Never will she know how much I needed to feel reassured even if only by a woman who has no idea what God's plans are. But it was two people in one day affirming my life. I'll take it.

Gloria spoke little English, and I understood almost no Spanish. Somehow, we managed to communicate volumes in our clumsy attempts at both languages.

"I love you, my friend."

"I love you, too, Gloria."

She asked for my number because she wanted to be able to check on me and see how I was holding up. She knew I had no other family in San Francisco apart from my son. She understood that one can't have too many friends while dealing with cancer.

My mind came back to the restaurant when the pretty Thai waitress, in her sixties with perfectly-coiffed hair and expertly-applied makeup, set down my spring rolls and said, "Enjoy." *It's been a full day*, I thought as I bit into the crispy crust of perfectly fried dough and savored the pleasure of eating vegetables deliciously spiced. I finished my dinner, packed some food for someone—I didn't know who yet—and headed out with a smile in my heart.

My mind wandered back to the homeless lady now warmed up in my old coat and thought to myself, *What a fitting way to end the year.*

I had a few hours before midnight. I had already planned on a movie and church. Buoyant with gratitude and newfound confidence after dinner, I bought tickets to see *Collateral Beauty* starring Will Smith. I had seen the previews, and they had looked depressing. Will Smith—with a perpetually haunted look on his face because he had lost his only child—should have warned me it was not going to be a light-hearted film. I cried through almost the whole movie. Even though I had known the movie was about death and loss, I didn't know the details, and as I watched scene after depressing scene, the joy of my heartwarming encounter with the homeless people slowly retreated, and the now-almost-familiar panic—birthed by the cancer diagnosis—returned. The film was all about cancer and its horrifying endings. The death of Will Smith's six-year-old from a rare form of liver cancer and the dying of his longtime friend and partner from melanoma were played out in full. The camera did a fantastic job of playing up the images of the progression of the disease by focusing on the grey, sunken cheeks and depicting, in slow motion, the character coughing up blood in bathrooms and collapsing in hallways. One practically witnesses cancer unfold, and my own shock, fear, terror, and panic all came rushing back. Was this my future played out for me? I was sweating and shaking all at once. Why had I done this to myself? It was bad enough that I was alone, hard enough to wrap my mind around the still-fresh diagnosis. What was I doing watching a movie like this?

Driving alone that New Year's Eve, although shaken by the horrifying movie, I noticed the absence of the familiar loneliness that had become a companion of mine on Thanksgiving, Christmas, and other occasions that call for the company of family and friends. This time, there were no tears, just a renewed urgency to go to church. I have done so every year for as long as I can remember. It is one of the few rituals of a life lived without the benefits of a stable family rooted in tradition. I drove first to one church; it was closed. Church Two closed. Church Number Three was closed, too, and there was no reasonable explanation in my mind for it. How was it possible that in a city that size, on New Year's Eve, there was no church lit up brightly with voices raised in praise as worshippers welcomed the coming year? I was just looking for a place to sit with myself and God, but the way things were looking, it did not seem like I was going to have much luck doing that.

Back home in Sierra Leone, New Year's Eve is perhaps the

most anticipated and celebrated holiday of the year. Muslims celebrate it in their own less-visible way. But, for Christians, the evening usually begins with attending the overly crowded services where you run into people who may not have stepped foot in church all year but would not miss New Year's Eve service if their life depended on it. It was a chance for the not-so-faithful to atone for sins committed all year round, and also a perfect opportunity to join the large groups of joyous people marching all over town singing the new year song.

"Api New year me noh die, api new me noh die oh, tell God tenki for me laif oh." *Happy New Year. I didn't die during the course of the year, and I am thankful to God for sparing my life.*

This would go on until daybreak when everybody would head home to continue the celebrations with friends and family, food and drinks, and more dancing.

I missed home that night, driving alone around San Francisco, and choked back tears at the thought that, with cancer as my new reality, I might never again make it back to Sierra Leone and sing another "Api New Year" song with strangers united in the celebration of this wonderful gift called life.

Still, I was determined I was going to experience the countdown into 2017 in a house of God. I had no place else I needed to be more. I pulled to the side of the road, plugged my phone in the car charger, and prayed the phone did not go off before I could google "New Year's Eve church service in San Francisco." Ten minutes later, I got lucky. One church was open: Calvary Hill Community Church. I breathed a sigh of relief, started the car, and looked at the time. It was 20 minutes past 11:00. I stepped on the gas, hoping there was no traffic and I would make it on time.

A quick negligible thought: the church was located in Bayview

Hunters Point. Some of San Francisco's more memorable killings, both by police and Black men killing other Black men, have happened there. Still, I did not hesitate. My need for God was far greater than my fear of being shot. A part of me felt I had already been handed a death sentence anyway, and the only hope I had of reversing it was making it to God's house to plead with him to spare my life.

I arrived at the church and drove around the block a few times to look for parking. There was none. Parking in San Francisco is impossible. Nearly as impossible as being able to afford a studio the size of a closet for $2900 a month. I was tempted to park in some mechanic's driveway, but that temptation did not last when I thought about the fact that I had not gone to my non-profit job in the past month. I had been busy running between tests, scans, biopsies, and everything else that makes fighting cancer a full-time job. I did not know where my next month's rent was coming from. Getting a towed car back from the impound would eat up half of my non-profit salary even if I had it.

I drove two or more blocks away from the church building and parked the car. There were bags filled with books and clothes I had thrown carelessly in the back seat from the pile of things I had put together to donate but hadn't gotten around to. I could not leave stuff in the car in that part of town, day or night. The clock was ticking, and time was running out, so I made a last-minute attempt to cover the things I could with a navy blue-colored sheet and prayed that I would not come back to find someone had broken a window to steal stuff that was worth nothing.

I ran up the street and dashed up the stairs two at a time. Well-dressed women standing by the entrance greeted me and ushered me to a seat as the preacher's voice boomed across the large room: "My time to rise. Tell your neighbor, 'this is my time to rise.'" I turned to my neighbor, but she seemed lost in a world far from church. The small child sitting next to her was calmly playing with a copy of the New Year's Eve leaflet as though she was used to being ignored and had learned to entertain herself. I turned behind me and told the young, good-looking Black man in his 20s: "It's my time to rise."

The preacher was a 300-lb. messenger of unbridled energy who exuded the kind of confidence that made you believe everything was going to be okay. I had made it to church. This was where I needed to be; these were the words I needed to hear as the year came to a close. Heaven-inspired sweat poured down his face as he moved and danced and exhorted the congregation to enter into the fullness of their destiny in the new year. His jowls danced in agreement each time he shook his head to drive his point home. For someone so heavy, he moved with surprising speed and grace, and one could not help but be captivated by his fervor. I jumped out of my seat, clapping, "Yes, God! Thank you, Lord!"

"These are the last few remaining minutes in 2016," he continued, "and if there is anyone here that wants to leave 2016 behind, come forward, come to the altar. Kneel, stand, do whatever you're moved to do, but bring it all to God."

I was among the first group of people to answer the call, people with burdens too heavy to bear. I fell on my knees as the preacher said, "Tell God! Tell him that whatever it is, it's too much for you. Give it to him." *Give it all to him*, his round face glistening with sweat implored. I heard shouts, murmurs, and sounds of weeping. I heard sounds coming from some place deep inside myself as I sobbed my heart out to God.

"Name that thing," he said in a voice brimming with authority. "Name it, whatever it is you want to give to God, name it, and tell him to take it from you." "Cancer," I whispered. "Cancer," a little more forcefully the second time. "God," I pleaded, "take this cancer from me. The weight of it is too heavy to bear."

I was broken in front of God. I was crying for things I couldn't put into words, and the things I could, I told him. I told him to heal the fear, the sickness, the doubt, the many shades and layers of pain that have colored my life so much that I can barely see anymore. I told him to spare my life for my son's sake. I begged him to let cancer be the last horrible event in a life that had seen enough suffering and bad luck to last me ten lifetimes. Sounds like an animal whimpering in pain came out of me, and I had no strength to make myself stop. I cried and cried, and it seemed like the tears would never stop and my heart would not stop breaking. Suddenly, I felt myself being wrapped up in a warm hug by the tall, big woman praying next to me. Perhaps it was my snot-covered face that moved her to me. Perhaps she had felt the anguish in my soul and could relate. Perhaps she had seen my unraveling and had reached out in compassion to hold me in place.

Tears. Sobs. More snot. It felt as if my whole being was weeping to God. The tall woman held me through it all, never letting go. After a while, I heard the preacher say it was time to pray for someone other than ourselves. I prayed for the people I love. My son, my brothers, my friends, Mimi, all those who have been kind to me. I even prayed for my mother. I prayed for their loads to be lightened; I prayed for grace to visit them and sit sweetly upon them. I prayed for them to be well in body, mind, and spirit. I prayed for them to be happy.

Then it was time to thank God for answering our prayers. Still sobbing, I thanked God for all the things that had led me to that moment in that church. I thanked Him for knowing I was too little in the face of my life. I thanked Him for my child and my friends and all the good things I still had that cancer had not yet taken. I thanked Him for bringing me into the new year just as the church erupted into "Happy New Year."

I got off my knees and, in a daze, walked back to my seat. Something was different. It felt as if I was floating. I felt so light. A box of tissue was passed on by one of the smiling ushers. I cleaned my face and did not wonder if I had streaks of mascara running down my cheeks like river tattoos, reminiscent of the past dark weeks. More "Happy New Years," more group hugs with strangers that have already become a part of me as we held each other and swayed to moving choir music. I thanked God silently for this very bearable lightness of being and drove home reborn, renewed, and ready to kick cancer's ass.

When they were well, my breasts were an enviable 36D, often the standard of perfect fullness and voluptuousness. By the time they became diseased, childbirth and crème brûlée had settled on triple D as my new normal. Words like "huge" and "wow" had taken the place of "voluptuous" and "perfect." I remember the reaction one of my dearest friends had when I told her I had been diagnosed with breast cancer: "But your breasts have been what you have been most proud of!" she said as she wept over the phone. We were thousands of miles away. She was back home in Africa, and I had just come from Kaiser Hospital in San Francisco. Later, after she had offered to leave her children and fly here to help take care of me and had enlisted every prayer partner she could find to beg God for my life, she would remind me of our days in college when I wore low-cut blouses that flaunted my chest. I remembered.

My friend and I laughed and cried and prayed that even though they were not a perfect D cup anymore, I still wanted to hold unto them and asked God to help me do so. I would go through scenarios in my head of having one empty space on my chest next to a very heavy lonely droopy boob hanging down from sorrow and defeat. I would imagine a brown silicone cone stitched on, unnatural to look at or touch. I imagined never taking my clothes off again in front of a man from feelings of shame and inadequacy. I imagined and imagined, each scenario more frightening than the last. It is so easy to go about our days grumbling and finding fault with our bodies. This is too that, that too this. I wish this were smaller, bigger, longer, rounder, thinner, thicker, lighter, darker-shorter-taller. It is only when we are faced with the idea or reality of losing a part do we plead to hold unto what we had despised, rejected, hated—the beautiful, miraculous machine that is our bodies. The heart that pumps 20 gallons of blood a day and never takes a break. Imagine if the heart decided it needed a vacation.

I wondered what particular lessons cancer was here to teach. I knew vanity was one of my deadly sins. I did not have much to believe in growing up. I never believed I was worth anything, no matter how many times I was told how smart I was, how many awards I won, how much I had accomplished. It never registered. My looks were no different. Looking back, I do not think I ever believed I was beautiful in spite of the many times I was told I was. Deep down, I didn't buy it. It always felt as though I was watching myself from a distance and trying to see what other people saw when they looked at me. I thought my arms were fat. I called them tree trunks. You could not pay me enough to wear a dress without sleeves. I may never have believed I was beautiful, but I look at my college pictures now, and the slender yet curvy and smiling girl in them tells a different story. She could not possibly be me. What I would give to have those arms back! *I most certainly cannot go sleeveless now,* I think sadly. Not after having arms three times the size of what they used to be.

If only I had truly seen myself. How many times have I been jealous of women who could wear whatever they want? Big women and small ones alike? I have envied their confidence and sometimes mocked the ones I thought had no business showing some parts of their bodies. Now I realize that perhaps, like me, some of those women do feel uncomfortable or scared but have the courage to do it anyway. Perhaps one day, I, too, will have such courage. Perhaps one day, I, too, will be unafraid to show off my arms that do so much to make my life easier and beautiful. Perhaps one day, I will have the courage to embrace them and love them just as they are now.

In some medical schools of thought, ductal carcinoma in situ is not considered cancer. DCIS, for short, is the presence of abnormal cells inside the milk duct in the breast that have not spread and become invasive. I thank God He has been merciful. I have chosen to believe that God has been merciful. When I compare myself to people like Kate Butler, who wrote *All the Lies I Told Myself,* a book about her battle with cancer at age 32 with a two-year-old, I am grateful. There have been times when I have been embarrassed to share about my own cancer diagnosis, especially after hearing "That's nothing" after hearing other women say they had stage two or stage four or had both breasts removed or whole reproductive organs removed. I feel sorry and bad for them, but sometimes I feel angry, too, at this easy dismissal because I, too, have felt the same terror at hearing the words "You have cancer." Two surgeries, six weeks of radiation, the threat of having a breast removed, pain, and burning the likes of which I have never felt in my life— I venture to say that I have at least had an introduction to cancer. The emperor's visit is real, alright. I have lived through the crazy thinking which accompanies a cancer diagnosis. *What's going to happen to me now? Will this come back? What did I do to provoke it?*

I, too, live with the guilt of eating sugar and flesh. Meat is said to cause cancer, as is alcohol, fried food, toxins in the air, cosmetics, cleaning products—the list is endless. And some days, I am hard-pressed not to believe the world is not one giant cancer-causing agent.

As a single mother with no lover, who shares custody 50/50 with my son's father, on the days when my son was gone, I was alone. Nights were the worst and being a chronic insomniac all my life, a cancer diagnosis while living alone is the worst. It was no better during the day as most of my friends had left San Francisco because they could no longer afford to live there. Now I understood the signs I read but did not really grasp fully on the buses all those years: "No woman should have to face cancer alone." But, for the most part, I did. My brothers flew to see me when they heard the news. They stayed for five days and then went back home to their lives. My mother came the day before surgery and stayed a week. I was grateful for her help that first week when my howling from raw pain frightened my son so much, and nothing could make me comfortable. Relief only came after I finally fell asleep from the pain medicines that got me throwing them right back up as soon as I woke up.

I am grateful my brothers came. For a few days, I got lost in their love. We were the Three Musketeers again, even though it was a scary and stressful time for all of us. I cried for days after they left, recognizing once again how much I had lost in America and in my life. I thank God for Mimi, who never got tired of picking up my late-night calls and held me in her love over the phone, assuring me that I was going to be okay. Those nights when I was too scared and too rattled to pray. I thank God for my friend in Africa who prayed and called and texted and loved me hard and long through it all. I suppose I fell in love with my third pastor because, even though he was thousands of miles away, I could pretend someone was there to dry my tears—if only over the phone. I loved him because he spared me the heartbreak of thinking I was still alone, in spite of the fact that there were people—strangers—who loved me through those first hard months. There's nothing like a real-life person to hold onto when things are falling apart, and I did not have that.

I missed Africa. I missed my friends. I missed love. I missed being wanted, and I missed having someone to make me tea and rub my neck when I was sitting up and propped up to sleep for a whole month after surgery made my neck and back muscles cramp and stiffen in protest. I missed having a loved one in whose neck I could bury my nose and weep when it all became too much to bear. Most of all, I missed hearing another human voice when I walked into my tiny apartment when my son was gone. America has many reasons the world considers it the greatest country in the world. It's a democracy (albeit an imperfect one). It has some great public schools, freedom of speech, and a capitalist market system that allows for the possibility of having the proverbial house with the white picket fence. And it has internships for high schoolers and college students, so they don't have to sleep with politicians to pay their school fees like 80% of young people are forced to do in Africa.

But America is the loneliest place on earth. Thankfully, doctors are beginning to call attention to the fact that most diseases and cause for suicide is the isolated lives most people lead just by virtue of the American culture that places individuality and independence above all else.

I wanted the doctor to tell me it was all over—everything had been cleaned up, every diseased cell was out, and I would not have to worry anymore. No talk of radiation or hormone therapy, that cancer was behind me. But that did not happen. In spite of the fact that the cancer hadn't spread, that one spot that required a second surgery six months after the first, was God's way of keeping me close to Him.

My son was a rock throughout the whole experience, although I wish he had never had to go through it. The first time I told him, I used the simple language the social worker recommended for parents needing to tell their child that their life is going to be turned inside out. He got on his knees and asked me to kneel with him. Dry-eyed, he prayed for the doctors to see everything and remove everything so that his mama will be well again. He never wavered in his faith, and never once did I see him cry. I know only too well that just because children do not show their tears to parents sometimes, doesn't mean they are not drowning in an ocean of grief. Because I knew this, I would check in with him at different times in different ways, trying to gauge where he was at all times. God has been merciful. I know there are things that went on in my son's heart that I will never know, but for now, I am grateful he has come out, if not unscathed, stronger, and more resilient than ever.

CHAPTER 18

Men of the Cloth

WHAT IS IT IN ME THAT ALWAYS GOES AFTER MEN OF GOD? Am I looking for God so much that I have fallen for three men of the cloth, each of whom, in their own way, broke my heart? The first was a newly converted born-again-on-fire-for God priest in his early 20s who wanted to make me a priest's wife. I was intrigued by the idea of someone who had married the church being so consumed with me. It thrilled me to have him feel torn between me and his calling; it was my first real taste of power. The power of a woman over a man. I was not as corrupt then as I would become when I met the other two pastors decades later. Except for the sexual innuendos that colored our attempts at "Christian conversation," our flirtations would remain unexplored. Still, my relationship with him only cemented the idea of my "wrongness" deeper. Why would I want a priest to want me if I was not a bad person? No wonder my stepfather; no wonder Kazim.

By the time I met my second man of God, I had been in America for 17 years, I had married, divorced, and was a single mother. We met at his friend's church on one of those occasions when my desperate circumstances forced me to run to God once more. It is the only place I can go when I can no longer hold myself together, when all my capacities to manage, endure, and try are depleted.

A man I had struck up a conversation earlier that week had mentioned a church that he said had changed his life. He was open with me about his struggles with his homosexuality and his faith and had found refuge in that church. I asked him for the name of the church since I knew it was only a matter of time before I had a big need for God again. I did not have to wait long.

The Sunday I met my second man of God, after the altar call, I went to the altar and told a room full of strangers that I felt so miserable and lost that it had become impossible to imagine another reality where I would ever feel safe and capable of living a meaningful, productive life. I needed an end to a life of misery with no apparent end in sight. Losing my home and sleeping days in my car had finally done it.

After Alexei and I had separated, he decided to put our condominium up for sale. I had nowhere to go. I could not go back to my math teacher and her family, though they had been thrilled that I had made a life for myself in San Francisco. I had seemingly checked all the boxes—a successful engineer for a partner, a home, a child, and a future. But most of the friends I had made over the years had left San Francisco. It had become nearly impossible to pay rent and raise a family there.

I learned a lot those few days, sitting in my car. I discovered the distinct and particular language of the night and a world with its own set of rules. I sat watching those lost like me wandering the streets traveling to nowhere. Then, of course, the proverbial selling of goods and services. I didn't really sleep. I could never sleep outside alone in my car on the street. My mind simply wouldn't let me. Not with its penchant for conjuring up one horrible scenario after another—hence my refusal to go camping despite my son's many pleas. He was shocked—it was one of the few things even my love for him was not big enough to overcome. He did not understand how a person born in Africa could be scared of sleeping outside. I tried to explain that sleeping under the stars in Africa is very different from camping in some remote place in America. I had watched the news and seen too many camper stories that have left me forever afraid of it. It's hard enough to fall asleep in my plush, king-size bed, a legacy of an earlier benevolent time. I do not need to go chasing demons on campgrounds.

Perhaps it was the fact that I looked defenseless, vulnerable, and broken, perhaps it was my "chocolate self" as he described me later that did it. He had always been drawn to people and things of the motherland. As usual, I immediately fell in love. This time, at the first show of kindness.

"You're fine now. You're in the house of the Lord. Everything is going to be okay. He told me in a voice which sounded like music to my tired, sad ears. He was a Reverend , sometimes referred to as "preacher" by the last few devoted members of a small church he pastored on the outskirts of the city. The peeling grey-gold paint of the walls and musty smell of the main chapel were tell-tale signs that the church had seen better days.

Preacher loved all things African. He wore dashikis every day of the week and on Sundays a western suit with pocket squares made of African-inspired prints. He had even learned to say "hello" in many African dialects and spoke a good amount of Swahili. He was in awe of the fact that I come from the Mandinga.

Hailing from the Malian Empire, known to be the home of the fiercest, strongest, and arguably the most good-looking among West Africans, Mandingas were prize slaves during the slave trade. Fetching the most money at auctions with their tall, broad frames and sinewy muscles, they made excellent bed toys for the white slave owners' wives and great breeders of field hands for their masters' cotton plantations.

We talked about Africa and America, their similarities and differences. We discussed African movies and American history and marveled at the great African warriors who went to war and did great exploits. Men who had been willing to fight and die for their women, children, and their people. They had not been emasculated like the descendants of the African American slaves in America, half of whom were in prison for small and not-so-small crimes , while the other half stand on street corners, smoking and drinking their miserable lives away.

Preacher had been married before and did not talk much about his past. He told me we should focus on now, on us. He wanted me to be his wife. From time to time he would say to me "God has a plan and purpose for your life. He is going to use you someday."

I believed him and was very happy to hear this. I wanted to be useful to someone other than my son.

For a while, things were okay between us. Mainly because we did not spend too much time together. I was a single mother busy raising my child and he, had many church duties to attend to. When we did spend time together, things did not always go smoothly. We had many disagreements about almost everything and it was clear we were both unhappy.

In the end, I was too much for the greying Reverend, in whose generation anything the man says goes, whose legacy of discrimination and Jim Crow had left many of our men too damaged to understand true masculinity and how to love a woman in the modern world.

He ended up hating the very thing he had loved so much about me. I was too independent, too proud- typical of the Mandinga.

Papa had never lived long enough to teach me what to look for in a man and so I would make the same mistakes over and over again.

When I met my next man of the cloth six years later, a lot had changed. He was younger than me by three years. It was a first for me. Alarm bells should have gone off then, but by the time I met him, my third pastor, I was pretty sure no man would ever want to date a woman like me. A woman dealing with cancer.

I had nothing like romance on my mind when we met. My diagnosis was fresh on my mind, and I still was trying to make sense of my new reality. We met over the phone. He was given my number by someone close to me. He lived on the East Coast, and I was told he was a good and anointed man of God and would pray for me. He did. For months. During those first horrible weeks, when I was still reeling from shock and terror, he would sometimes spend hours on the phone with me. Given my history, it was inevitable that I would fall for him. He had shown me care when I was most vulnerable. It felt wonderful to be wanted again, especially with my new reality of dealing with the unknowns of cancer, not to mention the many ways a cancer diagnosis undermined my sense of self and, of course, my sexuality. There are whole courses, retreats, books, and resources offered on the subject of dating and cancer. It felt good to hear, "I will never leave you." Were those not Christ's words?

"And if you're ever sick to the point where you can't wash your own shit, I will clean it for you." He said those things, and I loved the sound of them. He told me I was the kind of woman he'd always dreamed of but never imagined he would meet. He was married; they were separated. Later, he said he was divorced. His wife had gone back to Africa and was "never coming back." I believed him. I would have married a gorilla then if he'd asked me to.

Cancer was too big for me to take on alone. I strongly believe that basking in the sweetness of this forbidden affair was what possibly saved me from a depression and loneliness that might have killed me long before the cancer did. There were days when a phone conversation with a phantom lover thousands of miles away would not suffice. There were days when I needed to hold on to what and who were familiar: my mother, my papa, my beloved brothers, my closest friends, Africa. Home. They were all not there. I needed something physical, someone to hold on to reaffirm my existence. I needed someone to feed my hunger for human contact, to nourish me for all the days I would be alone when my son was gone and there was no one to even talk to. America can be a very lonely place.

I needed someone drinking from me again to quench my thirst for love. I needed to feel flesh against flesh, hips grinding into hips, fears dissolving in the pool of passion. I needed to feel like a woman. I started to feel the emaciated frame of my love-starved soul fleshing out each second I was engaged with him. He seemed the ultimate male to my female. Funny, smart, arrogant, knowing exactly what to tell me to make me forget reason. I found myself breaking all my own rules of restraint and caution. I was swept away by an impossible flirtation. I imagined him touching me, could feel him against me, inside of me, taste his kisses through the 4000-mile divide between us, making it physically impossible to touch in person. For this distance, I was grateful. I am sure I would have made a bigger fool of myself had we been physically nearby. I knew I was treading on dangerous ground, but I couldn't stop, didn't want to stop.

I tried hard not to respond to his calls, but I ended up picking up the phone and dialing him in spite of myself. When I said "No" to the telephone calls and video chats, they sounded hollow and unconvincing. I hated him for knowing I couldn't help myself. I loved that it was through him that I had once again discovered desire.

There was so much at stake: his marriage, my peace, his reputation, my heart. I knew I was not going to get out unscathed. I prayed for forgiveness and grace. I prayed for my very human need for love—to give it and be given it. I prayed for strength for what might come next. I chose to be seduced by my own hunger, and I braced myself for the inevitable punishment for my wayward heart. Situations like these always have one thing in common: a "never happily ever after" end.

I knew he was a distraction, but was he not a very welcome one? From the many years of loneliness, privation, sickness, fear, and constant worry? Do I not deserve to be in a state of forgetfulness from cancer, if only for a little while? I wondered if it was too much to ask of the universe.

I married him a month after radiation treatment, six months after I met him. It was the only way we could try to make an already wrong situation right. He was, after all, a pastor. Marriage gave us permission to touch.

Once I became his wife, my need for him grew bigger than my desire to be good, so I gave him all of me, all of my starved parts. His every touch lit a new fire before the flames of the old could grow. His kisses burned my brain; everything in me wanted him. Never had I wanted to be woman more; never had I wanted to feel more wanted. He kissed me 'til my lips swelled from his want and my desire. He loved me 'til I forgot cancer, hunger, and need. Ours was a passion I could not get enough of. My "bushman"—the playful name I gave him. Unlearned and unsophisticated, I knew I would never discuss Danté or Brontë with him. It didn't matter. I knew that he would never be able to woo me over discussions on Anna Karenina or the Bluest eye; still, I wanted him. He broke my heart along with the walls that hunger, loss, pain, despair, and loneliness had built solid around my sexuality. This was his gift to me after leaving me four months after we were married.

I spent a month on the East Coast, but I had to come back home to San Francisco. I was still undergoing treatment for cancer. We had talked about him moving since Alexei lived in San Francisco, and all my doctors were there, too. It was with this understanding—that he would come in the next couple of months—that I flew back home. He wanted some time to arrange his affairs before joining me. He needed to look at prospects for work since setting up a church was something that was not likely to happen overnight.

I came back to San Francisco, and the demons came, too, and chased my man of the cloth away. He broke every promise he had made to me. He would be gentle with my heart. He knew how much I had been hurt. He was going to erase every memory of pain I had ever had. He was never going to leave me. He was going to be there with me through the cancer ordeal. It had all been a lie. He who had been so happy just to hear my voice suddenly wanted nothing to do with me. He would not answer my calls, and, when he did, he sounded strange and distant. I who had been his "queen" became someone who annoyed and irritated him. To hear my voice was to risk his wrath. I did not recognize the monster that had taken the place of my kind and tender pastor.

Once again, I was left asking, *What just happened? When will this end? When will my luck change? When will I ever actually have and keep something good for once in my life?* In one year, I had gotten a cancer diagnosis, fell in love, had two cancer surgeries, gotten through radiation, got married, got divorced, and had my heart broken—again.

The heartbreak was the most painful of all. My already-fragile sense of self has been shaken further still. Was it me? Did he not want to be saddled with a woman dealing with cancer? Was it my past? Was it because I had no money to offer? Or because I was a single mother? The questions had no end, and all the answers left me with the same, cold fact. He no longer wanted me.

I could barely register it when he asked for a divorce. My doctor had just told me that, six months after my first cancer surgery and radiation treatment, my follow-up exams were showing more cancer. I had to have another surgery. He wanted a divorce. There was talk of mastectomy. He wanted his divorce. That was the only conversation we had in those weeks of this new devastating development in my cancer journey. I filed the papers just before I went in for my second surgery. He got his divorce; I got to keep my breast.

I was empty after all of it. For him to leave me at the time he did was a blow that was hard to recover from. For someone who had always said they would never get married because they were too damaged for it, two marriages and two divorces were plenty. I think I will put the earthly crosses down for now and cling to the heavenly one. Christ's "I will never leave you nor forsake you" is one I can count on.

CHAPTER 19

Close Encounters of the Not-So-Kosher Kind

I HAD MY FIRST COLON HYDROTHERAPY. I have been told that having clean bowels is a good way to start ridding the body of stuff it no longer needs, stuff that can even be toxic. The cleansing is said to help prepare it for healing.

In the few weeks after the diagnosis, I had nearly finished shedding my shame skin. Never in my life did I have to bare myself—body, mind, and soul—to so many people, all strangers, in so short a time. When the prospect of death looms, small indignities and other inconveniences like no privacy have little room to exist. So, when Svetlana, my Russian therapist, said, "Strip from your waist down and wear this gown with the opening in the back, use the bathroom and come back to the room," there is almost no hesitation to do as she tells me. Svetlana was a slender middle-aged woman with kind, knowing eyes and long dark-brown hair. I was shocked, pleasantly, when I entered the bathroom. The toilet had a bidet. I wish every bathroom in the world had one . No more pulling tons of paper towels to clean oneself after using the bathroom. One stack of paper towels with soap to wash and another stack to rinse off and make sure I was not leaving residue on my bottom and feminine parts from cheap commercial soap in public bathrooms. And yet another stack for drying properly. Pity the person who goes to the bathroom after I have been there. I am the reason you probably find no tissue or paper towels. The conservationists are going to hate me for this.

On the plus side, I am also the reason that, when you walk in, you do not have to sit on a wet seat or step into a puddle of piss at the foot of the toilet that some women leave behind after squatting to use the bathroom. I leave the bathroom clean for two reasons: I do not want anyone else to have to deal with the mess I walked into, and I do not want anyone to think I was the one making the mess. I can never shake off the feeling that if someone walked into a bathroom after me and found it messy, the color of my skin would become the reason for it. I refuse to let us be blamed for that, too. We are guilty of so much else in the world. So, I am a self-appointed bathroom ambassador for Black people everywhere I go.

"Lie on your back, knees up." She stood next to a square-shaped aquarium that looked like a small icebox from the 1950s. "I am going to connect these tubes together—one small and the other large. This one feeds the water in your colon. The other is where the stuff will pass through." I was shown a clear-plastic tube that could have passed for a dildo, which she told me had been lubed. The whole process was beginning to mimic something sexual. Why did my mind go to such weird places? The clear plastic gleamed like a magic wand from the substance it had been greased with. Svetlana interrupted my thoughts.

"Do you want to put it in yourself, or do you want me to?"

"Oh, I can do it myself," I said, smiling, slightly trying to see how much of myself I could hide from her.

"Bend your knees this way. I will help you."

No point in me trying to maintain any semblance of dignity when she pried one cheek open and handed me the magic wand. It is cold, and I am not used to this feeling.

"Yeah, it's in," I say, wanting the humiliation over.

She took a look, adjusted me on the table, and it felt a little less uncomfortable. My angle had been a little off. Wand in, knees bent, I was ready to receive two liters of slightly warm liquid, which she told me was chamomile tea and other cleansing herbs. I felt a coolness and then a weird sensation of something snaking its way up in me.

"You vill feel pressure. Don't push. Just tell me when you feel like you want to go."

A small okay from me.

"I am going to massage belly to get things moving."

For someone slight, her hands were surprisingly strong. She dug into my belly and sides, going round in circles, pushing down and out like she was kneading bread. It was not painful but not pleasant, either. As I watched her, I was struck by the wonder of our connectedness as humans. Here I was, an African Black woman having my belly manipulated by a white Russian woman to get rid of my decades-old kaka.

The whole process reminded me how, just the day before, I had almost vomited in the X-Ray chair while I was getting my mouth photographed because of my inability to stop my mind from wandering to certain places. My doctor had wanted to check to make sure that my wisdom tooth was not infected and would not require intervention while I was going through cancer treatment.

Something small and made out of foam was placed between my teeth to help get a good picture. I had bitten down too hard on the foam a couple of times before I was "encouraged" by the technician not to. I sat with my elbows resting on the arms of the swivel chair, and the technician would move the chair to adjust the X-Ray's arm and position it directly above the area he wanted to X-Ray. He adjusted the chair, moved the arm, and then looked in my mouth to make sure I was biting down on the foam correctly. I gagged a few times and nearly threw up my fancy $9.00 Green Juice Supreme that I'd just gotten from Whole Foods. *HEADLINES: Filipino Man Covered in African Woman's Green Slime While Trying to Do His Job.*

I struggle to keep my very expensive juice down. He told me to breathe, and I did, and surprisingly the gagging stopped until I thought, *What if the person in the chair before you had HIV or some other unwholesome disease? What if that someone, or the person before them, had just taken a shit and didn't wash their hands?* The thought that the technician had first adjusted the chair and only then put his hand in my mouth was almost too much to bear.

I had ingested someone's skin, their DNA, their shit, piss, or some other bodily fluid. I just knew it. I was sure the technicians do not wipe down the arms of the chair after every patient. Mine certainly hadn't wiped it down while I was there, and he had made several trips between the chair, the X-Ray machine, and my mouth.

We do not realize how close we are to each other, how very inter-connected we are. It became clear to me in that moment, that we are simultaneously depositing and eating each other's shit. Without knowing it, in this very moment, a Jewish man's DNA might be floating in an anti-Semitic being. A Black girl's Brazilian hair weave spray might be slowly poisoning a white supremacist's blood as we speak. As I laid there watching my shit travel through the clear plastic pipe, I imagined that my kaka was going through a space shuttle. The first African kaka floating away into space with a Russian cheering on.

With no idea what was going through my mind, Svetlana said, "You're doing good. Have you done this before?"

"I'm not sure," I stammer, embarrassed and grateful for the mystery of hidden thoughts.

"O, you wudd have rremembered." She seemed certain. "Where arr you frrom?"

"Sierra Leone."

"I saw movie *Blood Diamond*. Beautiful place."

"Yes. Used to be. Not anymore," I said.

Svetlana was easy to talk to. She rubbed my belly and coaxed things out of me that needed coming out years ago.

"My daughter is wrrriter like you," she said after I told her I was trying to finish something I was working on, and hopefully, get published.

"I am not exactly a writer. I don't have a degree in writing," I quickly try to explain. "I just write my thoughts down. Your daughter is the real writer."

"You should self-publish, "Svetlana continued, ignoring my refusal to call myself a writer. "You never know. Maybe someone vill discover you. Too bed Oprrrah doesn't have show anymore."

Models get discovered, I thought, smiling to myself.

"She does," I told her. "But it's different."

She asked me what the book was about.

"I am writing about this time in my life."

"You should, and you vill sign a copy for me."

I was touched. She had no idea how moved I was by her faith, how humbled I was that she wanted a signed copy of a book she was so sure I would write.

"You have a story to tell—most people wrrrite, but they don't tell story."

Confused, I asked, "But doesn't everyone have a story?"

"Yes everrryone does but not everrryone has the ability to tell it. It is a gift. You have gift to be able to do this."

I was quiet. I did not know how to respond.

In an hour's time, Svetlana and I had shared things about our lives most people don't get to, even after years of knowing each other.

"People, you know, people have rrrealizations on this table," she continued. "There is dirrrect link between the solar-plexus where I am pushing and ourrr emotions. People say that as they are passing out all that fecal matter, so also are they letting go of other non-physical shit." She paused, then, "I love my job."

"I bet you do, Svetlana." I smiled quietly to myself. Who knew shit held that much power?

I was curious that she wanted to be so intimate with people's waste, but I didn't ask further. I got it by the time I got home hours later. She was one of those ambassadors of life who know the truth that most of us spend a lifetime not knowing or trying to figure out—that on our own, we cannot survive. We need people like her to help us get rid of the shit we carry throughout our lives, the shit that holds us down and back. The shit that poisons us and, if not expelled, the shit that will inevitably kill us.

In my years in America, two major world events sent shock waves reverberating throughout the globe, reminding me that despite the many personal troubles keeping me occupied with my own survival, I was still very much a part of the rest of the world. The first was the attack on the World Trade Center in New York City on September 11, 2001. I cried along with the heartbroken families mourning their loved ones and thought to myself, if such senseless and cruel acts can happen in America, too, then where in the world is anyone safe?

The second was President Donald Trump's travel ban in 2017, which affected 135 million people, according to immigrant advocacy groups. It was disheartening watching doctors and other professionals on the news being detained and denied entrance into the United States just because they had been in some of the countries on the list. All of a sudden, every immigrant suddenly realized how precarious their status in America is. It was no longer just the Dreamers or those undocumented—it was all of us. Every immigrant now has the awareness, that no matter how "American" we consider ourselves, we can always be told to go back home.

CHAPTER 20

Marilyn Monroe is Black

WHAT DOES IT MEAN TO BE BLACK? From skin color to hair, from self-perception to social conditioning, I explore my own often-hidden uncertainties about myself as an African woman, as well as the experiences of other Black people in general. I am forced to confront the image reflected back at me in the mirror of Blackness, an image rife with controversy and despair, hope and beauty, an image the grown-up me can no longer turn away from.

I had always called myself the Black Marilyn. Since adolescence in Africa, I had adored and had a strange fascination with the white bombshell. When I turned fifteen, I resolved to become the Black Marilyn Monroe, and I read everything I could lay my hands on about her: her love affairs, her movies, her life, even her tragic end. I wanted to be her. It was my lifelong ambition.

It was not too long ago that I had an epiphany about the woman I had idolized most of my life. It happened quite unexpectedly one day after my cancer treatment.

I had the realization that taking on the persona of Marilyn would be to somehow live out her story. After all, we become what we believe.

Just a few weeks before, I had written "Become Marilyn Monroe" on my vision board under "Goals." That moment, divine clarity shone through me, and I realized there could only be one Marilyn and one me. She lived out her story—and it wasn't mine. I wanted my own story. I wanted to be in my own skin and be comfortable there. I pulled down the large poster I had made into a vision board and cut out the part where I had written "Become Marilyn Monroe." The cut left a gaping hole in the middle of my board, but I decided to leave it there. I will not patch it up and make it pretty; I will leave it there as a reminder of the messiness of life, a reminder of the hole in me brought on by self-hatred and lack of self-acceptance.

I had learned a lesson that day at age 44. A lesson no one had taught me: I can never escape myself, no matter how fast I run. And for the first time, I no longer wanted to.

I can teach my son the value of self-love and self-discovery; I can teach him the sacredness of self-acceptance as the beginning of the deepest and most fundamental relationship, after the one with Spirit. That day, after my epiphany, I knelt down and prayed out Marilyn and prayed in Hajah. I have finally put that dream to rest and said goodbye to both Marilyns—the Black one and the white one.

Can it be that a whole race of people has been taught to forever question themselves, perhaps even hate themselves? Shocked by my discovery after living Black for more than four decades, that, as adamant as I have been all my life about loving my Blackness, I might have been mistaken, perhaps even unwittingly lying to myself. Recognizing this and coming face to face with my own self-rejection by wanting to be Marilyn Monroe, a white woman, I am now forced to contend with my own issues with race. Yet, these are issues I had never even considered I had since on the surface, and, to my knowledge, I have always accepted my Blackness, even taken pride in it. I have no choice now but to examine certain parts of myself I never thought had any connection to my Blackness.

Hair is among the most controversial and most significant of issues in the Black African repertoire. There are camps for and against natural hair and weaves. Each camp passionately believes they have found the truth about Black hair and Black identity. The two are inseparable. For the die-hard "naturalists," maintaining the kinky curls of Black hair and doing without the perms and weaves is making a statement of self-acceptance. It is about preserving the legacy of movements like the Black Panthers, who advocated for and promoted Black consciousness, Black power, and the then-radical position that Black is beautiful. For this group, "white hair"—in the form of straighteners and hair extensions—is a betrayal and a rejection of self.

On the other hand, to the Brazilian, virgin-hair patrons and will-wear-nothing-but-hair-from-India believers, shelling anywhere from $300 to $3,000 to get hair from temples like Tirupati or Brazil is a small price to pay to look like the people who run the world: white people with fine hair. This camp argues that Black people who grow locks or keep their hair in its natural state are often discriminated against in the job market as well as other socio-economic forums, leaving them with one more battle to fight yet again. Black people already have many, in the form of discrimination, police brutality, unfair representation in the judicial system, and a host of other challenges people of color have to contend with. Why add furor to the fire, they reason, by appearing definitely, unapologetically Black?

Every day, Black people are faced with impossible choices since they can't take a break from being Black. There is a whole culture now around LWB—living while Black—to expose some of the harsh realities of Blacks in America. Some Black women take matters into their own hands, thinking, "Why not have a child with a white man—or any white man, for that matter, if the White Anglo-Saxon Protestant (WASP) is out of reach—so your child can have 'good hair'?" It is a choice some Black women make to help make life a little easier for their children, children who live in a world that still places a high value on whiteness and is still a place where Blackness has to be defended.

When we were young girls in Africa, just beginning to form our identities, we talked about the women we knew, admired, and wanted to look like. When asked who that was, I answered, "I want to be just like I am but have thick, Black hair like Persian women." I had believed them to be the most beautiful women in the world with their waist-length midnight hair, soft curves, and arresting sensuality. In my mind, they were the complete embodiment of the feminine. When I got a little older and discovered Marilyn Monroe, I wanted to be her. Having spent the first 20 years of my life in Africa as an African and the last 20 in America as an African woman living in America, I have made some discoveries and came to some conclusions. I am tempted to believe that, perhaps somewhere deep inside every Black woman, consciously or not—having been taught by the world that she is less than, not enough, and does not meet the standard definition of beauty—she wants to be something other than herself. Anything but Black. Had I chosen to idolize one of the most well-known white women in the world for her story—or for her race? Can you really separate one from the other? Wasn't being white part of her story?

What, then, did a young Mandingo girl and a bottle blonde in America have in common? What had I been drawn to in Marilyn Monroe? Why had I not wanted to be the "African" Maya Angelou? Or look like Dorothy Dandridge? Why had I not wanted to emulate Rosa Parks, Sojourner Truth, and other strong, beautiful, accomplished Black women? Could the reason be that I never heard of these women growing up in Africa? Could I have picked Marilyn Monroe simply because she was there and because something about the tragedy of her life had appealed to my broken child self?

Have I, like so many other Black women, in spite of my very definite conviction about loving my Blackness, subconsciously hated the skin I was born in?

Coming face to face with the possibility that I could hate my Blackness is shocking for me as I have always been critical of the African girls in college who bleached their skin and went to extreme lengths to do so. Sometimes they would travel to parts of Africa that are known for skin bleaching. They would have their whole body slathered in bleaching agents made of dangerously harsh chemicals, after which they are wrapped tightly in plastic sheets and made to stay in one place for days. The plastic then comes off and along with it, old skin. The combination of the heat from the plastic and the bleaching agents gives these breathing mummies new skin that would have taken years to get through conventional skin whitening routines. These African women, like their African American sisters in America—the privileged "high yella" or Black women light enough to "pass"—had bought into the notion that "light" is beautiful. I had scorned the very idea of trying to bleach my skin and would often say, "As black as I am, it will take me 50 years to get the black off my elbow," a particularly difficult area of the body to lighten. It is not uncommon to find dark spots or blotches on areas like knuckles, inner ears, knees, and other sensitive unbleachable areas on people who have tried to erase all traces of their Blackness.

I was greeted by a friendly radiation tech who had soft brown eyes and dark, longish hair that went past the collar of his white lab coat. He looked like an artist and seemed out of place here. He handed me keys to a locker like the ones you would find at a YMCA and asked me to put my belongings in there and then follow him.

I walked down the hallway behind him with my head bowed, wishing someone had come there with me. It was my first radiation treatment, and I was alone and scared. The tears welled, and I choked them down, closing my eyes quickly. We went into a room that that been set up for my treatment, and once some questions were asked to confirm my identity—name, date of birth—I was asked to get on the odd-shaped table that had side panels like foldable trays. The weight of the pillowcase covering my eyes was slightly unsettling. I had asked for one to shield my eyes from the red beams of light that shone directly into my face from the radiation machines. My heart started to race. I was alone on the table in a cold room, arms above my head. I was instructed to be still, absolutely still. I had seen this in movies: the dreaded image of a body lying on a table in a morgue. I have always been struck by the inescapable aloneness that image evokes. I was on a table now, too. Alive, yet feeling closer to death than I had ever felt before. Having to be so still while being covered up with a thin white sheet made me imagine myself dead. I wondered: *Will I know that I am all alone as I do now? Will I hear movement but be unable to speak or move? Will I be screaming silently as I am now: Don't leave me here alone! I am scared!* I could feel my confidence dwindling as my mind was assailed by such thoughts.

Weeks before, some friends and family had asked me how I felt about my upcoming radiation therapy. My responses varied. Sometimes I would say, "I have no thoughts on it." Other times, I said I did not know what to expect, and that made me a little apprehensive. A few times, I said I was fine, and when I did, I was taken back to the many times in my life I have pushed things away subconsciously in order to delay the pain of the harsh reality they presented. In the beginning, I had done the same thing with the radiation treatment, but over the last few days prior to the treatment, I had made peace with the idea. My friend had sent me a voice recording from Africa in which she prayed and told me the angels of God will be with me. Now, lying there scared out of my mind and playing out my own death, I channeled my thoughts to the angels. I gave them my attention and surrendered myself into their capable, heavenly hands. I imagined some gentle, whispering reassurances in my ear, others holding my hand, still more around the table, forming a protective, loving circle around me.

I smiled to myself.

"You're moving," said a nurse. "Let's try that again."

Even the slight movement of my smiling had registered to them, even though we were in separate rooms. I tried to remain calm.

"Breathe in. Hold your breath. Exhale."

I told my guardian angels not to distract me. I told them I have to be perfectly still so I don't change the settings of the carefully-positioned light that's directed to the spot on my breast, marked X, and have to start the whole process all over again. I wanted nothing more than to get off that table and run out of that cold, cold room.

"Last time, dear." Then: "We're done for today."

I closed my eyes and sank down into the table, knowing I was not alone even if there was no one waiting for me out in the waiting room, or even if there was no one at home to ask me how my first treatment had gone. I told myself to believe that, when all this was over, I had been radiated to unveil my true radiance.

I had managed to find a mechanic to fix my car and paid peanuts for work that could have cost me thousands. I was somehow able to buy, organize, and sort through over 200 pounds of clothes, shoes, cosmetics, perfumes, jewelry, and ship them to Africa. I had promised my friend that as soon as I got any money, I would do that for her so she would never have to wait for me again to send her money for food or her kids' school fees. I had been diagnosed and was being treated for cancer. Who knew what was going to happen to me? Who knew when I would have as much as $5,000 in cash again—my tax refund from my non-profit job?

I was grateful that God had made it possible for me to fulfill my promise to her, but I was tired. It had taken superhuman effort to do all that shopping just two weeks after my surgery. I was still swollen and in a lot of pain. Going from one store to another and only looking at things on clearance so I could stretch the money as far as possible had taken a toll. I did not want to wait since my days were filled with uncertainty, and I didn't want to just have the money lying around and use it for the many things that one always suddenly "needs" when there is money at hand. I was also able to make all my doctors' appointments and keep them.

I was proud of myself and happy my friend's dream of having her own business had come true. If she was careful and managed things well, she would never again have to ask someone for help or go without. It never occurred to me at the time to think of how I was going to live if I gave away all my tax refund since I was no longer working and had no other means of making money to survive.

The social worker at the radiation treatment center had shared with me that it always helps to bring something of sentimental value to the treatments, such as a scarf or anything of someone dear, as it seems to help a person stay connected to happier, easier times. She said she had taken her mother's sweater; I did not have to ask if she, too, had been treated for cancer. So, I went through my clothes, looking for something that had meaning, something that I wanted with me every day for the six weeks I would be getting radiation. I finally settled on my mother's wrap. I knew I was making the first choice of many. Perhaps if I carried my mother's wrap with me in the radiation room, I would be making a statement: I come with the one who gave me life, therefore, I am surrounded by life. I wanted to hold on to anything that gave me some kind of leverage.

I had made a very conscious decision to take her with me. My mother had not been my first choice, my granny had been, but there was nothing feasible of hers to bring. She was back home in

Africa. I had asked my mother if she had anything of granny's I could take, and she told me she had granny's gold bracelets. They would most certainly not be allowed in the treatment room, so I decided to sew an eye-mask to shield my eyes from the bright lights on the radiation table. I thought of using one of my own head-ties to make it, but I realized the point was to bring something from someone else close. I have been alone for so long, sometimes I forgot. I thought about using something of my son's, but I couldn't bear to cut up a shirt of his. So, I would use the brightly colored wrap my mother left with me after her visit for my surgery. I cut up the edge of it and got to work.

I weaved my mother back into the fabric of my heart one imperfect stitch at a time. Weeks before, when she had shown up at my door nearly giving me a heart attack because I wasn't expecting her, she had looked disheveled and almost unrecognizable. The old black wool coat I had bought her many years before had gathered so much lint it looked like she had picked it up from a discarded pile in a Goodwill store. I took her shopping even as I prepared for cancer surgery. I realized afterward that my care had been born out of shame and pity and the irrefutable fact that she was my mother. I have never been able to see someone suffering and remain unmoved. Perhaps I did not want the people who knew me to see her looking like a derelict when they came to visit at the hospital.

It was not until I began the process of attaching a piece of her wrap onto my eye-mask that it dawned on me that I had made room for my mother again. As I threaded the needle and put first one, then another stitch in place, it hit me: I had to have forgiven her if I wanted her so close to me at that particular time.

The act of sewing that little mask opened a new chapter for us, at least it did for me. I realized it was still a blessing to have a mother—something I never thought I would say or imagined I would feel. When I told her about the eye-mask and mentioned that the nurse had suggested I get something a little more substantial, like a gown that I would wear in the hospital instead of the one the hospital provided, she did not hesitate.

"Okay. I will have the alterations lady at my dry cleaner's sew one quickly," she said. It was only after the gown came two days later did it dawn on me that she could have said No. I could have been going through this most frightening time without any connection to the one person every child, no matter how old they are, runs to when they hurt. I did not realize my very human need for my mother; I had buried it so far into my anger, sadness, fear, and hatred that I had forgotten it was still there.

More than anything, I had always wanted to experience the maternal in my mother, and I had finally gotten it. I had to make peace with the fact that it had not come in the way I would have liked or chosen.

My mother is my soul's torment. How do I rid myself of her and still remain whole? She gave me life, yet she has slowly drained it out of me. I rail against the fact that she has put me in a prison I can never escape. Over the years, I have thought about why I made the choice to commit a crime in those early years of living with her betrayal. Perhaps I had just been bad and had been a criminal at heart all along. Perhaps I had wanted to be locked up so that the reality of a prison cell would reflect the prisoner I had become in real life. Perhaps I had wanted my external circumstances to reflect my internal ones. Like most things in my life, this, too, remains unclear. When a child is betrayed by the one person they should feel safest with—their mother—that child's sense of self breaks down, and there is almost no hope for healthy, normal relationships. Not with himself or with the world at large.

When I had my second surgery for breast cancer, my mother came and stayed for a month. It was the longest time we had spent in the same space in almost 30 years. It was bittersweet because there was so much between us, and yet, I was still her child, and I loved her. She slept in my bed, and, at night, I would crawl next to her and play at being her child. I wanted her to hold me. I would lift up her arm and put it around me. I wanted to feel I was a part of her. I did this knowing it was a game. Still, while she snored softly next to me, I silently asked her: "Why do I have this need to feel like I am your child? Why would I have the need to still feel like a child when more than half of the threescore and ten years God promised me have already gone?"

More and more, I see how different we are and how much I am like her, too. This part I resist with a passion—"I am nothing like her"—but I see her in me, and it hurts me. This is not a resemblance I want to claim. Is it possible to hate someone so fiercely, so unrelentingly, yet also want so much for them to be happy and at peace? I want to disconnect myself from her-cut her off like a rotten limb severed to preserve the rest of me, but I cannot. There is no way we can escape each other. We are forever bound by the men who had come between us.

There are always these conflicting feelings when I am around her. It is pity mixed with disgust then, always, disbelief. How does she do it? How can she bear it? What part of her is missing that she cannot register the wrongness of her marriage? What part of her is so dead that she cannot register my heartbreak and shame? What demons have chased her and stripped her of her essential core goodness? What secrets lie in the belly of her heart?

I finally bared my heart to my mother in a 25-page letter at age 45. Conversations do not happen with my mother. We discuss things, issues, family—but we do not talk about us. Our attempts often end in screaming matches, cold retreats, blame, bitter words—all widening the chasm between us.

When I once attempted to ask her how she wants me to show my face among people and how she expects me to bear the pointing and the whispering over and over again—because as long as she is with him, I do not get to forget nor do other people—she lashed out in such rage that I wanted to scream. "You never wanted me! You should have had that abortion! You should have had them scrape me out of you like they do burnt food at the bottom of a pot." I reminded her of something she had mentioned casually years before. She had been scared after she found out she was pregnant with me and considered having an abortion. It was papa who had stopped her.

To some relatives, my mother and I are two people who love each other very much. To my mother and I, that could not be further from the truth. She has wounded me the most. I think I have wounded her, too; after all, she has said so. I look at times in my life when I was betrayed by the father of my child and people I thought were friends, and I wonder why I should blame them. If my mother could, who wouldn't?

My mother remains an enigma to me. I often wonder who she was as a child. I know she likes pink and loves to chew on poached grains of rice like Krispies or other cereals that crackle. I have seen her dedicated to taking care of my grandmothers and other relatives, but I do not know my mother.

I have heard people say she is smart and beautiful , but I do not know what moves her or brings her joy. I do not know what drives her. I have seen her give up her children, her pride, and her dignity for her greatest need, to be in the company of a man. Certainly not for comfort, safety, love, and security, she has never had those . I have watched her give her soul away to the men she has loved and watched them use her and break her heart, but I do not know my mother.

I do not know my mother and doubt I ever will. Sometimes I wonder what if it would have been easier for me to lose her to death. I have her here as she is now and we are both living out a life sentence in our own private hell.

Over the years, I have begged God to help me forgive my mother and her husband, and, to a large extent, I have. But I am human.

I have learned that forgiveness is a process. The words "I forgive you" remain only words until a full healing of the heart takes place. That requires time, especially in cases of complex trauma like mine, where the sufferer is retraumatized over and over again, both consciously and unconsciously.

I have forgiven her, I know, but it still hurts to see her with him, to know she is still there with him. Perhaps there are parts of forgiveness we humans do not understand and can never under-stand beyond the "forgive 70 times 7" that Jesus commanded us to do. Isn't it easier to forgive an act that was done once, an act you never have to relive again? What about an act that keeps on repeating? "Go and sin no more, God commanded." Does it apply here, too? Doesn't God Himself require change after repentance? Though my mother has said she was sorry, her staying these 30 years with the man who raped me is a daily negation of me, and it leaves me with the kind of pain I do not yet know how to rid myself of. I have been told by some in the church that if I have truly forgiven her, it would not hurt to see her with him.

Perhaps I should ask God if the pain of reminder is unforgiveness.

CHAPTER 21

Me, Too

THERE IS AN UNBEATABLE POWER IN THE COLLECTIVE VOICE, and I am grateful for the #MeToo movement and the brave women who understand this. I know how much pain there is in sexual violation, and I also know how costly keeping those particular secrets are. I know about the lack of self-esteem and devaluation that become a second skin afterward. I know about living in fear of someone finding out and the fear of being judged and rejected. I know about the biggest cost of all, shame. Simply telling a woman or child it's not their fault that someone had hurt them in that way doesn't change or erase the shame that accompanies assault, and women have to live with it in addition to the other kinds of pain that go along with it. While hearing the stories of these women trigger feelings of sadness and other emotions, I have also found comfort in the fact that some of the world's most beautiful, most accomplished women had lived with rape and its devastation and survived it. It was a relief to know I was in big company. The movement has given me the courage I needed to finally say: it happened to me, too.

What is it in men that makes them take such liberties with women? Is it something about us that tells them we are nothing but something to be used, abused, and discarded at will? Is it because we find ourselves in situations where we need the help of men to get a job, to pay for medicine for a sick child, or to sign a check to ensure our survival—and they know it, so they take advantage of it?

Something happened to me in San Francisco when I had first arrived from the East Coast, fleeing from demons too large and real to fight. I was 25 but felt 80.

During those first few weeks, I took the train, bus, and street-car to explore the city. When I was let off the streetcar at Union Square one day, I immediately knew that part of my destiny was tied to it. I felt a certain excitement I hadn't felt in a long time. The girl who had had great dreams as a child woke up again, and I knew I needed to find and work in a place that made me feel that alive. I asked my math teacher and her husband to tell me how to look for work.

It was more than 20 years ago, and most jobs were advertised in the paper. For weeks, I scoured every newspaper I could find in the hopes I would find a job. I saw many listings, but they were not on Union Square—they were not for me. I was looking through the job section as usual one day when a little ad caught my eye. Saks Fifth Avenue was looking for "greeters." I did not need to read anymore. I had walked by Saks a few times, even ventured in on one occasion and thought, *If papa were still alive, this was the kind of place he would shop for me. Maybe someday I'll be able to walk in there and buy anything I want.* I took the trolley home to my math teacher and told her I needed a suit for an interview. I showed her the newspaper ad, and she told me it was a very fancy store, and if I wanted to do an interview there, I was going to need something other than my thrift store finds. I asked her if there were any stores that could possibly have "nice things" without a hefty price tag. She told me to go to Loehmann's downtown and check their sale rack. "You might get lucky."

I told her I needed to borrow some money and would pay her back as soon as I started working. She laughed and said, "You know, you haven't changed. You're still the little troublemaker you were back in my class. I am sure you will get the job if you're hell-bent on it."

I grabbed her, gave her a big kiss, and jumped on the train as soon as she handed me the money. I found a navy-blue suit that fit me to perfection and transformed me into a young woman who could go for an interview at Saks Fifth Avenue. I was amazed at the transforming power of clothes.

I have one photograph of me as a child. I was perhaps two years old or younger , and in the photo, I am smiling the same smile that people still remark on after all these years. It has not changed. I look now at the thousands of photos of my grown-up self, thanks to technology and selfies. In most of them I am smiling-and it's not that I am faking it either. Perhaps deep down I have reason to smile. Perhaps God knows to keep my smile on my lips even when my heart cries because I need my smile to survive.

B. Eisenberg was a tall, elegant woman who oozed confidence and a tempered sensuality that was arresting as well as comforting. I marveled at how she could pull off both. She was the kind of woman in whose presence you wanted to sit up straight and be your best self without feeling intimidated. I liked her immediately. Her large grey eyes assessed me quickly and gave her enough of what she needed to tell me the job was mine if I told her just a little about myself and could provide a resume. I told her that my math teacher, who had been in the Peace Corps in my country, had invited me to San Francisco. I was looking to start law school once I settled down and, if she hired me, that would of course hasten the process. She laughed and called over the general manager of the store.

"I just found someone I think you're going to love," she said to him. "She is charming and very smart and will make a great impression on our customers." She had the kind of laugh one would have expected from a man or someone less chic. But I liked it. It was warm and inviting.

I wanted to tell her I'd get her my resume, so I said, "I will get it to you if I knew what it is. "

She laughed her booming laugh and told me to write down the things I had told her about myself and include my education and the jobs I had done.

"Oh, you mean a curriculum vitae!" I said, a little embarrassed. I walked out of her office, knowing I had made my first friend in San Francisco. I also realized I was going to have to learn to speak the language of America. I was excited I had found myself a job. Although it was not intellectually stimulating, it was a great place to meet many different kinds of people—people with money and connections.

I was the first person you saw when you walked through the large glass doors of Saks Fifth Avenue. I was part of the Ambassador Service Department and part of the welcoming committee for John F. Kennedy Jr., although I never got to meet him. I had become the face of Saks. I loved my job and quickly devised ways to make my meager wardrobe work. I combined pieces from the clearance racks at Loehmann's, my finds from thrift stores, and some of my African prints that resembled Oscar de la Renta pieces. Sometimes a customer would compliment me on my outfit and ask if they could get it on the third floor of the store. I would laugh and come up with some response that didn't admit I got it at a thrift store, as one of the girls at the makeup counter told me I should never do. I wondered why. I was proud of the fact that I did not have to spend thousands of dollars to look like the customers who shopped at the store. On my days off, I went all around the city and combed through the better Goodwill stores located in Pacific Heights and other affluent neighborhoods. I always found great things. Sometimes I found new clothes with the price tags still attached.

I was happy to dress up and go to work each day. Being around well-dressed people gave me confidence and kept my mind on what I wanted to accomplish. Every day, I was reminded of why it was important for me to work hard and become successful. The only thing that made me uncomfortable and a little sad in my new situation was the coolness that African Americans, especially women, had towards me. I had my brightest smile when they walked in, I was happy to see them and glad Black people shopped there, too. Sometimes they were rude to me and would not respond when I greeted them. I did not understand the rejection. Growing up in Africa, I had been taught that Black people everywhere are my sisters and brothers—my people.

One morning, I was standing on Carl Street near where I lived, waiting for the streetcar to take me downtown to my job at Saks when a car pulled up and a not-unattractive man leaned out of the window and said in a heavy African accent—which I immediately recognized as Nigerian—"Hello, pretty lady. Wherever you need to go, I will take you." I hesitated, but got in the car, thinking he is "my people." He told me he was a professor and lectured at one of the top universities in San Francisco. We chatted about this and that—where I was living, what brought me to the United States. He asked was I a student, was I married? I looked too young to be—and on and on. Africans can ask you very personal things within minutes of meeting you with no qualms. It is all part of the blurry, oftentimes non-existent boundary lines in the African culture. I answered some of his questions briefly, and the ones I did not want to answer, I pretended I hadn't heard. I hated being asked to talk about myself and was grateful when he pulled up and let me out in front of the store. I thanked him and got out of the car, breathed a sigh of relief, and walked into the store, glad it was a sunny day, not the typical foggy San Francisco morning. The sun always improves my mood.

The next morning, as I waited for the streetcar again, he pulled up.

"Hello, pretty lady."

We did this for weeks. He was never inappropriate. He had, of course, expressed interest in me and admired me but was always polite and deferential in his treatment. I gradually learned to relax with him. One day, just before he drove off, he said, "I would love to cook you dinner. Please do me the honor and allow me, Princess."

He had started calling me that the week before, which both annoyed and amused me. I told him I would think about it. He kept asking and asking, and I finally said okay. He asked for my address, and I gave it and told him to come to the door and ask permission from the family I was staying with. It would be a gesture of respect since it is expected in the African culture; it would also mean that they would know who I was with and where I was going. He agreed.

When the day arrived, he picked me up and promised to bring me back safely. He lived in a large apartment on Lincoln Avenue, close to Golden Gate Park and the beach. It was neat and welcoming, and I noticed that he had gotten flowers. He had also written a card, which he had placed next to the flowers, and he told me to read it as he peeled plantains.

I relaxed in the aroma and gentle bubbling sounds of frying onions and garlic in palm oil. It was the smell of home. I was transported and happy in those few moments, inhaling Africa. I was also feeling good that this distinguished man was cooking for me. What is it about men in power that is intoxicating to women?

I chatted with him and laughed as we ate delicious stewed fish and plantains and rice and a small salad. He was a good cook. I was surprised; the role is usually reserved for women in Africa. I almost forgot we were in America. He was divorced and had two children with his ex-wife. I was sure he had learned how to live alone. One learns to expand one's thinking very quickly if one is to survive away from home. We moved into the living room, and he turned on the TV and then excused himself, saying he would be right back.

I asked to use the bathroom. I wanted to check it out. You can tell a lot about a person by their bathroom. After opening cupboards and looking behind curtains and inside cabinets, I was satisfied. It was spotless. I quickly ran back to where I had been sitting on the couch when I heard his footsteps. He walked purposefully towards me in a burgundy satin robe and sat next to me on the couch. I was shocked by the sheen of the robe, which almost blinded me, but I was even more shocked when he parted it and showed me how big his attraction was for me.

I sprang up and said, "Please cover yourself, doctor," reverting to a formal way of addressing him, hoping to dispel any ideas of intimacy he might have been harboring.

"Please, Princess, come sit with me. Please," he whimpered. How disgusted, scared, and disappointed I was. What was a big man like that doing begging a young girl with such little disguised desperation? How embarrassed he would be if his colleagues back home were to see him like that, looking almost ridiculous in his seducer getup, like a grown man forced to wear women's clothes as punishment for ego crimes.

"Please take me home, sir. Thank you for dinner. It was nice of you, but it's late, and I must be getting back."

I had already made my way to the front door of his apartment. Kazim's violation had taught me never to be too close to men under these kinds of circumstances—when you might not be able to physically defend yourself should the need arise. I was taking no chances.

"You really are not going to stay with me?"

"No, professor. It's not going to happen. Please take me home."

"Really?" in a tone that implied "No" was not a response he was familiar with.

"You want to leave, there's the door," he said, all warmth gone from him. "You're taking me home, right?" I asked. Wanting to make sure I had not misunderstood him when he had shown me the door. "You're not going to drive me home?" I repeated in disbelief. "I can't go out there by myself. It's late."

It was almost midnight, and cell phones were not as available to everybody as they are now. "If you want to leave, go. I am not driving you," he said.

I picked up my purse, which I had left hanging on the dining room chair, and walked towards the door backward, my eyes never leaving his. I did not want to push my luck. He had not made a move to attack me or force things. I figured I had gotten off easy—if finding my way home in a city I wasn't very familiar with late at night was the only problem I had. I unlatched the door, flew down the three flights of stairs with the sound of my high heels echoing behind me, as though mocking me. I did not breathe until I was out in the street. I took off the offending heels and started the long walk home.

I got there at about 1:40 in the morning. I have never walked and run 35 blocks so fast. I would run a little, stop and look behind me to see if anyone was following, walk, then run again until I got home. My feet were blistered, and my nerves were shot, but I was home safe. Grateful. I learned a lesson that night, two and a half decades ago. I never go out anymore without having cash on me. I may need to catch the bus or take a taxi home.

Do men think we're worth only as much as a cup of coffee? Dinner? A dress? A job contract?

I was sent to a renowned dermatologist and infectious disease doctor for pruritus a few years ago—after I had managed to strip off the membrane in my vagina with every soap and feminine cleansing product I could find. A thin, attractive Chinese doctor in her 60s with a quick wit and dazzling sense of humor, Dr. Cheng asked me questions about my skincare regimen and how often I showered or took baths. She asked me why I was washing myself excessively. I told her it was because I didn't want to smell.

"That thing has a smell," she countered. "No amount of washing is going to get rid of the vagina's natural odor. You will only succeed in removing all the good stuff down there and leave yourself unprotected against infection. Stop washing. The vagina has its own way of cleaning itself."

Perhaps I want to erase every mark on my womanhood, I thought to myself. I walked out of her office, knowing I have to live with the fact that soap and sanitizer are never going to wash away the memory of being taken against my will.

Most days, I wonder what happens to the millions of children like me all over the world who have to wake up each day in their prisons where they have been sentenced to life. Their prisons of incest, rape, molestation, physical and emotional abuse? Prisons whose walls are colored by self-hatred, rage, distrust, shame, and betrayal? What happens to the children living in their private hells, serving out a sentence for which they have never been guilty? I think of my love for literature, of books, which had me lost in worlds far from my own and made me dream. I think of being gifted with a soul so easily moved by beauty—one that can be overcome by the sight and smell of a flower, or how a piece of music or poetry sounds. How do the children survive without the many small talents and skills that have made it possible for me to have varied experiences and meet the many people who have nurtured and somehow shaped my life? Like my smile, which has never stopped inviting people in, even when I was dying inside, and no one could see? What do these children do if they do not have all of what I have had to survive life?

I know that, in spite of my many blessings and reasons to be grateful, for the first 33 years of my life, I woke up each day asking God to let that day be my last. I only stopped praying for death after my son was born. I knew that I did not want him to navigate life without me here to help him. But how do the children survive who do not have someone or something like I do to give them reason to fight? How do they live through each harrowing day without something bigger than their misery to sustain them? I know, without a doubt, the only reason I am still alive is because of my son. God knew the day would come when all other reasons to fight would be exhausted. He knew that only this love for my child would keep my heart beating, so he gave him to me.

CHAPTER 22

Full Circle

NEW YEAR'S EVE 2017. It had been a whole year, and I had lived a lifetime in 365 days. Grateful I had my son with me this time, I prepared to do the one thing that had been on my mind all day—going to the church where I had gone the December before and implored God to heal me. It was hard to believe it had been a year already since I was diagnosed with cancer. I was strangely excited and nervous, too. I debated whether I should give testimony in front of the whole church or just go quietly back to the altar where I had knelt and cried to God. I could not decide , but I did easily decide on the look I wanted. I wore a long, flowing, pale-pink skirt, a filmy white blouse, and a headband with gold filigree and crystals. I wanted an angelic look. In the photos that were taken afterward, I was told I looked sensuous and like a "queen," not an angel.

Getting dressed was symbolic this New Year's Eve in more ways than one. Last year at this time, I had just wanted to make it to church. Nothing else mattered. I had been broken. This time, I was going back whole and victorious, and I wanted to look the part. My son and I drove to the church, and it was packed. I sang every song with gusto and danced along with the praise dancers with abandon. I was happy. Last year, I had been on my knees, weeping. This time I am on my feet, praising. The pastor prayed and thanked God for all he had done for the church over the past year. Did anyone have anything to thank God for? If they did, let them thank Him that they had made it through the year, let them thank Him that their families had made it, let them thank Him that God had provided for and kept them. Let them thank Him. He had done all those things and more for me. He had healed me from cancer—twice in one year.

I knelt at the altar and thanked God for a year that only His grace had seen me through. I thanked Him for all the things He had done and for all the prayers He had answered. I thanked God for Tanis, who had started a GoFundMe and raised enough money to tide me over several months when she found out I had no income after losing my job during treatment. We had met in the waiting room at the radiation center. This time, my tears were tears of joy.

After the jubilant countdown to the New Year, amid all the hugs and Happy New Year's, I went up to the pastor. I told him that the previous year, I had gone to the altar and told God to "take that thing away" like he'd asked the congregation to do. Did he remember? He said Yes, he remembered. I wanted him to know that God had taken it away, and I had come back to thank Him. I told him that two weeks before that New Year's Eve service, I had been diagnosed with breast cancer and had come to church to ask God for a miracle. He was surprised and happy and wrapped me in a big hug after hearing the story.

"Praise God! Praise God!"

My son and I both hug him again and say goodbye.

"You look different," he had told me with a big smile as I walked towards him to tell him why I had come to church that night. Now he knew why I looked different. I was cancer-free.

CHAPTER 23

Realizations

IT HAS TAKEN TWO DECADES OF LIVING IN AMERICA to understand the complicated relationship between us African immigrants and our African American brothers and sisters. There are spoken and unspoken rules, codes of conduct in place in Black communities in America that are unknown and unfamiliar to a newly arrived African. In my first years in America, I never gave the color of my skin and the friends I made much thought until I learned that being Black in America requires careful planning. One's speech, approach, dress, hair, and the company one keeps can on any given day make a difference between life and death. I now understand the term "living while Black." Africans come to America with a certain naiveté about white America, which is often reinforced by the phrase "you're not like the Blacks here." It's a statement often made by whites to give an African a false sense of superiority. Not until the police pull you over do you realize that, to the white person in America, you're just another Black person. Not until you're confronted with the ugly truth that a white police officer can hose down little Black girls, that women can be dragged out of cars and shot just like Black men. Not until you're in the back of a police car for a minor traffic violation do you realize you can no longer buy into the illusion "you're not like the Blacks here." Thanks to social media and cell phones, these incidents, which were before now hidden, are now made public. Africans are getting an education on being Black in America. I now have a clear understanding of why the Black women who came to Saks had snubbed me. They had been angry. In their eyes, I was nothing but a well-dressed doorman in a fancy white establishment. A sight they are awfully familiar with.

I used to scoff at the saying "our secrets will kill us"—until I spent four decades living as a prisoner of mine. How many times have I told myself I cannot tell anyone about my life because that would mean hurting my mother and hurting my brother? How many times have I asked myself what is my story and what is theirs? In the telling of mine, have I not told theirs? I know that there is no getting around the parts where all of our stories intercept. I am telling my story, and they are a part of it. I know if there is to be any hope for me to find some peace in this world, I must speak my heart—because I know that the silence from my effort to cover, protect, and hide has cost me my sanity and peace. Perhaps those I have hurt—because "hurt people hurt people"—will understand how I have come to be as I am and forgive me.

I am weary of my chameleon-like existence. Decades of living the many personas I have perfected over time, of wearing disguise after disguise, of protective armor after protective armor, have worn me out. I have no more capacity to continue living out my many names. Neurotic Nyla had nearly ruined my enjoyment of Cancun. It's time to put her and her sisters out of work: Fix-it Felicia, Worrywart Wilhelmina, Plan it Prudence, Do it Dorothy, Tantrum Tatiana, Angry Ann, Frantic Francine, Talkative Tina, Perfectionist Patti, Fearful Philippa, Lifeless Leila, Jealous Jasmine and her twin, Envious Eva, Grouchy Gretchen, Judgmental Judy, and Ruthless Ruth.

My French friend, Madam, told me years ago that starving myself is the ultimate expression of self-hatred. We had been talking about why I would go hours without eating, and when I did finally eat, it was nothing that nourished. Though I have been called overweight, even obese, I have been starving myself on starch and sugar—white rice and ice cream. I am trying now. Eating chia, chlorella, and kale. Drinking water and running a little, even if I am tired. Taking Chinese herbs, cleansing my body, and surrounding myself with more whole people. All this requires time, effort, and money. Self-care does not come easy or cheap. It would be hard for poor people with three jobs, five children, a mortgage, and a car note to be good.

I have learned to meditate and quiet my mind. It is helping me manage one of the most difficult symptoms of the traumatized brain—the constant waiting for the other shoe to drop.

I am also saying No—even to my son. Loving him the way I do, I thought I could make up for all the things that are wrong in his life—not giving him a mother and father who live together raising him, not providing him with a more secure financial environment, for seeing me sick one too many times, and all the ways life has broken his heart already. But I am saying No now because I recognize my need for rest and self-care. I know now that there are some things I just don't have the power to fix in his life; the most important gift I can give him is my unconditional love and the effort I am making to try and be here longer for him.

I am also asking for and accepting help. That has changed everything.

I have always believed in magic, and I had grand ideas about making magic for people growing up. Over the years, trying to survive my life occupied so much space that there was little room left for dreams. Yet, there was one dream even the harsh grip of my life has never been able to pry from my heart—building a sanctuary for children. A place where we would nurture the land, and in turn, she would feed us corn, cassava, and herbs. A place where children would share their dreams, knowing they would be nurtured. A place where we would bare our wounds and love each other into wellness.

One day, feeling especially discouraged that I had not been able to make this happen yet, I asked myself how else can I make magic while I wait? Time has gone by, and I am beginning to notice a few grey hairs. Then I realized that I did not have to be a millionaire from my "successful careers" to make magic. I could use what I have now.

I have always been told I have a beautiful smile. I can start with that, I decided. I could start smiling in places and at people who didn't expect it. My sunshine smile might perhaps bring a little sun to someone. Once I made up my mind, I started doing different things. Small things with what I had. I took a huge bouquet of flowers to the waitress who let me use the bathroom in the restaurant where she worked on Valencia street. No one does that for free in San Francisco. You have to buy something or, at the very most, be white—especially in certain parts of the city. I couldn't count the number of times my little boy has been told No when he badly needed to go. No one would let us use their bathroom until I paid five dollars for a cup of tea or ordered French Fries or something else that would give us access.

Sometimes I was told he is too young. "We can't allow him in here," they said, as though my five-year-old was going to walk up to the bar and order Smirnoff, straight. I can't help wondering if they turn away little white boys and their mothers, too. When I brought the flowers, the waitress had tears in her eyes and said they were the most beautiful flowers ever, and she would never forget the thought. They had not cost me too much. I had gotten them at the farmers' market. She insisted she had done nothing special by letting me use the bathroom, but I knew better. Isn't it the most wonderful thing when people do good things and never think much of it?

I have always been a good tipper, but I have taken it up a notch. I have an exceptionally wonderful time seeing the reactions of people when they're not expecting much, then, suddenly, get it. Like the 15-year-old boy that I gave a $20 bill to for a $2.75 scoop of ice cream and told him to keep the change. The way his eyes opened in disbelief was beautiful. He kept asking, "Are you sure? This is a lot!" He went from being slumped over and dragging his feet to having the biggest smile on his face as he handed small spoonfuls of samples to customers trying out flavors before settling on one. There was a new quickness in his step that was heartwarming. I stood outside and watched him through the glass windows for a while and walked away, smiling. My little change had made a big change. It is a great feeling knowing I am able to do it with who I am and the little I have. All around me now, I see possibilities to make magic, and I am making it more and more each day. I no longer have to wait until I am rich. I wonder why it took me so long to discover this.

I had some realizations after going through one of my dark spells. Resistance was one of them. I was confronted by my own resistance. I realized that my exhaustion, albeit due in great part to the circumstances of my life, has also been fueled by me. Resisting requires force.

I have resisted sadness because somehow I have not wanted God to think I am not grateful for all He has done for me, knowing fully well how much worse things could have been. looking back, I realize this kind of thinking only made things worse. I see now how I was always swimming against the current instead of just going with the natural flow of things. I recognized my resistance to love because I really never believed that anyone would love me if they knew the real me.

I also came face to face with my unwillingness to give in to joy. The fear that it will not last or that things always undoubtedly end badly for me has left me looking at joy like an exotic animal: beautiful and dangerous and best-observed from a distance.

Growing up, I held my mother's love so tightly, my father's memories so fiercely, and my need to have a normal, happy family so desperately that I could never fully enjoy the gift of the love and care I was given by strangers. I don't remember having anything or anyone constant or permanent in my life. I have lived and grown up wild and without tradition, except for what my soul is learning to develop.

Trying to hold onto people and things too tightly and for too long has caused me great pain throughout my life.

When she was a child of about six, my mother was sent to live in another city, having been given to her aunt who could not bear children. My grandmother had done this to spare her barren sister the shame and pain of being childless. Perhaps this explains why it has been so easy for my mother to leave me and my brothers. How can she give us what she never had for herself?

I am learning to hold things lightly. People too. Perhaps the Buddhist monks have figured this out, spending hours making spectacular creations of beauty called *mandalas* and then purposely destroying their creation, knowing the impermanence of things, and being okay with it.

Recently I was gifted with an all-inclusive ten-day trip to Cancun, Mexico with my son—a gift given by his father. It was my first real vacation ever in my life, yet even there, the demons reared their ugly heads. I was trying to stay open, but I had a moment of panic when I thought I had been poisoned for sure by the room service staff because we had ordered room service twice in a day. I took a bite of the key lime pie we had ordered and decided it tasted bitter, even for key lime pie. *They hate me, that is why they've poisoned me even though they have never met m*e, I thought. Why would total strangers, catering to hundreds of people at a resort each day, have poison, especially for me, lying around? It sometimes does not take much to trigger the trauma brain. But more and more, I am recognizing the triggers and managing them better.

In spite of that incident, I had the most glorious time. Restful days in the sun, swimming in the ocean, meeting new people—beautiful people, rich people, well and not-so-well people, ordinary people—all extraordinary in that place. There, money is the currency for happiness, but for once, I can't fault it. The soul needs that kind of rest from time to time; I know my soul does. After everything we had been through the past year—to be with my son, cancer behind us, other troubles behind us, money worries forgotten for the moment, all of the weights of my life laid aside, thrashing about in the blue-green waters—was heaven. All around me, there was the hum of the music of life, and I was finally a part of it.

I left Cancun with my belly full, my soul full, and my heart full, in awe of how good God is. I was also amazed at the fact that the father of my son—the man who had caused me perhaps the greatest pain of having to deal with CPS— had also given me one of the most extraordinary healing experiences of my life.

I have one photograph of me as a child. I was perhaps two years old or younger, and in the photo, I am smiling the same smile that people still remark on after all these years. It has not changed. I look now at the thousands of photos of my grown-up self, thanks to technology and selfies. In most of them I am smiling and it's not that I am faking it either. Perhaps deep down I have reason to smile. Perhaps God knows to keep my smile on my lips even when my heart cries because I need my smile to survive.

CHAPTER 24

Joy

I WAS SITTING ON THE TOILET, THINKING, AS I OFTEN DO, since some of my best thinking and epiphanies have happened in the bathroom. I was feeling a feeling I wasn't familiar with. Upon reflection, I realized it was joy. I was feeling joy. I had felt happiness before, pleasure, too. I had even felt joy from time to time, I'm sure, but I couldn't readily place it that day because I had not asked for it. I've prayed for peace and for healing, never for joy. I have always thought that if I have peace, it would be my greatest happiness. But as I sat on that warm toilet seat that night, I resolved to have joy, to seek it, since, according to Rumi, "that which you seek seeks you."

I love the feeling of being content with my life right now, as it is, and, having been freed from cancer, I want to be free of the old shackles of pain, joylessness, stagnation, fear, and anger. I want to be free from the habit of holding on to things that no longer serve me. I want to do different, feel different, be different. I am grateful for and enjoying many new relationships and some old ones, and through them, I have begun to understand how empty my life has been these many years. How devoid of safe, healthy relationships it has been and how vital those are for the soul. It was only after the holes in my life started getting filled did I realize how many there were. Toxic, manipulative relationships no longer feel comfortable to me.

It is almost as though I have been asleep; it's been a long nightmare-filled sleep, and I am waking up and recognizing real life. Never have I been more focused and clearer. Never have I accomplished more. Never have I set goals and seen them through. I am watching myself become. God is making me. The closer I get to him, I am realizing, the less angst and fear I feel, and the more positive changes I see in me.

The more I live life, the less I read. These past few months, I have observed myself rarely touch a book other than the Bible, which I am asking God to help me read every day. I simply do not have the time nor the desire to read. Perhaps it is time to put other people's stories down for a while and embrace my own.

I am busy. I am engaged with people, relationships, projects, life. I praise God that each day I see how he is healing my broken-ness and showing me what is possible for me.

Decades of sorrow, shame, hiding in the shadows, not daring to show my face and risk *being*—all these I am putting behind me now. I pray for God to help me focus only on the relevant. I have lost so much time already. I want to guide my son to be the best he can be. I want to support his dreams and pray them into realization.

I want to travel, write, dance, and try. I want the best love yet. I want to help others and make my life count. I want to live.

Lately, I have been reflecting on one of my favorite books about the Holocaust, *Night,* by Elie Wiesel. His unveiling of the horrors people suffered then and continue to suffer today in so many ways leaves me in awe. I look back on my own journey through life and all the heartbreak I have seen in this world, and I am astounded by the capacity of humans to survive.

I never did get to star in my own blockbuster movie but, who knows? One thing I have learned and know for sure: anything is possible.

Perhaps one day, I will even wake up and see myself through God's eyes—fearfully and wonderfully made—a quilt whose fragments have been made into a one-of-a-kind piece. A masterpiece.

About the Author

HAJAH KANDEH fled the conflict diamond war in her country of birth, Sierra Leone, where she had suffered tremendous violence. She credits her survival to all the strangers who have "loved her into being."

At 16 She won a scholarship to France after placing first in the national exams for best French language students. In college she won a "Best Actress" award for The Revelation, a play she wrote and starred in. She graduated First Class from Fourah Bay College, University of Sierra Leone where she majored in Political Science and French literature.

After college, she worked for the BBC as a freelance writer in Sierra Leone. Upon arriving in San Francisco, she struggled to establish herself in her new home working retail, customer service, nannying, and other jobs most immigrants do to get started in

America. After working in the hospitality department of Saks, and later getting her certification, she secured a position as a mental health counselor for a local non-profit.

She actively engages in women's writing groups and conferences, including "Writing Ourselves Whole," where women of all backgrounds come together and connect through writing and telling their stories.

Hajah loves poetry, smart movies and great conversations and has been afraid of snakes most of her life. She is fluent in several languages including French, Russian, and Krio and dreams of traveling the world someday.

She is the Founder of "Do Tell", an organization which aims to educate and empower children to speak up in a safe space about sexual abuse and other forms of violation. Her passion is to help them through the long journey of healing necessary to becoming healthy whole adults capable of living fulfilling lives.

Hajah lives in San Francisco with her son and a feisty black cat named Luna where she pays it forward by making magic wherever she goes, one person at a time one day at a time.

Made in the USA
Middletown, DE
18 April 2024

53178799R00182